All scriptures are from the King James Bible

© All rights Reserved 2013
Publisher
Good Shepherd Writing and Publishing LLC
A subsidiary of Shepherd Ministries
Dr. Willie B. White

Monthly Topical Discussions
- ◊ A New Birth A New Creature
- ◊ New Converts In The New Community
- ◊ Called To Christ's Church
- ◊ Revelations From God
- ◊ Witnessing Christ
- ◊ God's People In Strange Places
- ◊ Follow God
- ◊ God's Chosen Leaders
- ◊ Christian Growth And Maturity
- ◊ Communication With God Through Prayer
- ◊ Harvest Time
- ◊ The Joy Of Christmas

Audience

This devotional is designed to inspire all readers the world over and point non-believers to Christ and give believers a deeper love, devotion and affection for God.

The aim of this devotional is to provide daily inspirational thoughts with Biblical background for practical applications as well as promoting Bible study and meditations on God's Word. Daily readings from this devotional will establish a deeper and a more intimate relationship with Christ our Savior.

At the conclusion of this devotional it is the author's desire that the reader will proclaim the good news of the gospel beginning in his or her Jerusalem, Samaria, Judea and the world over in obeying the great commission that was issued by Christ Himself (Matthews 28:19-20). In doing so others will come to Christ and God's kingdom will grow; thereby further winning this spiritual warfare against Satan and his army.

Read, meditate, pray and be filled with the Holy Spirit.

A New Birth A New Creature

Day 1

Washed in His Blood Through Redemption: Titus 3:5

Not by works of righteousness which we have done, but according to his mercy he saved us, by the washing of regeneration, and renewing of the Holy Ghost.

Regeneration within it self is all believers' new birth which is made possible with Christ's death on the cross and as we accept His atoning works in reconciling man back to God. In the regeneration process believers become new creatures in Christ, a fellowship is restored and once again believers can live in harmony with God. Why? This is because all believers' sins have been washed away in the blood of Jesus Christ our Lord through His death on Calvary's cross. Therefore, believers have been cleansed from the stain of sin that prevented us from being acceptable in the eyesight of God our Father.

As stated so eloquently in our scripture verse that our works of righteousness did not and couldn't have saved us because we have no righteousness besides that of God, but because of His love and mercy Christ saved us from eternal alienation from God.

It is through His blood that mankind is made new and the newness is sustained through the presence of the Holy Spirit who dwells in each believer. If the question were raised, Why is a constant renewing necessary? It is necessary because there is the constant temptation of sin that will hinder our walk in the newness of Christ.

Redemption is a precious commodity.

Day 2

Born Into a New Life: Romans 8:10-11

And if Christ be in you, the body is dead because of sin; but the Spirit is life because of righteousness. But if the Spirit of him that raised up Jesus from the dead dwell in you, he that raised up Christ from the dead shall also quicken your mortal bodies by his Spirit that dwelleth in you.

Our scripture lesson packs a powerful message in that it speaks to the works of the Holy Spirit who gives life to all believers the moment each of us accepts Jesus Christ as Lord and Savior the Holy Spirit takes up residence in each of us. It is noteworthy to say that not all believers have been baptized in the Holy Spirit which empowers the believer with charismatic gifts to perform different ministries as gifted (Acts 1:8).

If the question were raised, **What is the significance of this verse?** Verse 1 has two connotations as it relates to believers, which are (a) "ye shall receive power", which is more than an ability or strength to perform a task. It is the authority to drive out evil spirits and the anointing to heal the sick and to perform many signs and wonders. (b) "ye shall be witnesses", which means that believers who have been baptized in the Spirit will boldly witness Christ the world over as well as the power to manifest Christ and His righteousness. In manifesting Christ, spirit-filled believers carry the life of Christ, hope and forgiveness of sins to a lost world so that every man, woman, boy or girl may be saved, as this is God's plan for all mankind. Another point to be made is that spirit-filled believers who have been baptized in the Spirit allow the Holy Spirit to work to His fullness in our lives.

Now that we have discussed the significance of Acts 1:8, let's look at the work of the Holy Spirit in raising Christ from the dead and all who believe is likewise raised from the death of sin to that of a new life in Christ. Jesus Christ came to give us that new life and for all who believe to have it more abundantly here and now (John 10:10). In our mortal bodies we can experience this abundant living by yielding to the Holy Spirit who gives this new life (8:2) and He empowers us to do great things such as kingdom building. However, we will experience the full affect of this new life at Christ's second coming (1 Corinthians 15:50-54; 1 Thessalonians 4: 13-16). **What a blessing it is to be born into a new life of Christ?**

If were to answer the above question, it would be that all believers are no longer dead to a life of sin, separation and shame, but to a life of righteousness, holiness and the power to witness Christ. Also, a new life in Christ carries the blessing of spending eternity with Him.

Born into a new life of Christ we are made heirs to the kingdom of God. What a life!

Day 3

A Transformed Mind: Romans 12:2

....be not conformed to this world; but be ye transformed of your mind, that ye may prove what is that good, and acceptable, and perfect, will of God.

The word transformed means a change has taken place inwardly or outwardly or both (Romans 12:2; 2 Corinthians 3:18). Today's lesson discussion is on the transformation that occurs first in the heart and manifest in outward actions and or expressions. The heart is the core of our being, thoughts and actions. An evil heart is one of destruction whereas a loving heart is one of righteousness, good and godliness.

Let's take a deeper look into being transformed; first, the believer has accepted Christ as Lord and Savior and is willing to be governed by the Holy Spirit who is our guide, teacher and protector. Second, a transformed mind/believer is no longer affected and or confirming to this world and it satanic systems. Third, a transformed mind is one that is truly committed to Christ, His righteousness and kingdom building. Fourth, a transformed mind is one that obeys Christ's command to love and His Great Commission (Matthew 28:19-20). Lastly, a transformed mind is one that is renewed daily by the indwelling Holy Spirit and has embraced the will of God as the highest and only way of life that leads to perfection.

A transformed mind is one that depicts the heart and will of God. "Be ye transformed" to that of God and resist conforming to the world and its destruction.

Day 4

A New Birth: Ephesians 4:23-24

..Be renewed in the spirit of your mind; and that ye put on the new man, which after God is created in righteousness and true holiness.

Yesterday's discussion focused on a transformed mind which leads to a new birth or a new life in Christ, which is supported by today's scripture text which speaks to the renewing of your mind through the spirit man in each believer. It goes without saying that once a person is born of the flesh/physical body it cannot be reborn again, but through the spirit all believers have a new birth which is one of righteousness and true holiness after God.

Our new birth begins with the atoning work of Christ and the convicting work of the Holy Spirit who convicts each believer of his or her sins and convinces each of us the need for a Savior-Jesus Christ.

What does a new birth entail? This new birth entails a change in lifestyle as the old nature in each of us no longer controls our actions, thoughts and desires. In the old life we were enemies with God whereas in the new life we live in harmony with God. **What a difference!** A new birth encompasses all the works and benefits/blessings of regeneration, which is preparing each believer for God's kingdom and spending eternity with Him.

A new birth/regeneration gives each believer the ability and desire to obey and please God. **What a life altering experience! Thank God for a new life.**

Born A New Creature: John 3:6

That which is born of the flesh is flesh; and that which is born of the Spirit is spirit.

For the past few days our lesson studies have been focused on new beginnings or new birth which encompasses regeneration. Regeneration is the foundational teachings of the Christian faith that in order to see and experience the kingdom of God we must be born again in the Spirit.

What is the meaning of "born again in the Spirit"? It means that there is a re-creation of the person to a spiritual life one that is guided by God the Holy Spirit. Part of the regeneration process is where the believer is not alienated from God to becoming part of the family of God where the heart of God is imparted to each believer. This transitioning process the old sinful nature mortified (put to death) and the new nature comes to life.

It is noteworthy to say that a new birth/regeneration and a mind transformation is predicated on ones' faith in (a) God and His plans of salvation, (b) Jesus Christ as the Son of God and His atoning works and saving powers, (c) the convicting works of the Holy Spirit, and (d) the fulfilling promise of spending eternity with God; at that point a new creature is born into the family of God.

Given the blessed benefits from regeneration begs the question, Who wants to remain in sin with no hope of tomorrow and being eternally separated from our creator?

Born Into The Family Of God: John 1: 12-13

...A many as received him. To them gave he power to become the sons of God, even to them that believe on his name. Which were born, not of blood, nor the will of the flesh, nor of the will of man, but of God.

Our lesson study outlines how believers are born into the family of God, which brings about a new beginning in the life of believers. The first action required is faith because it is through faith that we believe in God and accept His Son Jesus Christ for who He is.

Fleshly desire of men has no part in the believer's rebirth; this is predicated solely on the will of God and His desire for all men to be saved and become His children (sons). The will of God expresses His love for all humanity as depicted in John 3:16. **What love!**

Accepting Christ as God's Son is the "receive" component of our faith and Christian walk. Our faith is a lifetime commitment to Christ and His atoning work, which constitutes self-denial of our own wills but one that yields to the will of God. Being sons of God is a benefit as the result of our belief which carries a royal family heritage, which surpasses all other royalty. Being sons of God also makes believers part of the holy nation of God, a set aside people.

Believers, what a rich heritage we have? Believe and enjoy.

Day 7

Two Families-Satan's Or God's: 1 John 3:6-10

He that committeth sin is of the devil; for the devil sinneth from the beginning. For this purpose the Son of God was manifested, that he might destroy the works of the devil. Whosoever is born of God doth not commit sin; for his seed remaineth in him; and he cannot sin, because he is born of God.

Our scripture text and topic begs the question, which family do you belong? This question desires an answer because it tells the world which family we belong by our obedience. If we chose to obey Satan then those persons are considered children of Satan whereas those persons who obey God are Sons of God as they have been born of Him and cannot sin. His seed, the Holy Spirit dwells in each believer to aid in making our decision of family choice as His convicting work is ever present.

Verse 10 solidifies our discussion regarding which family you belong by stating, "In this the children of God are manifested, and the children of the devil; whosoever doeth not righteousness is not of God, neither he that loveth not his brother." This verse implies the teaching found in John 2:28 which warn believers that they cannot continue in sin and remain in fellowship with God. The very nature of salvation is love because God is love and He commands us to love Him first, others second and then self.

Choose your family-God and live forever or chose Satan and die.

Results Of Repentance: Matthew 3:2

....Repent ye, for the kingdom of heaven is at hand.

What is repentance? Repentance is the changing of one's mind/heart and turning away from something to something. In this scenario the repentant person is turning away from a life of sin to a life of righteousness in God. A repentance person realizes that life without God is wrong and hell bound with no hope of salvation whereas life in Christ assures the person of spending eternity with God.

A repentant person has the blessings of being born into the family of God and co-heirs with Christ our Lord and Savior as well as being part of His church---the bride of Christ. Repentant persons have the assured hope of wearing a golden crown and a white robe washed in the blood of Jesus. Most importantly, a repentant person has the indwelling Holy Spirit who is our guide, teacher, and protector as He is our road map to heaven as believers travel the road of righteousness.

It is noteworthy to say that to repent is a free choice made by the sinner who hears the Word of God and accepts the grace of God through the works of the Holy Spirit which enables the sinner to believe the gospel of Christ and accept salvation. While making the wise choice to repent, the person has decided to sail on the sea of God's love as our salvation is predicated on God's love.

Repent and enjoy the unquenchable love of God.

Day 9

A Tale Of Two Lives: Galatians 5:19-24

...The works of the flesh are manifest, which are these, Adultery, uncleanness, lasciviousness, Idolatry, witchcraft, hatred, variance, emulations, wrath, strife, sedition, heresies... they which do such things shall not inherit the kingdom of God. But the fruit of the Spirit is love, joy, peace, longsuffering, gentleness, goodness, faith... And they that are Christ's have crucified the flesh with the affections and lusts.

Today's discussion is the focus of a life in Christ and the one out of Christ which depicts the vast differences which begs the question, Which do you choose? In choosing your family (Satan or God) indicates whether or not we will live in the flesh and be controlled by Satan or live in the Spirit and be controlled by God. This is because a life of Satan represents a fleshly desire which is contrary to God and His Spirit. The works of the flesh is about self and will go to any lengths to achieve and or satisfy the flesh whereas the works of the Spirit emulates the love of God and His humility shines through in all that we as believers do.

It is noteworthy to be reminded of the scripture which states that persons who live in the flesh "shall not inherit the kingdom of God". This is because to live in the flesh says we have rejected the goodness of God and the atoning work of Jesus Christ. Let's take a comparative look at of some the character traits from living in the flesh compared to living in the Spirit.

    A. "Adultery" is the sexual activity outside of the marriage union whereas people' living in the Spirit of God value and honor the consecrated institution of marriage as it was instituted by God Himself. Temperance is on display as one masters his or her desires in regards to marriage.

    B. "Uncleanness" and "lasciviousness" is ones passions and desires to the point there is no shame in his or her public conduct. Whereas persons living in the Spirit of God is mindful of his or her conduct as him or her is representing

God and His righteousness must be manifested in our lives daily.
C. "Wrath" is an explosive anger that explodes in some type of violence in either words or deeds, whereas the "gentleness" of God is shines through not wanting to hurt anyone. Longsuffering is also on display because it means being slow to anger as this too represents God.
D. "Strife" is the divisiveness among people or congregations whereas the peace and love of God is the order of the day as there is no strife in God and His people. *This is because God is a God of peace.*

It can be concluded then that a life of the flesh is one of death and destruction whereas the life of Christ is one eternal to the heaven; one that will live forever depicting all the character traits of our heavenly Father.

Choose a life of the Spirit and inherit the kingdom of heaven. God has left the Holy Spirit to help us resist our fleshy desires.

Regenerated To Love: 1 John 4:7

Beloved, let us love one another; for love is of God; and every one that loveth is born of God, and knoweth God.

In our scripture text John is exhorting us love one another as God is love and all who are in Christ is born of God as love is one of the fruits of the Spirit (Galatians 5:22). As all believers show their love is evidence of his or her rebirth. Developing a love everybody relationship is the believer's responsibility and is accomplished with the aid of the Holy Spirit. This love is the care, goodwill and help to those persons in need as God is very concerned for the needy as He made provisions for all as well the needy. **God's love at work!**

If the question were raised, Why are we as believers commanded to love everybody? Three reasons come to mind, which are (a) God is love and it is His very nature (vv 7-9) and He showed His love by giving His Son Jesus to die on the cross for the sins of the world. As believers we share in God's loving nature. (b) The nature of God being love we share in His forgiveness, His love and acts of kindness toward others. (c) Verse 12 provides the third reason of loving everybody, which states in part, "If we love one another, God dwelleth in us, and his love is perfected in us." *What perfection!*

Through our rebirth, God's love is manifested in us.

Commanded To Love: 1 John 4:11

Beloved, if God so loved us, we ought also to love one another.

Yesterday John encouraged all believers to love one another, but in today's scripture he is commanding us to love one another because of the love God shown to mankind. It was God's inescapable love that He gave His only begotten Son to die on the cross for mankind bridging the spiritual divide that existed between man and God, the Father. Who would have shown any greater love than that of the Father that He would give His best and all for sinful man and then who would be born with the sole purpose of dying on the cross as man's propitiator? Lastly, who would give part of Himself to live inside of each believer as our guide to keep us safe and from falling to the temptation of Satan and sin? Only the Godhead, God the Father, God the Son and God the Holy Spirit all working in harmony for His beloved creation--man would display such love.

Given the magnitude of God's love is the motivation behind John's command and Jesus issued the love command Himself; with the fact that God loved man while he was enemies with God. With that being said then if we as believers fail to love one another, we are being disobedient to Christ's command.

Reciprocate love to God, others, and then self. Love! Love!

Converted To Season And Light the World: Matthew 5:13-14

Ye are the salt of the earth; but if the salt have lost his savour, wherewith shall it be salted? It is thenceforth good for nothing; but to be cast out, and to be trodden under foot of men. Ye are the light of the world. A city that is set on a hill cannot be hid.-

Jesus in His many parabolic teachings used every day commodities and or situations to make His point clear to His audience. In this scenario, Jesus uses salt and light to make His point of believers being the salt of the earth which are commissioned to spread the good news of the gospel of Christ to others the world over. The analogy is that salt is used for seasoning food to give flavor; whereas sharing the gospel of Christ we as believers are seasoning the world so that the unsaved may be saved. Another point is that if we failed to spread the gospel, then we become useless and the world will cast us aside and walk (trodden) over us as just another person residing in this sinful world. It is noteworthy to say that for believers to remain seasonable we must remain in fellowship with God.

Regarding the city setting on a hill is believers letting their light shine brightly for Christ in words and deeds. Believers are light in a sin darkened world reflecting the brightness of God's glory.

Salt and light are precious commodities represented by all believers.

Commissioned To Preach And Teach Christ: Matthew 28:19-20

Go ye therefore, and teach all nations, baptizing them in the name of the Father, and of the Son, and of the Holy Ghost. Teaching them to observe all things whatsoever I have commanded you, and lo, I am with you always, even unto the end of the world.

Believers are not saved just to keep his and her encounter with Jesus him or herself. Believers are saved to share this glorious encounter with everyone beginning in his or her respective Jerusalem, Judea, and Samaria and then to the uttermost parts of the world.

Obeying the Great Commission is an individual responsibility of each believer as well as being the goal and mission of the church. This is known as soul winning for Christ.

What are believers to teach and preach? Believers' message is "the repentance and remission of sin (forgiveness)" (Luke 24:47), which carries the promise of receiving "the gift of the Holy Spirit" (Acts 2:38). All believers are encouraged to separate his or herself from the world (Acts 2:40). This is to be done as we wait for Christ's return (Acts 3:19; 1 Thessalonians 1:10).

What is the purpose of preaching and teaching Christ? The purpose is to make disciples so they too can make other disciples thus furthering the kingdom of God. There is a difference in adding to the church role and in making a disciple. Disciples are students of Christ who have dedicated his or herself to Christ and His message and are sharing this message with all.

Believers are commissioned-obey.

Day 14

Created In His Image: Genesis 1:27; 2:7

So God created man in his own image, in the image of God created he him; male and female created he them. And the LORD God formed man of the dust of the ground, and breathed into his nostrils the breath of life; and man became a living soul.

Looking at the creation process we find that man was the last to be created by God and what is most important is that man is created in the image of God. With that being said begs the question, what is the image of God? God is a person Being though infinite, eternal and a self-existent. God is a personal Being who caused everything that ever existed and will exist. God has no beginning and no ending, and He is revealed as a moral Being who created all that is good and without sin.

God's attributes has two categories which are unique and moral. The unique attributes of God are He is omniscient, He is omnipotent, He is transcendent, He is unchangeable, He is eternal, He is perfect and holy, and He is triune, which means He exists as three persons in one. There are moral attributes of God which makes Him superior to any other god. His moral attributes are He is good, love, merciful and gracious, compassionate, He is longsuffering, He is truth, faithful and just. Man being created in the image of God has the ability to exhibit the moral attributes of God as He put part of Himself into man.

Man is three in one-body, soul and spirit-the triune God, the Father, Son and Holy Spirit.

Day 15

New Creatures In Christ: 2 Corinthians 5:17

...If any man be in Christ, he is a new creature; old things are past away, behold all things are become new.

How do believers become new creatures in Christ? Believers become new creatures in Christ by accepting Jesus Christ in faith and the creative command of God the Father (4:6) have been made new and now totally belong to God and His world which is ruled by His Spirit. Romans 8:6 states that "to be carnally minded is death and those with spiritual minds is life and peace." This peace is the peace of God which rules supreme. Also, being born new creatures in Christ allows believers to walk in the spirit as opposed to that of the flesh (Galatians 5:25).

The blessing of becoming a new creature in Christ is that all believers become new persons (Galatians 6:15) renewed in the image of God so that we may share in His glory as well as a renewed knowledge and understanding of Him to that we as believers can live a life of holiness (Ephesians 4:24).

If the question were raised, How did this come to be? God has reconciled us to Himself by Jesus Christ (v 18) who was made sin so "that we may be made the righteous of God in Him" (v 21). This was accomplished on the cross at Calvary. *What a righteous Lord!*

Being new creatures in Christ, believers become ambassadors for Christ (v. 20) as all believers are to continue His work.

A Life Of Holiness: Ephesians 4:24

And that ye put on the new man, which after God is created in righteousness and true holiness.

In today's discussion let us define two words from our scripture text, "righteousness" and "true holiness" to give a glimpse of the life of believers. The Student Bible Dictionary defines righteousness (P.203) as the "rightness of God's standards, justice and fairness (Isaiah 41: 10; 2 Corinthians 5:21)". It further talks about man matching his life with that of God's commandments, God's love, and purposes for man's life. Man's actions should be based on his love for God and his relationship with God. God's love is agape love and God wants an intimate relationship with man.

How does man establish an intimate relationship with God? This can be established through daily scripture reading and meditating on His Word as well as having a meaningful prayer life; one that is based on faith, honesty and sincerity.

Let's look at "holiness" which refers to "the pure, loving nature of God", as this is one of His attributes (Zondervan's Pictorial Bible Dictionary (P.357)). As believers live a life of holiness we too become separated from evil and the world with the aid of the Holy Spirit. It is noteworthy to say that all holiness originates with God; therefore, all believers are to live holy lives as members of God's family. Believers are set aside as "a chosen generation, a royal priesthood, a holy nation, and a peculiar people" (1 Peter 2:9).

Why are believers set apart for such royalty? Believers collectively as a holy nation are set apart for God and His kingdom to proclaim the gospel message of salvation (Isaiah 42:1). As God is holy so are believers. Through Christ's atoning death all believers have been a priest before God (Revelation 1:6; 5:10; 20:6) and believers can come boldly to the throne of God. believers being of the royal priesthood have the obligation to live holy lives (vv 5,9; 1:14-17) as well as offering they bodies as living sacrifices unto God (Romans 12:1-2). Believers are to make intercessory prayer for others as Christ is our intercessor. Lastly, believers are to declare the Word of God as believers are commanded to do so in Matthew 28:19-20. It is noteworthy to say that believers are set apart for such royalty to tell the world that we are members of God's family and our life standards are what we live by.

Believers can live a life of holiness with the aid of the Holy Spirit who resides in each of us. However, believers must yield to the leadings of the Holy Spirit who is the third person in the Godhead. His role in the lives of all believers is to guide, teach, lead and protect.

It can be concluded then that a life of holiness is one of right standings with God as all believers are dedicated to living according to God's will and ways.

Day 17

Believers Reconciled To Christ: 2 Corinthians 5:18

And all things are of God, who hath reconciled us to himself by Jesus Christ, and hath given to us the ministry of reconciliation.

The term "reconcile or reconciliation" means to bring something into balance. In regards to believers we have been brought into balance with God through the atoning works of Christ at the cross. The need for reconciliation was made necessary by the disobedience of Adam which caused a spiritual divide and the once harmonious fellowship between God and man was broken. Christ's death restored man's fellowship with God the Father. Man now has a renewed fellowship with God (Matthew 5:24; 1 Corinthians 7:11) and from this reconciliation we have unity as all believers can operate/live and minister according to God's holy Word and will.

What is a ministry of reconciliation? Having a renewed fellowship with God we now can minister/tell the unsaved what God has done in our lives and the blessings received from being in harmony with God. In the words of a song by the William Brothers, "Tell somebody about the goodness of the Lord." With full knowledge of what God through His Son Jesus Christ has done in the reconciling process is worthy of a continuous testimony of praise and worship.

Think of this as a check register, what's in the bank should equal what's in our check registers.

Believers are no longer alienated/out of balance with God for we have been reconciled.

Day 18

Born Into Righteousness: 2 Corinthians 5:21

For he hath made him to be sin for us, who knew no sin, that we might be made the righteousness of God in him.

Let us look at the characters in this verse as it will tell us who did what for whom and why each action was done. The "he" in this verse is God Himself who gave His only Son Jesus Christ with the sole purpose of dying on the cross for man's sins. Jesus is the "him" as it is well documented that Christ remained sinless because He was God in the second person and could not sin as He was both God and man. It was through Christ's death on the cross that mankind was made right/justified with God. When God looks at man He sees the righteousness of His Son.

It goes without saying that in order to be made right with God; we must accept Christ's work of salvation and believe that He is God's Son. In doing so all believers are no longer in the sinful state of alienation but are born into the righteousness of God where we are no longer an enemy of God but a family member.

Being born into righteousness brings justification, sanctification, regeneration and salvation; all because God reached out to humanity because of His love.

Thank You Lord for Your love, grace and mercy, I am now in a right relationship with You. Amen.

Day 19

Saved To Eternal Life: John 3:16-17

For God so loved the world that he gave his only begotten Son, that whosoever believeth on him should not perish, but have everlasting life. For God sent not his Son into the world to condemn the world, but that the world through him might be saved.

John 3:16 reveals the heart of God as it provides the reason for His action. The word "love" gets to the very core of God as He is love and His love encompasses everyone with the term "whosoever". God's love is so deep that it is His desire that all mankind be saved from eternal damnation.

The "whosoever" is not limited to a certain race, gender, social status, creed, or religious affiliation. This encompasses the phrase "come as you are"; it matters not your condition because all mankind was once destined to perish through the condemnation that sin brings. **Thank God for Jesus!**

In God's declaration that all mankind be saved He issued some assured promised/guarantees, and they are (a) "gave" which means no one forced God's hand in this action He willingly provided His Son as the sacrificial lamb. (b) "Believe" man must believe that Christ is God's Son and accept Him as such and Savior. (c) "Should not perish" this gives all who believe and accept an assurance of where their final resting place will be--heaven. (d) "Everlasting life" this is another assurance that all believers will spend eternity with God and will live forever. **What an assurance!**

Christ came for our salvation (v. 17).

Day 20

Born To Serve: Deuteronomy 11:13

And it shall come to pass, if you shall hearken diligently unto my commandments which I command you this day, to love the Lord your God, and to serve him with all your heart and with all your soul,

All month our discussion topics have been centered on a rebirth and a new creature in Christ, therefore, as believers are born into the family of God we become His servants. Being servants of God, believers are to carry the gospel message into the entire world as well as serve the needs of others just as Christ Jesus did during His earthly ministry. Jesus always met the earthly needs of those He encountered so He could meet their spiritual needs. We as believers are to do likewise as all believers are God's workman left here on earth to carry on His kingdom building ministry.

Believers are to view our respective ministries as a promotion from God to serve others and not to be served, neither expecting self-aggrandizement. True servantship is an honored but humble position while being ever so mindful of who is to get the glory from our service. Jesus Christ is our perfect example of being a servant and serving all to the glory of God. Jesus washing His disciples' feet was to provide a visual example of what being a servant is to look like.

Believers are born to serve even if it means suffering through persecutions, trials and tribulations, because Christ is our perfect example who suffered much at the hands of man whom He came to save.

Christ served through it all, so must we.

Day 21

Born Into A New Community: John 4:31-42

...many of the Samaritans of that city believed on him for the saying of the woman, which testified, He told me all that ever I did...when the Samaritans were come unto him, they besought him that he would tarry with them; and he abode there two days. And many more believed because of his own words.

From the Samaritan woman's encounter with Jesus, she became a believer in Him and through her testimony a whole town was saved. As more of the towns' people came and heard Jesus expound on the Word of God, more souls were saved. What is represented is that there is power in the "Word". Look at Paul when he encountered Jesus on the Damascus Road his life was changed forever. Paul's life mission changed from persecuting the church to saving souls for Christ and His church. Whatever situation Paul found himself in he never ceased to preach Christ; the Roman jailer was saved through Paul's preaching Christ.

Encounters with Jesus lives are changed forever, as well as when the gospel is preached and or taught souls are saved. The two depictions of Jesus encounters resulted in new communities of Christian believers being formed all to the glory of God. As God's Word is shared with others, new communities continue to be formed. The new converts are born into a new community of faithful believers- -*God's family united in love.*

Join Christ's community and share in His love.

Believers Righteousness And Faithfulness: Isaiah 11:5

...Righteousness shall be the girdle of his loins, and faithfulness shall be the girdle of his reins.

What is the meaning of this verse? The NIV version of this verse reads as follows, "Righteousness will be his belt and faithfulness is the sash around his waist." The true meaning of this verse is that righteousness and faithful are integral qualities of the Messiah--Jesus Christ and all leaders/believe as believers are to follow the foot steps of Christ. From Christ's earthly ministry He maintained both qualities to the end as He was God in the flesh. Believers have the indwelling Holy Spirit who is God to aid in our efforts to remain righteous and faithful as we are children of God and are to represent His holiness at all times. It is God's righteousness that all believers are judged and are encouraged to persevere in faith to the end as this equates to a long distant runner.

It is noteworthy to say that all believers are the light of the world and it is His holiness and righteous standard that the world will see of Him reflected in us. Also, believers are called out of darkness into light of righteousness to be the living Bible (God's Word) for the world to read. Collectively, believers are the bright city that is set upon a hill that cannot be smothered by the darkness of sin.

Righteousness and faithfulness are must have qualities for all believers.

Day 23

Hope And Faithfulness: Lamentations 3:22-26

It is of the Lord's mercies that we are not consumed, because his compassions fail not. They are new every morning; great is thy faithfulness. The Lord is my portion, saith my soul; therefore, will I hope in him. The Lord is good unto them that wait for him, to the soul that seeketh him. It is good that a man should both hope and quietly wait for the salvation of the Lord.

The prophet Jeremiah's writing may have been to the nation of Israel during their time of captivity, but the phrase "It is of the Lord's mercies that we are not consumed", speaks volume to today's society and believers in that we are to be grateful for the Lord's mercies, because they are witnessed daily. It has been well documented of God's longsuffering and mercy for mankind. This is because man does not deserve saving or a Savior, but through God's loving compassion and mercy He provided a Savior--Jesus Christ. Justice demanded that man be consumed by the wages of sin-death (Romans 6: 23); through His love and faithfulness to all humanity mercy prevailed.

Through the mercies of God man has three reasons to be hopeful and they are (a) God's anger lasts only a short time, but His love is everlasting. (b) God has not and did not reject His covenant people (Israel and all who believe) for God has a purpose for mankind. (c) God is good when He is forced to punish His people to bring about His purpose and His goodness is witnessed by all who wait upon Him in humility.

In the midst of trouble and calamities what can be said for God's presence? Psalm 46:1 states that "God is our refuge and strength, a very present help in trouble." This verse supports verse 24 which states in part "Lord is our portion", which is to be believed with our very souls. The phrase means that the Lord's help is enough and with the His help there is no need for anybody else. **What must we as believers do?** The question can be answered in two parts; **(1)** "Be still and know that God is God" (Psalm 46:10) and He will fight your battles. **What did Paul say?** "But my God shall supply all my needs." Whatever your needs are they will be met by God. If you need deliverance He is a deliverer, if you need a comforter, He is a comforter, if you need a Savior, He provided His Son. The "all" is complete just as the "whosoever" in John 3:16. (2) Part two of our question is that all believers must remain faithful to God and His Word and know that He cares. He asks mankind to "cast all your cares upon Him"(1 Peter 5:7). Then we must remain hopeful in God. Why? Because great is thy faithfulness--God's and hope in God is never in vain or wishful thinking.

Hope in God is a sure thing.

Day 24

Faithless And Unsaved: Matthew 17:17

...Jesus said...O faithless and perverse generation, how long shall I be with you? How long shall I suffer you? Bring him hither to me.

In this setting Jesus is assessing the state of His disciples and churches who fail to minister and or tell others about the saving power of God's Word and His kingdom. All those who are in the body of Christ and fail to minister/tell others about God will be chasten with many stripes, but when the unsaved are told and they fail to listen then they will be whipped/chastened with a few stripes. It is the mission of the church to win souls for Christ which adds to God's kingdom.

Another point of view is that failure to teach and preach is a failure to deliver the unsaved from the demonic powers of Satan and his followers and it speaks to a lack of faith in the power of God's Word.

Verse 20 speaks of the impossibilities for all who have true faith. Christ's disciples (all believers) have the power to cast out demons with the power of the Holy Spirit and faith. Acts 1:8 talks of the power given to believers after the Holy Ghost has come upon them. There will an endowment of the Holy Spirit to perform "many" miracles, signs and wonders.

The faithless includes both the saved and unsaved because the saved must operate in faith in order to testify to the unsaved of God's amazing grace which He freely gives to all who believe.

Faith is essential to our belief.

Day 25

Be Converted: Matthew 18:3

...Verily I say unto you, Except ye be convert, and become as little children, ye shall not enter into the kingdom of heaven.

What is the meaning of this verse? The central theme is humility, because Jesus was outlining the requirements to gain entry into heaven. The term "converted" means to change and the change Jesus is speaking of is that one must be of a humble spirit as little children are humble, they are unpretentious. Whereas grown ups have the attitude and you cannot teach and or tell them anything. Little children are teachable and dependent upon their parents for all their needs to be met. The same principle applies for adults, because God our heavenly Father provides all our needs both directly and indirectly.

The question now becomes, **What is the conversion process?** Conversion process incorporates a change of heart (repentance) one that is dedicated to totally and obediently following Christ. Conversion is an outward human expression of response to God's gift of salvation and this is accomplished through the power of the Holy Spirit and is received through faith in Jesus Christ. Also, conversion involves our relationship with God as believers are no longer enemies with God, but are now adopted into His family. Conversion brings about a change in a person's habit, commitments as his or her entire view of life is different.

Conversion is essential to faith as it the basis of ones salvation. What a change!

Day 26

Stumbling Blocks Removed: Isaiah 57:14

....Cast ye up, cast ye up, prepare the way; take up the stumbling block out of the way of my people.

What is a stumbling block? According to Zondervan's Pictorial Bible Dictionary (P. 813) "the term "stumbling block" is referring to anything that causes a person to trip or fall. In a figurative sense it means a cause of material or spiritual ruin." It was Israel's idolatry and iniquities that were stumbling blocks to her. Ezekiel 14:3 and 4 supports the figurative definitions for stumbling blocks as the nation of Israel was guilty of idolatry in their hearts and was not loyal or committed to God. God being a jealous God and when other gods are placed before the one and true God He will withhold His blessings and or refuse to guide or answer prayers. This is what happened to Israel. An idol is anything that takes precedence before God. This was common during Israel's early history and is prevalent in today's society because man will attend a Sunday sporting event or participate in other events before attending church and worshipping God.

Jeremiah 18:15 talks about God's people turning aside from Him and the activities that caused some to walk in ways not pleasing to God. In Romans 14:13 Paul urged Christians to be mindful of being a stumbling block our Christian brothers and sisters. We as true believers in Christ are to be mindful of how we judge, correct and or address the issues/concerns of our brothers and sisters, because if done without love can become a stumbling block.

Love for God and others removes all stumbling blocks.

Contrite Heart And Humble Spirit: Isaiah 57:15

For thus saith the high and lofty One that inhabiteth eternity, whose name is Holy; I dwell in the high and holy place, with him also that is of a contrite and humble spirit, to revive the spirit of the humble, and to revive the heart of the contrite ones.

A contrite heart is one that is sorry for the sins committed by the person and humility is the freedom from pride. A humble person is one who has the right view of self, God and others; in other words a person who has put things in perspective.

With that being said, a contrite heart is to recognize that I am a sinner and am in need of a Savior and God through His Son Jesus Christ is the only who can and will save anyone who comes to Him with a humble spirit. Scripture tells us that if we believe in our hearts and confess with our mouth then we shall be saved (Romans 10:9-10), because "with the heart man believeth unto righteousness" (v 10).

Another point on having a contrite heart and a humble spirit is that believers can be sorryful for the oppressions and or sins of others and will cry out to God for deliverance. God hears the cries of the righteous and will respond with mercy and in love.

To the unsaved, have a contrite heart and be humble in your spirit, for the saved be sorryful for the sins of others and pray--God hears.

Seek The Lord: Isaiah 58:1-2

Cry aloud, spare not, lift up thy voice like a trumpet, and shew, my people their transgression, and the house of Jacob their sins. Yet they seek me daily, and delight to know my ways, as a nation that did righteousness, and forsook not the ordinance of their God; they ask of me the ordinance of justice, they take delight in approaching to God.

What is happening in this scenario? The prophet Isaiah was crying out against the sins of the nation of Israel because of their transgressions and hypocrisy against God. Isaiah being a true prophet of God was genuinely concerned for the people's spiritual welfare as they were only pretending to follow God and His ways.

Verse 2 makes it plain the hypocritical actions of the people of Israel as they would seek out the Lord daily in prayer and worship, but the sincerity required was omitted as the people continued in their sinful ways. From all outward appearances their worship appeared genuine, but judging from their lifestyles they continued to live indifference to God's ways and will. This kind of action is lacking true repentance and a humble spirit and a contrite heart. Hypocritical worship is an insult to and an abomination to God and punishment is sure to follow for such actions.

What does this say for today's society truly seeking God? To truly seek God and worship Him with sincere praise and daily Bible reading, then a change is manifested in ones daily lives.

Seek the Lord with sincerity.

The Breastplate Of Righteousness: Isaiah 59:17-18

For he put on righteousness as a breastplate, and a helmet of salvation upon his head; and he put on the garments of vengeance for clothing, and was clad with zeal as a cloke.

Who is the "he" in this text? The "he" is Jesus Christ who would come to earth with a specific mission as He met all the necessary requirements to fulfill His mission that God required.

The prophet Isaiah describes Jesus' dress as He would be clothed with two important pieces of clothing that all believers are to wear, and they are the breastplate of righteousness which is the righteousness of God because Jesus is God. It is His righteousness that all humanity will be judged. Salvation was worn as Christ's helmet just as it is to be worn by all believers. A helmet is a head covering that is worn to protect our head from injury; the injury in this scenario is the fiery darts of Satan and his warriors. Another point on the helmet of salvation is the full knowledge of God, which Jesus knew because of who He is. Jesus dressed Himself in vengeance because sin had to be dealt with on a permanent basis. In the end times sin and all who continuously commit sin will be punished with the wrath of God. In Jesus eagerness to fulfill His Father's mission of brining salvation to all who believe and punishing the wicked at the end time (Revelation 19). He was clothed in the zeal of a cloke.

Your reward or punishment is assured by God Himself.

The Redeemed: Isaiah 52:3

....Ye have sold yourselves for nought, and ye shall be redeemed without money.

This is a powerful statement being made by the Lord as it speaks to the issue of sin and its magnitude, because it costs nothing to commit sin, but its consequences are great. The beautiful part about sin is that all who sin have the opportunity for deliverance by one who loves mankind so much that it costs humanity nothing, but it cost God the Father His Son and Christ His life.

God used the nation of Israel in delivering them from their captivity to show the world just what He will do because of His love for all mankind. An analogy of our text is that God told Israel "just because you have sinned, you do not have to remain in sin. Get up put on the garment of righteousness because I am your redeemer. You do not have to remain a captive to Satan and his lies, learn of me and know the truth as I am here to set free the captives-Israel."

These prophesy not only applies to Israel during their day of captivity, but to future generations when Christ our Redeemer would come and set free the captives from the bondage of sin. The redeemed would become free from sin and delivered into a life of righteousness and holy living. *What a beautiful transformation!*

What is our role in the redeeming process? It is simple, just say "Lord I have sinned before thee, forgive me of my sins." Accept Jesus as Lord and Savior, you shall be saved. **What a Savior!** Faith is at the core of this process.

The question now becomes **who are the Redeemed**? They are all persons who have confessed his or her sins and believed within his or her heart as each have been bought with the price of Jesus' blood at Calvary's cross.

Now that we know who the redeemed are, there are benefits from being redeemed, and they are (a) the redeemed become regenerated (born again) persons, (b) the redeemed are sanctified, justified, and saved by the blood of Jesus. (c) The redeemed have been

assured of their salvation by the indwelling Holy Spirit who serves as all believers' guide and sealer. (d) The redeemed will spend eternity with God and will be spared His wrath during the end-time judgment. (e) The redeemed will return with Christ and will rein with Him in the New Jerusalem. (f) The redeemed will have been given a crown of life, golden slippers, and white robes to wear as there will be no more tears, sorrows, pain and suffering as all things as we know it today will have been done away with. Lastly, the redeemed shall participate in one long heavenly feast of praise and worship where money is no good at this feast.
The redeemed of the Lord shall live forever.

Day 31

Their Redeemer: Proverbs 23:11

For their Redeemer is mighty, He shall plead their cause with thee.

The Redeemer in this case is Jesus Christ Himself as He is the perfect propitiator for the sins of man. "Their" in this text are all believers who have accepted the atoning work of Christ as all who believe have been bought with a price--the blood of Jesus Christ. This gives Him the blood bought right to be man's Redeemer.

The love of God through His Son Jesus has reconciled man back to God the Father and restored the broken fellowship that exist due to sin. Jesus our Redeemer having the powers that He does pleads our case before God as he took on our sin stains and presents us faulty before God. Jesus knew that His Father cannot look on or tolerate sin so He-Jesus makes intercessions for us and hides us behind His righteousness. Therefore, we as believers are seen as righteous in the eye sight of God (thee).

Questions, Isn't it a blessing to have a heavenly Father who is mindful of man that He would make such a sacrifice? Isn't our Redeemer worthy of all praises and honor for His work in our redemption process? Thank God for the Holy Spirit who once believers are redeemed keeps believers in fellowship with the Father. Just look as God and His love for man; the Triune God working together in unity in man's redemption.

Hallelujah, Hallelujah praises His holy name.

New Converts In The New Community

Feeding New Believers: 1 Peter 2:2-3

As newborn babes, desire the sincere milk of the word, that ye may grow thereby; If so be ye have tasted that the Lord is gracious.

The apostle Peter is using an analogy of newborn babies desiring milk as his or her food so the baby will grow, and with this growth the new convert will and can digest solid food. This applies to newborn believers in Christ. A new believer in Christ is considered a babe in Christ and is eager for the Word of God because his or her spiritual thirst must be given in regular intervals just as you feed a newborn to aid in his or her physical growth. Case in point, when a child begins Church School they are taught with pictures corresponding with scripture that the child understands; as the child grows so does these lessons.

While feeding the new convert, the baby must be fed the truth regarding the Word of God, which includes faith, humility, obedience to God's Word and trusting God for all his or her needs and to cast all cares and worries on God (1 Peter 5:7). **Why are these teachings necessary?** Total dependence on God is necessary to prevent the new convert from becoming weighted down with the cares, riches and pleasures of this life (Luke 8:14) as this will prevent the new convert from bearing fruit for Christ as he/she grows in Christ.

Feeding new convert/believers the truth of God's Word is essential.

Feb 2

Growth Of The New Believer: Ephesians 4:15

...Speaking the truth in love, may grow up into him in all things, which is the head, even Christ.

Yesterday we discussed feeding newborn babes in Christ; today we want to focus on the growth of the newborn and what constitute that growth. Truth is essential in feeding a newborn babe in Christ, but it must be done in love as we adult believers are to emulate the love of God in all that we do. This includes the nurture of newborns in Christ, which encompasses our words and lifestyle.

Many times while a new convert is growing in Christ the world will place many tempting lures to prevent his or her growth, but it is our, the seasoned converts responsibility is to lovingly correct the new convert using scripture to support our teachings. New babes in Christ as well as seasoned converts are to remain faithful to scripture even if it means separating oneself from love ones and or Christian institutions that are failing to hold fast to the Word of God and its truths. An important message for new convert/believers is that we "walk by faith and not by sight" (2 Corinthians 5:7), as faith is the key to ones accepting Jesus Christ as Lord and Savior. Hebrews 11:1 states that faith "is the substance of things hoped for, the evidence of things not seen." Faith can be termed as believing the impossible, seeing the invisible and thinking the unthinkable.

Faith is essential to a believer's growth undergirded by love.

Feed God's People: Psalm 28:9

Save thy people, and bless thine inheritance; feed them also, and lift them up for ever.

Our scripture makes a profound statement with regards to Christian leaders feeding the people of God as they are God's spokes persons. Many of the OT prophets spoke directly to God's people saying "what thus saith the Lord". This theme is carried over into the NT as God has chosen His spokes persons to continue sharing His Word with all who will hear and adhere. Ephesians 4:11 outlines the ministerial leadership Christ left for His church so that His people can continue to be fed for their salvation. It is noteworthy to say that all leaders who are feeding the people of God through imparting His Word there is growth in Christ's church--His body.

Feeding God's people gives growth to the kingdom of God as it is His desire that all mankind be saved, though many will be lost for one reason or the other, but is His spokes people's responsibility to diligently proclaim God's Word. Being obedient in proclaiming God's Word new converts will be added to the church daily.

God's Word serves as a lamp to the feet (life) of all humanity as it lights our way in a sin darkened world. All believers are to share God's Word whether in leadership or laity as we all has a story to tell.

When Christ is missing from ones life there is a constant hunger and thirst and a feeling of being unsatisfied; spiritual food is needed.

Growth Of The Righteous: Psalm 92:12

The righteous shall flourish like the palm tree; he shall grow like a cedar in Lebanon.

Our scripture text talks about the growth of believers which is the result of God's goodness and for that all believers are to express an attitude of gratefulness.

The analogy used in our scripture text is comparing the growth and boldness of the palm tree to that of righteous growth of believers and the spread of the gospel of Christ overall. Believers grow in the righteousness of Christ with holy living in total obedience to Him, reading, studying God's Word and meditating on His Word. As believers grow spiritually so does the Christian Community and this growth bears fruit even in the believer's old age (v.14).

It is noteworthy to say that both the cedar and the palm tree represent strength, steadfastness as their roots are planted firmly in the soil as they do not bend or sway with every strong wind. On the spiritual plane, believers who are firmly planted in the Word of God and remain faithful to Him and His mission are viewed as cedars and palm trees. As these believers are not tossed to and fro by every wind or doctrine that appear on the scene. Just as there were false doctrines during Biblical times, they exist today.

Who are the Righteous? They are believers who have been washed in the blood of Jesus and have been made right (justified) with God.

Be right and grow in His righteousness.

Feb 5

Beauty Of God's Messengers: Hosea 14:5-6

I will be the dew unto Israel; he shall grow as the lily, and cast forth his roots as Lebanon. His branches shall spread, and his beauty shall be as the olive tree, and his smell as Lebanon.

Here again the prophet Hosea uses poetry in his analogy of presenting his message to God's people Israel to repent. Repentance was necessary because the nation of Israel had turned away from God and His punishment had come down upon them. But in His mercifulness He promises to love them freely if they return to Him and stopped their backsliding (v.4).

Verse 5-6 express God's love for His people and the beauty of their lifestyles will be once restored. Dew is wet moisture that appears in minute droplets, but it resembles purity, freshness or the power to refresh (Merriam-Webster Dictionary P. 244). Through the Holy Spirit, God will refresh Israel and all believers to purity each morning and with the refreshing Holy Spirit residing each believer has the opportunity to grow into a lovely branch of God Himself as all believers have been covered with the red blood of Jesus Christ (red flower of the lily).

Lebanon is symbolized as both beauty and strength designed by God Himself and the olive tree served several purposes such as fruit for a family's fat source and the oil from the tree was used in temple lights.

Therefore, God's messengers are sharing the beautiful message of His love for His people. Repent and receive God's blessings.

Feb 6

Growing Into The Image Of God: Ephesians 4:17-29

Having the understanding darkened, being alienated from the life of God through the ignorance that is in them, because of the blindness of their heart. Be renewed in the spirit of your mind; and that ye put on the new man, which after God is created in righteousness and true holiness.

If the question were raised, **How does one grow into the image of God?** The best answer is the repentance process by first admitting that he or she is a sinner, then confess his or her sins and lastly turn away from the old way of life to that of Christ. Growing into the image of God requires humility, faith, steadfastness, obedience to God's Word and a willingness to live according to His holy standards.

Our scripture text outlines the differences of a life alienated from God and a new life in Christ. In the old man all manner of sin is committed, but when Christ is preached and the gospel messages take root in the heart of the hearer a change occurs. Where the devil once ruled the unbeliever's life is now replaced with the love and peace of God. Where taking from others is now replaced with giving to all those in need. The old man-the sinner who once lived in a community of sinners is now part of the Christian Community (believers).

Verses 22 and 23 sums up the process of what one must do to grow into the image of God, which states the unbeliever must put off the old man and clothe him or herself with a renewed spirit in his or her mind.

Romans 12:2 talks about Christian conduct which is believers' lifestyle by encouraging all to "be not conformed to this world but be ye transformed by the renewing of your mind, that ye may prove what is that good, and acceptable, and perfect will of God." Believers cannot grow into the image of God by remaining in love with the world and its systems. Even though believers are left here in the world but remain separated from the world as this sinful world hinders our spiritual growth and walk with God. Once a convert accepts Jesus as

Lord and Savior he or she becomes part of God's family. The person then become a set aside people, a holy nation and a royal priesthood because believers are a chosen generation (1 Peter 2:9).

To remain in royalty, Ephesians 6:11-18 outlines all believers' suit of armour when properly dressed will keep all believers from falling prey to Satan's temptation. Also, believers are to yield to the voice of the Holy Spirit as He resides in each believer guiding and directing our path as we travel this heavenly journey. Believers are encouraged to commune daily with God through prayer and scripture reading. This develops the believers' relationship with God as He wants a close fellowship with His children. The more believers walk and talk with God we grow more like Him.

A closer walk with thee O Lord is what I desire so Your image the world will see.

Servants In The Faith Community: Matthew 20:17-18

Behold, we go up to Jerusalem; and the Son of man shall be betrayed unto the chief priests and unto the scribes, and they shall condemn him to death.

The setting of today's lesson study takes place with Jesus traveling with His disciples and foretelling His death. Jesus knowing of His eminent date with death, still He served in spite of what lay ahead for Him.

In the Garden of Gethsemane Jesus asked His Father if it was His will to remove the bitter cup, but in obedience to the Will of God, Jesus persevered to the end. The question now becomes, What do Christ's actions say to all believers? Christ is the perfect example of being a true servant and how we as believers are to serve. Believers are to remain committed to the mission that God has given each of us. Christ remained committed to His mission and doing the Will of His Father as expressed when Christ stated "not my will but thy will."

Verses 26-27 we see Jesus explaining to His disciples the meaning of being a true servant, as He came "not to be ministered to but to minister", this He did. Christ is God in the second person who humbled Himself for humanity's sins. **What a servant!**

Believers (servants) do not have to die for others sins, but we die to sin in order to serve God in His kingdom building.

Servants serve in spite of obstacles.

Feb 8

Serving Christ In Humility: Philippians 2:1-11

..Made himself of no reputation, and took upon him the form of a servant, and was made in the likeness of men: And being found in fashion as a man, he humbled himself, and became obedient unto death, even the death of the cross.

Looking at the word "Christian" it means being Christ-like, which carries a deeper meaning than just following Christ or belonging to the Christian Community. Being a Christian means that all believers have taken on all the characteristics of Christ and is now dedicated to serving Him in total humility just as He served His Father in humility.

Verse 7 makes a profound statement on humility and how Christ served as He is the Son of God who in His own right was worthy of all reputation, but instead reputation and praises wasn't what He sought. Christ became a servant to save mankind from the sins of the world in doing so He paid the penalty for mankind--**death on the cross**.

If the question was raised, What are some of the characteristics that Christians have to have to be like Christ? Christ-like character is love, faithfulness, humility, no-reputation seeking, obedience, commitment to serving others and witnessing while promoting God's kingdom and all it blessing--**spending eternity with God our creator.**

Christian's serving in humility have the right view of God, self and others, because what comes into play are the first two commandments, loving God first and then others as thyself.

Serve God in humility and He will do the exalting.

Feb 9

Conduct Of The Christian Community: 1 Peter 3:8-22

..Be ye all of one mind, having compassion one of another, love as brethren, be pitiful, be courteous. Not rendering evil for evil, or railing for railing; but contrariwise blessing; knowing that ye should inherit a blessing.

Yesterday's discussion we talked about serving Christ in humility, for today we will focus on the proper conduct for the Christian Community as all believers collectively are to have a conduct that exemplifies Christ. Our lesson text outlines the proper conduct that the Christian Community both individually and collectively should possess. It would be difficult for the world to see Christ in the Christian Community when evil for evil is practiced, while showing no compassion on others. The Christian Community is the city that is set upon the hill for the world to see as it points others to Christ and the blessing that follows.

As a member of the Christian Community we suffer for the good of others and for righteousness' sake or just merely being a Christ follower. Verses 14 and 15 provide the response as it should be, as this is the proper conduct of Christians. **"Sanctify the Lord in your hearts"** provides insight to the reverence and commitment to Christ as Lord of our lives, because as believers we must always be ready to explain his or her faith in God to others-**a personal testimony**.

What conduct does the world see in the Christian Community? Does it resemble Christ's character? Doing good for evil and having compassion on others represents Christ.

Feb 10

Steadfastness In Christ: Colossians 2:5

...am I with you in the spirit, joying and beholding your order, and the steadfastness of your faith in Christ.

Paul's writing to the church as Colossian he expresses his concern and love for the church while encouraging them to remain steadfast in Christ through their faith. Paul's writing to the church at Colosse was to combat the false teaching that was threatening to confuse the minds of the Christians at Colosse. He wanted to make crystal clear that Christ is God's Son, and "to stress the true nature of life in Christ" and the fruitful blessing for believers (KJV). Also, Paul wanted the Colossians to know and remember that Christ is the center of the gospel message and His supremacy in the creation process as He was present during creation as well as Christ being revealed by the OT prophets and NT apostles, His redemption of all who believe in Him and Christ being the head of the church.

With those factors firmly implanted in the minds of the Colossian Christians, Paul encouraged them to remain steadfast in Christ, because in doing so they would be made complete in Him (v. 10).

What does this say for Christians today? Christians today are to possess the same like steadfastness in Christ while maintaining our covenant relationship with Him. Why? This is because Christ is the author and finisher of our faith and without Christ we as believers have no hope for tomorrow.

Remain committed as Christ has committed Himself to us.

Feb 11

Good Stewards In Christ: 1 Peter 4:10-11

As every man hath received the gift, even so minister the same one to another; as good stewards of the manifold grace of God. If any man speak, let him speak as the oracles of God; if any man minister, let him do it as of the ability which God giveth; that God in all things may be glorified through Jesus Christ, to whom be praise and dominion for ever and ever.

What is being said in these two verses? What these two verses are saying to us is that God has given every one of us a gift to minister to the body of Christ in kingdom building. All are ministers in some right according to the gifts given by God as there are different gifts that are to be used to edify the church-Christ's body. Just as no two people are the same neither is our abilities to do what God has called us to do through our gifts; neither is one gift superior to another when given by God. This is because God will receive the glory through His Son Jesus Christ.

Regarding speaking "as the oracles of God" is to speak with authority as divinely revealed by God through the Holy Spirit. Speakers/stewards have nothing to fear because God promised in His word that He would be with you to the end of the world (Matthew 28:20). **So what's to fear?**

Manage (be good stewards over) your gifts because God's grace is sufficient (2 Corinthians 12:9).

God's Grace Is Sufficient: 2 Corinthians 12:9

....My grace is sufficient for thee; for my strength is made perfect in weakness. Most gladly therefore will I rather glory in my infirmities, that the power of Christ may rest upon me.

Grace has been defined as **God's Righteousness At Christ's Expense**, therefore, Christ is ever present in all believers through the Holy Spirit. Let me remind you that Christ is God; therefore God's grace is His presence, favor and power in all believers and is revealed in our weakest moments.

Paul had a condition that he asked God to move when God replied "my grace is sufficient for thee" and it was God's strength that Paul was made perfect. God will do the same for you and I today only if we trust God in every situation. This is because the greater ones weakness and trials the more God's grace is seen to accomplish His will in our lives.

Reflect with me for a moment on God's grace and its sufficiency in our daily lives, He wakes us each morning, causes us to move performing our daily tasks, breathing fresh air and soaking in the rays from the sun that is beneficial for all life substance.

Given the magnitude of God's grace, **What is our response?** "I take pleasure in infirmities, in reproaches, in necessities, in persecutions, in distress for Christ's sake: for when I am weak, then am I strong" (v. 10).

God's strength is all that is needed.

Feb 13

Living By Faith: Romans 1:17

For therein is the righteousness of God revealed from faith to faith; as it is written, The just shall live by faith.

Hebrews 11:1 provides a Biblical definition of faith, but faith is the Christian belief all believers who have accepted Christ as his or her personal Savior and His atoning works on Calvary.

It is ones faith in Jesus Christ in meeting God's requirement for receiving His free gift of salvation which is freely given by God through His Son Jesus Christ. It is ones faith that causes one to believe first that there is a God who loves mankind so much that He would give His best to save humanity from the clutches of sin and redeem man back to Himself. It is faith that causes one to believe that Christ was crucified on the cross at Calvary and on that Sunday morning was raised from the dead by the power of God through the Holy Spirit. It is ones faith that causes him or her to realize that I am a sinner and is in need of saving; repentance comes into play. It is ones faith that causes one to live in total obedience to Christ as Lord and Savior and have personal attachment of devotion and expresses gratitude of love, trust, and loyalty to Him. It is ones faith and steadfastness that cause all believers to persevere to the end. It is ones faith that causes all believers to live in hope of spending eternity with Christ. It is faith that the OT patriarchs believed the promise of God (v 13) and their faith was counted as righteousness. It is through faith that we believe and understand that the world was formed by the Word of God (v 3; Genesis 1:3). As this brings in humanity's intrinsic spiritual understanding and the natural mind is unable to comprehend that the world was formed only God's Word and even believing that there is a God. it is noteworthy to say that the unsaved is failing to believe the Genesis story, neither John 1:1 or 3:16, but the saved believe without a shadow of a doubt that God exists. **He is real!**

Who are the ones living by faith? These are the saved (believers/Christians) that have accepted all the spiritual aspects of

faith and have been made right with God as well as believing the creation story and the Bible and Christ is its center focus. The unsaved must believe in John 3:16, then they too will begin to walk with Christ in faith--the new just. All who live by faith have accepted Christ's shed blood as our atoning sacrifice so when God the Father looks on us He see Christ's righteousness in all believers. Lastly, living by faith is all believers who have an understanding of the true meaning of grace. God gives His grace to the unbeliever so they too can believe in Jesus Christ and live by faith.
    Faith is a powerful component to salvation.

Feb 14

Faith The Key To Salvation: Romans 10:9-10

That is thou shalt confess with thy mouth the Lord Jesus, and shalt believe in thine heart that God hath raised him from the dead, thou shalt be saved. For with the heart man believeth unto righteousness; and with the mouth confession is made unto salvation.

Yesterday we held a lengthy discussion on living by faith and what causes all believers to do so; today's discussion focus on faith as the key to salvation which our lesson text summarizes faith as the essential element to salvation.

Let's revisit why salvation is necessary; it was because all had sinned and come short of the glory of God (Romans 3:23) and humanity's payment for sin was death (Romans 6:23), but through God and His love for humanity provided a free gift which is eternal life. In order to have this eternal life certain steps must be taken as outlined in our text.

Our scripture text carries future implications that one day all will confess that Jesus is Lord and will bow at His feet. Upon accepting Jesus as Lord and Savior is to recognize that God's wrath is promised to all unsaved, which results in being cast into the lake of fire where torment will last forever. Whereas being in the family of God is to be spared God's wrath on judgment day.

With that being said, the question becomes, Where is your faith? All who believe faith have taken center stage.

Have faith, believe and be saved.

Feb 15

Righteousness Of God Revealed By Faith: Romans 3:21-23

...The righteousness of God without the law is manifested, being witnessed by the law and the prophets. Even the righteousness of God which is by faith of Jesus Christ unto all and upon all them that believe; for there is no difference. For all have sinned, and come short of the glory of God.

The term "righteousness" is the rightness of God's standards (2 Corinthians 5:21) which means for man to match his or her standards of living with that of God's out of love for Him, obedient to His commandments, and a willingness to live according to God's purpose. God in His love for humanity willingly gave His Son (Jesus Christ) to be sin for us (2 Corinthians. 21) so that the righteousness of God would be revealed in us (all who believe). Believers' righteousness is revealed by remaining in Christ Jesus as we died to sin with Christ and rose with Him to righteousness. **Thank God for Jesus.**

Remaining in fellowship with Christ puts us in a right relationship with God the Father and His continuous redemptive activity through the Holy Spirit keeps us liberated from the power of sin.

Verse 23 explains why God's righteousness and His plan of salvation were necessary because man within himself has no righteousness and his (man's) standards are null and void. ***If man has a right standing on its own, then why was Christ's death necessary to pay man's sin debt?***

Feb 16

The Potter And The Clay: Romans 9:21

Hath not the potter power over the clay, of the same lump to make one vessel unto honour, and another unto dishonour?

The characters in this setting are God and humanity as God is the potter and humanity is the clay where God is shaping humanity into usable vessels where He will get the glory and honor. Picture in your mind if you will a potter taking a rough piece of clay and mixing it with water and begin to mold and shape the clay into the desired object. The rough surfaces/edges are pealed away until the vessel is smooth. This is the method God uses in bringing about perfection in all believers. When the smoothed vessels are completed they come forth as pure gold as all believers will have been shaped in the image of God Himself. These are the vessels of honor as they have heard the Word of God and willingly obey His calling. God in His infinite wisdom knows who will be His select and who will not because He knows the hearts of all mankind.

What happens to all who refuse to hear and adhere to the Word of God? Those persons will be cast off unto eternal separation from God-vessels of dishonor as they become the "vessels of wrath" (v 22). God's longsuffering gives the unrepentant time to repent and follow Christ (vv 22-33).

Which vessel are you, one that honors God or dishonor Him?

Feb 17

Believers A Chosen Vessel: Acts 9:15

But the Lord said unto him, Go thy way for he is a chosen vessel unto me, to bear my name before the Gentiles, and Kings, and the children of Israel.

The setting for this text is during the time of Saul's conversion when he met Jesus on the Damascus Road while traveling to Damascus to persecute the church for believing in the risen Savior Jesus Christ. Saul had a notorious reputation for persecuting the church and was very dedicated to what he was doing, but when he encountered Jesus his mission changed from persecution to witnessing Christ throughout the region of Asia Minor.

Many in the town of Damascus was afraid of Paul because of his reputation, but in obedience to God, Ananias did as directed (vv 13, 15), because when one becomes a chosen vessel of God they no longer a threat to the church or its message. The life of Paul changed drastically to where he established many churches in Asia Minor and suffered many hardships for preaching Christ. **What a change! A chosen vessel of God!**

Becoming a chosen vessel of God just like Paul's rough edges was peeled away God will remove all believers' rough edges of sin and all ungodliness so that believers become the set aside people to do His will--to preach and witness Christ the world over.

Believers being chosen of God, we hear, respond to the call and then begin the ministry.

Chosen vessels builds God's kingdom.

Feb 18

Prepared For Good Works: 2 Timothy 2:15, 21

Study to thyself approved unto God, a workman that needeth not to be ashamed rightly dividing the word of truth. If a man therefore, purge himself from these, he shall be a vessel unto honor, sanctified, and meet for the master's use, and prepared unto every good works.

How must believers prepare his or herself for works in the master's kingdom? God left everything that is needed to become sanctified people working to build God's kingdom. He left the Bible His holy Word as our road map and the Holy Spirit as our guide to successfully accomplish our assigned tasks.

Our scripture texts explain the process of preparation which begins with studying God's Word for His approval. Verse 21 encourages faithful (purged) vessels (believers) of Christ to purge him or herself of the weight of sin and all ungodliness that hinders our effectiveness in being an honored vessel for the Master. It is paramount that these two steps be taken as there are challenges ahead in Christian ministry. This is because purged vessels/believers are the human workmen that have been sanctified for good works in the Master's kingdom.

Why it is necessary for honored vessels be sanctified? One is that the Holy Spirit resides in all believers and He cannot live in an unholy place. All believers are to separate themselves from all worldliness and the world's corrupt systems as they are enemies of God.

Sanctified people are prepared for good works in ministry.

Feb 19

Believers Earthen Vessels Of God: 2 Corinthians 4:7

But we have this treasure in earthen vessels that the Excellency of the power may be of God, and not of us.

Paul uses an analogy of believers as being earthen vessels which are precious treasures because of the sanctification they possess. In believers' humanity we sometimes become perplexed with the troubles of this world, we become weary, we experience sadness, troubled and sometime fearful, but through it all believers have dwelling on the inside of each of us, the precious treasure of the Holy Spirit who has the power to enable all believers to overcome all adversities. Case in point, Christian weakness is not removed, but strength is gained through divine intervention of the Holy Spirit. Through the workings of the Holy Spirit our troubled waters are calmed.

Another point to this scripture is that "the Excellency of the power of God" the Holy Spirit is a treasure worthy of all praise and honor. All humanity is nothing within ones self, but through the power of God we as believers are special treasure to Him. **What power we possess through the Holy Spirit!**

Verse 8 talks about the calmness Christians experience the victory we have while living a life in Christ simply because Christians are not defeated foes. Christians have the assurances from God that He will never forsake His faithful children (Romans 8:35-39; Hebrews 13:5).

Believers an earthen vessel chosen by God, victorious in Him by His powers.

Feb 20

Purpose Of Scriptures: 2 Timothy 3:16-17

All scripture are given by inspiration of God, and is profitable for doctrine, for reproof, for correction, for instruction in righteousness. That the man of God may be perfect, thoroughly furnished unto all good works.

There are those (unbelievers) who question the fallibility and purposes of the Bible as the written Word of God. Our scripture verses makes it very plain that all scriptures are given by God Himself as the Bible is the final authority on how all mankind is to live. Being that God wrote the Bible through holy inspired men there can be no error in His Words as they are designed to teach man how to live godly lives as God set the standards by which all should live. Both the OT and NT writers of the Bible were very conscious of what they wrote was the Word of God (Deuteronomy 18:18; 2 Samuel 23:2) as in most instances in the OT, the prophets would preference their statements with "Thus saith the Lord" this was so that their audiences would know that God was speaking. In Matthew 5:18 Jesus expressed the authentication of God's holy inspired word and its smallest details would be fulfilled, while stating the all His words were received from His Father God (John 5:19, 30-31; 7:16; 8:26).

Therefore, to deny that scriptures are the inspired Word of God is to deny the fundamental witness and teaching of Jesus Christ (Matthew 15:3-6; Luke 16:7; 24:25-27; 44-45; John 10:35, the existence of the Holy Spirit, and the apostles who were eye witness to Christ and His earthly ministry. To deny that the Bible is the Holy inspired Word of God is to deny that it is the expression and character of God and its ability to provide wisdom and a spiritual life through faith in Jesus Christ (Matthew 4:4; John 6:63; 2 Timothy 3:15; 1 Peter 2:2). Regarding the wisdom of God, which is far superior than that of man as its doctrine is profitable-meaning living right, and it corrects us when we are wrong while showing man how he is to live and lastly provide instructions in becoming righteous. It is noteworthy to say that one must submit and obey the whole Bible as opposed to selective parts as the entire Bible was written addressing the whole man. One cannot submit to Christ as Lord and Savior with submitting to God and His Word because it is the ultimate authority. Submitting to Christ as our Lord and the Bible as our guide is an expression of our love for God and His redeeming work of salvation. All members of the Godhead are active in man's redemption; God gave, the Son died for us and the Holy Spirit keeps us all to the perfection of man (believers) so that believers can bear fruit.

The final analysis, all scriptures are given for the betterment of man as they are God's Word for they express His love for His people.

Feb 21

Believers Having The Form Of Godliness: 2 Timothy 3:5

Having a form of godliness, but denying the power thereof, from such turn away.

Paul in his writing to his son in the ministry Timothy was encouraging him to stand fast in the Lord through preaching of the gospel of Christ, and to endure the hardships he were sure to face while fulfilling his charge/mission. Paul was in prison when he wrote this letter and false teachers were rampant as well as persecution of Christians from the emperor Nero. Nero was practicing the same persecution of the church as Paul was before his Jesus encounter on Damascus Road.

Verses 2-4 outlines the sins and immorality that was being practiced during Paul's day as many of the same immorality exist today that Christians have to contend with. What are Christians to do? Christians are to be prepared to face the deluge of immorality that we will face as the end approaches. Also, Christians are to stand fast on the Word of God and His godly principles regardless of who practices immorality and where it comes from. Christians are not to tolerate sin in any format in the church, home, the community or in high places. Christians are to be godly, which is taking on the attributes of God as we have been born into righteousness through the blood of Jesus Christ. There are many who profess to be Christians, but continue to live in sin and or practice sinful activities. These are they who only have on a form of godliness or living hypocritical lives.

True Christians use the power within to overcome all ungodliness.

Feb 22

New Converts Standing For God: Psalm 119:9

Wherewithal shall a young man cleanse his way? By taking heed thereto according to thy word.

Our scripture asks a question and then answers by stating that believers and especially new believers in Christ must stand fast and take heed to God's Word regardless of his or her surroundings. Society can be an overwhelming place for new converts, but with a firm Biblical support system where the person is constantly being taught that society is an enemy to God and His ways, believers have a chance to win this spiritual warfare (Ephesians 6:11-18) .

How can new converts and believers win this battle? The new convert and all believers must make a firm decision and commitment to remain loyal to God and His Word and righteousness. As this is an ongoing battle because Satan, through society's fads will have Christians participating in his lies. Secondly, new converts and believers must commit God's Word to memory and have an active prayer life; for this is believers' communication with God. Third, new converts and all believers must look to God for guidance as the Word and the Holy Spirit is available. Fourth, new converts and believers must stand on God's Word and its truths. Fifth, new converts and believers must delight in the Word. Sixth, new converts as well as believers must weight the consequences of the choices that one makes--God's blessing or the world's condemnation. Lastly, always make time for God, make Him first.

Stand fast for God; He is not a fad, but a fashion wear, Him well.

Feb 23

Blotted Sins: Acts 3:19, 21

Repent ye therefore, and be converted, that you sins may be blotted out, when the times or refreshing shall come from the presence of the Lord. Whom the heavens must receive until the times of restitution of all things, which God hath spoken by the mouth of all his holy prophets since the world began.

In today's lesson study, Luke is encouraging all to repent and come to God so that your sins will be blotted out or done away with, because the time will come when God will pour out His Spirit (times of refreshing)--the Holy Spirit. This scripture coincides with Joel 2:28 which is a promise made by God of an outpouring of the Holy Spirit.

Perilous times will come toward the end of the ages and there will be a great falling away from the faith (2 Thessalonians 2:3; 2 Timothy 3:1), but God still promises a refreshing revival to His faithful believers as Christ's presence, spiritual blessing, miracles and the outpouring of the Spirit will come upon His remnant of believers who the world and all its demonic plagues cannot sway.

The time of restitution speaks of the day of reckoning when all that was promised will be fulfilled. What was promised in both the Old and New Testaments as restoration will be seen for Israel, the church and all nations. This is an end-time occurrence and the question to be answered is which side are you on, God or Satan? With God our sins will be blotted out, with Satan no such luck.

Salvation blots sin.

Feb 24

Confidence In God: Philippians 1:6

Being confident of this very thing that he which hath begun a good work in you will perform it until the day of Jesus Chris;

What Paul is saying to all is that we are to have confidence that Jesus Christ through the Holy Spirit who resides in each believer will never leave nor forsake us. Because this is a promise made and God has been true to His Word in keeping all promises from the beginning of time and will continue until the end of time.

The Holy Spirit is the "he" and His good works is convicting all unsaved that they need a Savior Jesus Christ, because when Christ died on the cross it was for the sins of the world. To the saved, the Holy Spirit is the guiding force that keeps all believers in harmony and perfect peace with God, because through Christ's death a broken fellowship has been restored. His good work will continue until Christ returns and rules the world through the establishment of His kingdom here on earth.

The question now becomes, What good works we as believers must do? All believers must maintain the zeal and drive for Christ as this dedication will enable all believers to remain steadfast in faith and continue to witness, preach and teach Christ. All believers will be called upon to make some sacrifices for Christ and will face persecution for His name sake, but considering what Christ has done for humanity.

God is a sure foundation.

Feb 25

Persevering In Faith: Ephesians 6:18

Praying always with all prayer and supplication in the Spirit, and watching thereunto with all perseverance and supplication for all saints;

The term perseverance is defined as endurance, lasting to the end with consistency, not giving up or keeping on. From our definitions that define perseverance means to continue in what ever task that one begins. Therefore, persevering in the faith of Jesus Christ is what is required to complete our journey to heaven, because it represents our commitment and loyalty to God.

Our lesson text tells us how we as believers should pray as prayers should be an integral part of believers' Christian walk. Prayer is our communication with God and builds and intimate relationship which is what He wants. We are to pray for others as well as ourselves and make petitions to God in the Spirit that He will keep us focused on Him and refresh our spirit daily.

All believers are entrenched in a spiritual warfare (6:11-18) where prayer is seen as part of the warfare itself and not just a weapon that Christians use to combat Satan's attacks. Moreover, it is our prayers where the victory is won, because Christians are working together with God and if Christians fail to pray constantly and with sincerity we fall or surrender to Satan.

To fulfill the will of God, Luke 18:1 encourages Christians to always pray and pray with consistency and effectiveness this is counted as faith. Faith is the key to our prayers, because in praying to God we believe that God hears and will answer.

Pray, keep the faith.

Feb 26

Christians Are Conquerors In Christ: Romans 8:37

..In all these things we are more than conquerors through him that loved us.

What is the true meaning of our scripture text? The meaning here is that Christians are victorious in all that we do through Christ Jesus simply because Christ Himself has conquered all. There is no reason to fear any adversities that we encounter in this life or be apprehensive of any battle that we are to wage, because Jesus gained a decisive victory for us and through the power of the Holy Spirit, we as believers are "more than conquerors" in life's struggles (vv 28, 33-39).

If the question were raised, **What are Christians to do when facing persecution for Christ's sake?** Matthew 5:10 states "blessed are they, which are persecuted for righteousness' sake; for there is the kingdom of heaven." This means that followers of Christ will face persecution from the world and all who refuse to compromise on God's principles and standards are blessed, and are to rejoice in our suffering simply because we know that victory is ours.

When Christians/believers are facing adversities and anxieties over different situations, 1 Peter 5:7 encourages us to cast all our cares on the Lord and in His caring love He will take care of the situation.

In regards to our physical needs being met, Philippians 4:19 gives God's assurances that He will supply all our needs; then what's the fuss (worry).

Believers we have the victory so live victorious.

Feb 27

Understanding God's Word, Ways, Percepts And Laws
Psalm 119:1-4

Blessed are the undefiled in the way, who walk in the law of the Lord. Blessed are they that keep his testimonies and that seek him with the whole heart. They also do no iniquity; they walk in his ways. Thou hast commanded us to keep thy percepts diligently.

What is being said in these scripture verses is that all we do as believers is to be done in total obedience to God, because He is the creator and sustainer of our souls. The heart is the centerpiece of the matter as all feeling, emotions, and actions begin in the heart. In totality this psalm expresses the love for God's Word, His promises which He has kept and continues to keep, His commandment, which are God's directives for the life of all humanity, His teachings as presented in His holy inspired written word, His wisdom which supersedes man's, His truth as God cannot lie, God's righteousness, for He is holy and man's righteousness is as filthy rags before Him (Romans 3:23), and lastly, God's reproof, which comes through the Word of God as it provides a measurement of how we are living and what adjustments are needed.

Now that a summary of this scripture has been provided, let's look at some important words in our verses. Let's begin with "blessed" which is to say that God promises to pour out His blessings upon all believers who have chosen to live by His standards and obey His commands as all believers have the personal presence of God in each of us (Genesis 26:3) as He provides strength, protection and help in the time of need. God's laws are His instructional guides for all believers and were prevalent in the OT as they pointed to need for a Savior (v 1). Verse 2 in regards to His testimonies is the covenant conditions by which God's people are to obey as they are to declare the Will of God. The ways of God are those principles and how God operates as it relates to His people in the advancement of His redemptive process here on earth. We know that God's ways differ from those of man as His ways are far beyond those of man, but we are encouraged to acknowledge Him in all that we do, simply because human understanding is what we think and feel as opposed to that of God's (Isaiah 55:8-9; Proverbs 3:5-6).

Lastly, the precepts of God are His more detailed instruction from God so there will be no mistake as to how He wants things (actions) carried out. Case in point, the institution of marriage, God specifically stated that it is to be between man and woman as He created the two Adam and Eve and any other form of marriage is an abomination to God. Another example of God's percepts is His specific instructions on being saved. God said the "He that salvation is free, but to have this gift you must accept my Son as your personal Savior as there is no other way to the God the Father but through His Son Jesus Christ."

So to understand God's way, testimonies, and percepts is to study and know His Word as He has given the Holy Spirit to provide divine understanding as well as His ministerial leaders to proclaim and expound on His Word.

Understanding God is knowing Him and having a willing heart is key.

Feb 28

Believers' Gifts: Ephesians 4:11-12

And He gave some apostles, and some prophets, and some evangelists; and some pastors and teachers. For the perfecting of the saints for the work of ministry, for the edifying of the body of Christ.

If the question was raised, What is the purpose of the many gifts that God gave to His people? Verse 12 provides the answer as believers are the body of Christ, which is His church and it is to be edified-lifted up. Christ's body-the church is based on the fundamental principal of the human body, which is comprised of many different parts that make one body.

However, God in His divine wisdom knew that His church needed to continue growing. Therefore, He left five different ministerial gifts in leadership roles to lead and proclaim His holy Word. Each of these ministerial leadership gifts is essential to kingdom building. These leaders have been gifted by God Himself to carry out each perspective assignment, and each assignment is given to perform in total obedience to God's call.

Let me just say that all believers have been gifted with a gift of ministry in some capacity in edifying the church-Christ's body. Some believers have been given the gift of ushering/serving, and some nursing, some singing, some speaking in tongue, the gift of healing, the gift of prayer and deaconing all to the glory of God.

Whatever your gift is glorify God as He is the giver of the gift and thank Him for the gift!

Called To Christ's Church

Mar 1

A Called Vessel: Ephesians 1:4-5

According as he hath chosen us in him before the foundation of the world, that we should be holy and without blame before him in love; Having predestinated us unto the adoption of children by Jesus Christ to himself, according to the good pleasures of his will.

The two terms in our lesson study provides definitions as to who we as believers are in respect to being servants of God. Scripture tells us that a call is "to be summoned or appointment from God to serve Him in a special way for a specific service "(1 Samuel 3:4 Isaiah 6; 49:1). Samuel answered God's call and became great in his service to the Lord as he was one of the first persons to hold the position of prophet. Moses is another person who did great things for the Lord and is recognized in Biblical history as one of the nation of Israel's first leaders. Our other term vessel, which is a container or utensil (Exodus 25:39; Matthew 25:4) and we know vessels carry its content whether it is water of some other material.

Therefore, believers are called vessels for Christ because we have been called by God Himself to carry the message of the gospel of Christ the world over. Just as God called us from the foundation of the world to be His vessels is because He knew who would answer as Samuel did by saying "hear am I". The phrase within itself says a lot about being a willing and humble servant of God. It says that Lord, I hear You and I am willing to do what You want me to do and I will serve where You want me to.

Answer the call willingly because as a vessel we carry the Spirit of God--the Holy Spirit delivering God's message.

What a blessed container!

Proclaimers Of The Gospel Message
Ephesians 4:7; Malachi 3:1

Behold, I will send my messenger, and he shall prepare the way before me; and the Lord, whom ye seek, shall suddenly come to his temple, even the messenger of the covenant, whom ye delight in; behold, he shall come, saith the Lord of hosts.

Just as the people during Malachi's time were skeptical of God keeping His promise of sending the Messiah-Jesus Christ, many today are skeptics of Christ's return for His people- His church, the baptized body of believers.

Let me remind you of a few facts, which are, (a) God always keeps His promise. (b) A Savior was promised and God delivered with the birth of His Son Jesus Christ, who fulfilled His mission here on earth. (c) His promised return is assured. The question is Will you be ready to go with Him when he comes? (d) All believers are commissioned to share the gospel of Christ the world over (Matthew 28:19-20). The question now becomes, Are you proclaiming the gospel to others? In obedience to our call we are. In retrospect, someone shared the gospel with you and I and we are to proclaim the Word of God with others, because it is God's desire that all be saved. How will the lost/unsaved be saved unless they hear the Word? The unsaved will miss God's blessing of salvation if we as His proclaimers fail to share the good news. *Luke 4:18 provides the answer to our call which is to "preach the gospel to the poor, heal the broken hearted, preach deliverance to the captives, sight to the blind and set at liberty them that are bruised."*

You've answered the call now preach the gospel.

Called To Believe: Luke 1:1

Forasmuch as many have taken in hand to set forth in order a declaration of those things which are most surely believed among us.

Our scripture verse begs the question, what was declared and what was it we must believe? We are to believe that Jesus is the promised Messiah as it was declared by many OT prophets hundreds of years earlier, but in God's appointed time He delivered. There were many who gave eye witness accounts of Christ's deity as they witnessed His many miracles authenticating His deity. All of us living in the age of grace are to believe that yes Christ was born as God's Son; He died for our sins and rose for our justification, and is now residing in heaven with His Father making intercession for us serving as our high priest. **What a Savior!**

It is noteworthy to say that faith is the underlying factor in all believers' belief, case in point the OT prophets had enough faith to believe God and the willingness to act on that faith and proclaim "what thus saith the Lord" to others as their messages were repentance because salvation is at hand. This theme is carried throughout scripture and is continued today.

Do you believe that God is the creator and sustainer of all that exist? Do you believe in God the Father, the Son and the Holy Ghost? Believe, because He is real and is alive today.

He was, is and always will be for He is God; just believe.

Mar 4

Called To Worship: Psalm 66: 1-8

Make a joyful noise unto God, all ye lands: sing forth the honour of his name; make praise glorious. O bless our God, ye people, and make the voice of his praise to be heard.

The writer of our scripture text is encouraging the people of his day to show forth their heart-felt love and devotion to God by worshiping Him with loud voices of praise and lifting of holy hands to Him because of His worthiness.

The Lord is worthy of all honor, praise and sincere worship because of who He is, what He has done, is doing and what the Lord will continue to do in the lives of all mankind and especially believers. Therefore, our praise to the Lord should be heard from the highest mountain top and even in the lowest valley. If we had ten thousand tongues they would be insufficient to give God His due praise, but worship Him in spirit and truth in spite of our inadequacy (John 4:24). **True worship is what God requires.**

Verse 5 answers the question of why worship God, while all believers have the working of the Holy Spirit living on the inside who enables us to say "come see the works of God" for they are many and spectacular. We know God gives many different gifts to believers to continue manifesting His glory so that many unbelievers will believe on the name of the Lord and be saved.

Worship God for what He has done in your life, and then tell others so they too can worship Him.

He is worthy.

Called To Praise The Lord: Psalm 95:1-8

O come, let us sing unto the Lord; let us make a joyful noise to the rock of our salvation. Let us come before his presence with thanksgiving, and make a joyful noise unto him with psalms. For he is our God; and we are his people of his pasture, and the sheep of his land, To day if ye will hear his voice, Harden not your heart, as in the provocation, and as in the day of temptation in the wilderness.

The writer of this Psalm is calling the nation of Israel to praise and worship service to God with a heart of obedience and commitment to Him. They were to reflect on His goodness and His delivering them out of slavery. Their wilderness journey that took forty years because of their rebellion against God and His punishment was that many who began the journey failed to see the Promise Land. This call is prevalent for all today as it warns us against failing to hear and adhere to the Word of God (v. 8). This is because the more we refuse the Word of God we become desensitized to His Word and become less sensitive to the voice and desires of the Holy Spirit.

There are several reasons why we are to joyfully praise God with a heartfelt thanksgiving is because it was God who saved us from the bondage of sin and all the devastation that sin brings as well as the assurance of spending eternity separated from Him. After this life who wants to be separated from our maker?

If nature can bow to His wonders and praise Him why can't you and I. Praise Him! Praise Him!

Mar 6

Rejoice In The Lord: Psalm 96:1-13

Sing unto the Lord, bless his name, shew forth his salvation from day to day. Declare his glory among the heathen, his wonders among all people. O worship the Lord in the beauty of holiness; fear before him, all the earth. Say among the heathen that the Lord reigneth; the world also shall be established that it shall not be moved; he shall judge the people righteously.

Here again the Psalmist is encouraging the people to worship the Lord with a heartfelt praise and thanksgiving while encouraging all believers to shout daily what God has done in your life. This is to say that daily praises to God should be the order of the day because His glory is witnessed each morning as He has given each of us victory over death and all believers have conquered sin through faith in Jesus Christ. This alone is to rejoice and shout victory, victory.

All believers are to shout glory to His name among the unsaved (heathens) as a living testimony of God's goodness and His grace. Verses 8 and 9 state why we should glorify God and sing praises to His name. Case in point, for those of us who have received God's salvation and experiences His wonderful blessing, one must be eager to share the good news with others. I am reminded of the OT prophet Ezekiel who said that the good news of God's salvation "is like fire shut up in my bones." Equate this feeling to that of arthritis when the pain is so great and there is no relief until some pain medication is taken. The same is true of salvation; telling others is the medication. It is noteworthy to say that this burning fire will cause all believers to obey the Great Commission and go into the entire world proclaiming Christ (Matthew 28:19-20). Another reason to shout for joy is because the salvation brings about a peace that neither the world gives nor understands. **What joy!**

Salvation brings an unquenchable joy for both now and in the future when we will meet in heaven at God's heavenly feast and walk around heaven all day touring His heavenly mansion that is being prepared by Him for His children. **What a time for rejoicing!**

The question now becomes, what would happen if all who believe fail to rejoice in God's goodness? Verses 11-13 give the answer which states that the heavens, the earth, the trees and the wood will rejoice in His goodness. Observe nature and see how it praises God because He created nature and it is grateful to Him. A popular phrase which states that if man fails to worship and praise God then the rocks will cry out; personally I do not want the rocks crying out in praises because I wouldn't.

It can be concluded that just as the call went forth at the writing of this Psalm the call is still in effect; therefore, rejoice and worship God for He is worthy.

Rejoice! Rejoice!

Mar 7

A Called Servant: Isaiah 49:1-7

Listen O isles, unto me; and hearken, ye people, from afar, The Lord hath called me from the womb, from the bowels of my mother hath he made mention of my name...And said unto me; Thou are my servant, O Israel, in whom I will be glorified.

Our lesson study has a messianic overtone in that it references the birth of Jesus Christ who was called to be the Messiah or humanity's Savior delivering mankind from the bondage of sin. What this says about believers who have accepted Jesus Chris as his or her personal Savior and are living in obedience to God's call is that God knew from our birth who He would call to be His spokespersons. This is because believers are chosen from the beginning of time to be His people. It is a wonderful blessing to be chosen by God to continue the work of ministry, which is calling others into redemption.

Verse 3 depicts Jesus Christ as God's perfect example of what Israel and all believers are to be like. Jesus Christ served God in humble submission all the way to the cross and beyond. Israel is God's chosen people to be an example for the world portraying His love and blessings that come as the result from being His chosen ones.

Therefore, believers being a called servant of God is to labor in His vineyard because the harvest is great-bringing others to Christ. Believers as God's called servants receive strength through the Holy Spirit which enables us to continue our work for the Lord.

It is a blessing to be a called servant.

Believers Witnessing Christ: 1 John 5:10

He that believeth on the Son of God hath the witness in himself; he that believeth not on God hath made him a liar; because he believeth not the record that God gave his Son.

What our scripture verse is saying to us today is that for all who say they are Christian have accepted Jesus Christ as Lord and Savior and His atoning works and therefore, witness to others God's love for all humanity only we just believe. This is because every believer has a testimony of what God has done in his or her life. Because since Adam's sin all born after him was born with a sinful nature and was out of fellowship with God; acceptance of Jesus as Lord the fellowship is restored.

This also speaks to our faith as faith is the center of our salvation because without faith there is no salvation. Why is faith is the epicenter of our salvation, because of the OT patriarchs who lived and died before the birth of Christ; they believed God. It also speaks to the issue of the OT prophets who spoke for God trusting Him as they carried His message to the people. They had faith that whatever God said was true. Then there are those who were an eye witness to Christ during His earthly ministry; faith was essential because they too had to believe that He was the promised Messiah. Lastly, those of us living in the age of grace our belief is strictly on faith.

Believers can witness Christ because we see Him with our spiritual eye.

Mar 9

Believers Commanded To Love: 1 John 4:7

Beloved, let us love one another; for love is of God; and every one that loveth is born of God, and knoweth God.

What makes our scripture verse so important? There are several reasons this verse is important and vital to the Christian walk. First, God is love as it is His very nature, and all who say they are Christians and have no love for his or her fellowman is being untruthful with himself. Second, love is virtual (God first) and then it becomes horizontal (man second). The question becomes, How can we love God and not man when God put His Spirit in all of us. Third, love is one of the fruits of the Spirit (Galatians 5:22), then how can one say that he is a Christian and have no love? Fourth, God first loved us and all believers have experienced His love, forgiveness and His help, so then we as believers are obligated to love others even our enemies. Sometimes this may come as a great sacrifice to us, but love anyway--God did. Reflect on the great sacrifice God and His Son made because of love. Fifth, if we as believers continue to love as commanded, then God continues to live in us and His love is perfected in us (v.12).

It is noteworthy to say that in order to obey God's love command, we must rely on the Holy Spirit as we grow in Christ.

Love so the world can see God in you.

Mar 10

A Covenant Relationship: Daniel 1:8-20

...Daniel proposed in his heart that he would not defile himself with the portion of the king's meat, nor with the wine which he drank; therefore he requested of the prince of the eunuchs that he might not defile himself.

The story of Daniel is well known throughout the ages, but it carries a significant meaning as it relates to Daniel and his walk with God. See, Daniel trusted God and worshiped Him with a sincere heart; even when he was exiled in a foreign land Daniel refused to adopt the customs of the land because they were contrary to those of God. Daniel's refusal to obey the customs of his present surroundings resulted in his eminent death at the hands of the king, but Daniel's relationship with God caused him to say to the king "put me in the lions den, for my God can deliver if it's His will." We know the story's results--Daniel's life was spared.

What does this say for you and I today and our covenant relationship with God? We are to trust God in all situations because He has the power to deliver us from any situation if it's His will. It also speaks to our faith in the all mighty God who created and sustains all and in His love for His people He delivers.

Daniel's lions den experience encourages all believers to have lion's den like faith; trust God for He is our deliverer.

What a covenant relationship to have!

Mar 11

Keeping God's Covenant In A Strange Land
Daniel 3:8-30

And he commanded the most mighty men that were in his army to bind Shadrach, Meshach, and Abednego, and to cast them into the burning fiery furnace. And these three men fell down bound into the midst of the burning fiery furnace.

Continuing our lesson study on our covenant relation with God and our trust of Him in our most trying times; yesterday we looked at Daniel and his situation while residing in a foreign land, today our focus is on the three Hebrew boys who were cast in a fiery furnace for failing to bow down and worship idol gods.

Both lessons serve as a reminder of the idol worship that existed then and idol worship still exist today, but we as believers are to trust God for His deliverance and remain true to Him as He is the one true God. Then we can say like the Hebrew boys "If it be so, our God whom we serve is able to deliver us from the burning fiery furnace, and he will deliver us out of thine hand, O king" (v. 17).

We know God is a deliverer from our lesson study and personal experiences because God allows circumstances to test our faith and trust in Him.

Believers are a set aside people who have been called out of the world while remaining in the world to be a light in a sin riddled world. Just as Daniel and the Hebrew boys remained true to God so must you and I today. God will get in the fiery furnace with you and cool the fire. ***Trust Him!***

Mar 12

God Delivers His People: Psalm 125:1-5

They that trust in the Lord shall be as mount Zion, which cannot be removed, but abideth for ever. As the mountains are round about Jerusalem, so the Lord is round about his people from henceforth even for ever.

If anyone ever wondered about God and Him delivering His people, our scripture verses make it plain of God's deliverance.
    Let's look at what these verses are saying, first, we see trust as the central theme in these verses as we have been discussing for the past several days. Second, "shall" in verse 1 is God's guarantee of His deliverance. Third, the writer of this Psalm uses an analogy of a mountain to make his point of God's deliverance and protection for His people. The writer plainly states that mountains cannot be moved, which solidifies the surety of God and as the stability of a mountain is the same principle of God and His protection around His people. Fourth, the writer further authenticates God's protection and deliverance by stating that the mountains that surround Jerusalem serve as a protection to keep out the enemy. On a spiritual plane, God's protection through the Holy Spirit serves as our mountains and Jerusalem is the dwelling place for all baptized believers. Lastly, there is no need to wonder about the time limits of God's protection and deliverance, because it lasts forever. His record speaks to His deliverance and protection.
    There is no failure in God; He delivers.

Mar 13

Believers Edifying Christ
1 Corinthians 10:23; Ephesians 4:12-13, 29

For the perfecting of the saints for the work of the ministry, for the edifying of the body of Christ: Till we all come in the unity of the faith, and of the knowledge of the Son of God, unto a perfect man, unto the measure of the stature of the fullness of God.

The term edify means to build up, encourage, strengthen, and unify others in the body of Christ (Ephesians 4:12, 29). Paul in his writing to the church at Ephesus was encouraging the believers there to lift up one another as each had been gifted with different gifts to equip and prepare the whole body of Christ--the church. How do we build up the whole church through our gifts? Some may have the gift of prophecy then we are to prophesy to the congregation so they too can know what thus saith the Lord. If our gift is singing, then we are to sing to the glory of God so that He may be glorified and not the singer's glorification. If your gift is teaching this too should be done to the glory of God. The teacher is to train others so they too can minister to others as we are about the business of winning souls for Christ.

Every member is to be trained and released into the world to perform ministry for Christ to build His church. This promotes church growth as well as growth for the individual believer. As believers grow in the grace of God and through the works of the Holy Spirit there is unity in the church and community overall. This is because all is on one accord working for the Master--Christ. Growing in the grace of God brings about spiritual maturity in all aspects of Christ (v. 15), which includes being filled with the fullness of Christ Himself and God (v. 13; 3:19) as this gives all believers the knowledge of the truth. With the true knowledge of God we then can live in "righteousness and true holiness of God" (v. 24, cf. vv. 17-23).

If the question were raised, What is the goal of edification? It is to be made whole in Jesus Christ and with others as stated in Romans 14:19 which speak of the following things that make for peace and the

things that edify one another. Another question that begs an answer is where does edification come from or how do we become edified? Edification comes from the other believers, the Holy Spirit and our daily activities. We get there by humbly submitting to the will of God and living daily for Him. If the world can't see Christ in you then who does He see? Are we building up self? Is our lifestyle strengthening our community or is it a hindrance? Lastly, How often do we encourage others to seek Christ and His saving powers?
   Self edification is not of God.

Mar 14

Believers Called To Be An Example: John 13:12-17

If I then, your Lord and Master, have washed your feet; ye also ought to wash another's feet. For I have given you an example, that ye should do as I have done to you.

The example Jesus set for His disciples and all believers is that humility is the hallmark for all believers. Jesus was constantly plagued by His disciples with the human problem of position of one wanting to be superior to his fellow disciple. A perfect example is when the mother of James and John requested of Jesus to give her sons position of power when He came into His kingdom. The message Jesus wanted His disciples and all followers of Him to see was that the desire to be first or in a position of honor is contrary to God and His spirit.

It is noteworthy to reflect on the life of Christ and everything He did was in humility. He was born in humility, entered Jerusalem in humility, and healed all manner of diseases in humility without questioning one's pedigree or why you are in this situation. He did everything in humility and in total obedience to the Will of His Father, and this was setting the example of how we as Christians are to live in obedience to Him and with one another.

If believers portray an I'm better than you attitude, then what kind of message are we sending to the world? Follow Christ's example so the world will see Christ in you.

Be an example.

Mar 15

Doers Of The Word: James 1:17-27

..Be doers of the word, and not hearers only, deceiving your own selves. For if any be a hearer of the word, and not a doer, he is like unto a man beholding his natural face in a glass: Fore he beholdeth himself, and goeth his way, and straightway forgetteth what manner of man he was.

Why is it so important for believers to be doers of the Word, not just a hearer? There are several reasons for believers to be both a doer and a hearer of the Word. Some are:

(a) Believers have been commissioned by God to go into the entire world sharing the gospel message of Christ (Matthew 28:19-20). The question now becomes, If someone had not shared the gospel of Christ with you, how would you have heard? The apostles of Christ shared the gospel with others in spite of difficulties.

(b) Believers are the salt of the earth seasoning the world with both our witness and telling others about Jesus Christ and what He has done in your life. It is important to note that believers are a peculiar people who have been set aside to do the work of the Lord which is to witness Christ to others.

(c) Believers are to live holy lives before men so the world can see Christ in you. This is because the life of a believer may the only Bible others are reading. Then there is the unspoken word as 98% of our communication is nonverbal, therefore, the life we as believers lead leaves a lasting impression on others.

Share the Word of God; He shares His blessings with you.

Mar 16

Disciples Of Christ: John 8:31

Then said Jesus to those Jews which believed on him, If ye continue in my word, then are ye my disciples indeed; And ye shall know the truth, and the truth shall make you free.

To be a disciple of Christ is to be a follower of Him and a student of His Word. What it means to be a disciple of Christ one must continue in God's Word by submitting ones self to do as the Word says. Being a disciple of Christ is to leave family and friends if necessary just as the early disciples did when asked to "follow me"; they left family and occupation to become "fishers of men for Christ." This is not saying that in today's society we are to leave our occupation, but instead believers are taking on a new occupation as we have been called by God to do His work. It is noteworthy to say that in some instances being called into the discipleship requires one to leave present occupation as one may be called into ministerial leadership positions where compensation is rendered.

Disciples of Christ often time suffer persecution for the sake of Christ, because as disciples deliver the true Word of God many will despise the truth. Paul suffered many persecutions for preaching Christ while facing eminent danger. Peter like Paul was jailed for preaching the true gospel of Christ. They both were delivered through God's divine intervention. God will do the same today for you and me--His disciples.

Disciples of Christ persevere.

Mar 17

Believers Are Sons Of God: 1 John 3:1

Behold, what manner of love the Father hath bestowed upon us, that we should be called the sons of God; therefore the world knoweth us not, because it knew him not.

Our scripture verse carried a profound connotation in Christians being Sons of God, which express the true love of God as our Father through His Son Jesus Christ and His atoning work to make our Sonship possible.

If the question were raised, What are some of the implied facts of this verse as it relates to being Sons of God? Being children of God is one of the greatest revelations that result from accepting Jesus Christ as ones personal Savior. This is because God saved us to become part of His royal family which carries inherited blessings. Another fact from our scripture verse is that because of our faith and trust in God we have a glorious hope of the future which includes spending eternity with God our Father. Being Sons of God gives us the desire to be led by the Spirit of God. This is the basis for our being disciplined by God our Father and the reason we live to please Him. Being Sons of God we conform to His Will and ways as we become more like Him. God disciplines His children out of love as we continue our God-like transformation. Believers' transformation is completed when we see our Savior face-to-face.

We are blessed to be called children (sons) of God.

Mar 18

Called To Reveal Christ: Ephesians 3:1-13

....To make all men see what is the fellowship of the mystery, which from the beginning of the world hast been hid in God, who created all things by Jesus Christ.

Just as the OT prophets revealed God as our creator, sustainer and deliverer, so did the NT apostles who preached Christ throughout the land. The apostolic message is the responsibility of all believers today. Those who spoke for God during the Bible days lived a godly life so the people could see the glory of God manifested in their lives. Modern day believers both laity and leaders are to reveal Christ through sharing His Word and living holy lives that manifest Christ.

Let's pose a question, which is, What does it mean to be called by God? First, to be called by God is a blessing within itself because He has predetermined who will be His spokespersons. Believers' predestination was determined before the foundation of the world. This is because God knows the heart of all men and God knew who would be his elect. Second, God chose us to be His elect to have fellowship with Him and to serve Him in kingdom building. God's kingdom is built by increasing Christ's church, which is comprised of a body of believers. As believers witness Christ and the unsaved come to know Christ and accept Him as their personal Savior the church grows. Lastly, believers are called or elected to salvation as it was made possible by Christ Himself.

Does the world see Christ in you?

Mar 19

Called To Bless Others: Ephesians 1:3-10

Blessed be the God and Father of our Lord Jesus Christ, who hath blessed us with all spiritual blessings in heavenly places in Christ:

How has God blessed us? God blessed all humanity by putting His Spirit in us and all who believe there is a God and accept His Son Jesus Christ as Savior is blessed again because we have salvation. Upon accepting Jesus as our personal Savior the Holy Spirit takes up residence in each believer and becomes active in the lives of all believers guiding, teaching and protecting us. Also, the Holy Spirit enables all believers to remain committed to Christ and His mission. In carrying out Christ's mission of finding and saving the lost is why Christ came to earth. This is the mission (Great Commission) of all believers-the called.

With that being said, we as believers are blessed to bless others because all believers have the spiritual blessings that salvation brings and we are to share with others. Two things occur when we fail to share our blessings, one is the act of selfness and two disobeying the directives recorded in Matthew 28:19-29. God shared His love for man and desires that all will do likewise.

It is safe to say that God blesses us with material things so that we may bless others. This is God's provision for the less fortunate; He always replenishes what is cheerfully given to others.

Has God blessed you today? Who have you blessed today?

Believers Called Into God's Priestly Kingdom
Exodus 19:1-8

Now therefore, if ye will obey my voice indeed, and keep my covenant, then ye shall be a peculiar treasure unto me above all people; for all the earth is mine.

Throughout the Bible, the nation of Israel is known as God's chosen people and His love for them is seen in His protection of Israel. Because of His love for His covenant God entered into numerous covenants with them, which they would break. When a new covenant was renewed God would remind them of His loyalty to them and how He cared for them (v. 4). Each time Israel would promise to obey God's covenant, but verse 5 contains the condition of God's covenant and the obedient theme is central to the new covenant which was implemented by Christ.

If the question were raised, How does the nation of Israel relate to being called into His priestly kingdom? The nation of Israel is His chosen people and there were a notion of believers within the nation itself just as the body of believers is His chosen people because on a spiritual plain there is no nationality. The common thread that holds all believers both Old Testament and New Testament believers is our love, commitment and gratitude to God for His saving grace. Love is the motivating factor that leads to obedience to God our creator and sustainer which results in a harmonious relationship with Christ.

What makes both Old and New Testament believers peculiar people to the rest of the world? All believers from both Testaments are a sanctified people as they have been set aside to God for special purposes and the unique relationship with Him because He was their redeemer before the coming of Christ. It is noteworthy to say that the purpose of Israel foreshadowed God's purpose for the church, which is to be the bride of His Son Jesus Christ. 1 Corinthians 3:16 describes believers as His temple. The entire congregation of believers is His temple which sits in the midst of a corrupt society and is to be a light to the world. Given that all believers are of royalty by association with

God we are to refrain from fraternizing with the world. Also, believers as the temple of God must be holy as He is holy. Therefore, being holy is the goal of all believers and is the purpose of election in Christ (Ephesians 1:4).

1 Peter 2:5, 9 describes the essence of all believers being in the royal priestly family of God, which carries the following blessings and duties, (a) all believers have direct access to God, (b) believers are under obligation to live holy lives, (c) all believers are to offer "spiritual sacrifices" to God, (d) believers are to offer our petitions of sacrifices of praises, (e) believers are to serve Him with our whole hearts and willing hands, (f) believers are to present our bodies as instruments of righteousness, (g) believers are to intercede for others and pray for one another and all humanity, and (h) believers are to share the word with others and pray for its success; believers are planters and God waters.

Blessings! Blessings abound being in God's family.

Mar 21

The Eternal Inheritance Of God: Matthew 19:23-30

Then said Jesus unto his disciples, Verily I say unto, That a rich man shall hardly enter into the kingdom of heaven. And again I say unto you, it is easier for a camel to go through the eye of a needle, than for a rich man to enter into the kingdom of God.

The setting for today's discussion sprang from a rich man in Jesus' day wanting to know how to be saved? Needless to say the young man didn't like Jesus' answer and went away sad. This was an opportunity for Jesus to teach His disciples a lesson on the difference of material wealth and spiritual wealth. Material wealth has no salvation as all material goods come from God as He owns everything.

For all who have salvation have an eternal inheritance that money cannot buy because Jesus Christ paid the bill with His death on the cross at Calvary. The cost to us is accepting Him in faith and dedicating our lives to Him in holy righteousness.

What do believers inherit? Believers inherit all the richness of God while becoming His children born into a family of holiness. Also, believers become co-heirs with Christ which carries bountiful blessing as Christ is God's Son.

The prodigal son story gives a vivid picture of believers inheriting what God has as all were alienated from God before salvation. *What an inheritance!*

Eternal inheritance is more precious than rubies. Believe and receive your portion.

Mar 22

Guided By The Holy Spirit: Galatians 5:16-18

...Walk in the Spirit, and ye shall not fulfill the lust of the flesh. For the flesh lusteth against the Spirit, and the Spirit against the flesh; and these are contrary one to the other; so that ye cannot do the things that ye would. But if ye be led by the Spirit, ye are not under the law.

For the purpose of this discussion, let us establish who the Holy Spirit is? The Holy Spirit is the third person in the Godhead who has been active in all phases of humanity since creation. The Holy Spirit is a living breathing person and not an "it" as so often referred to. The Holy Spirit is the Spirit that is recorded in Genesis as "moving" over the face of the deep (Genesis 1:2). He was preparing creation for God's future works.

The Holy Spirit is active in the lives of all humanity as in the unsaved He is seen as the one who convicts or reminds us of our need for salvation. The saved He resides in each of us leading, guiding, teaching and protecting us from all harm both seen and unseen. He teaches God's truth because He is God in the third person. He is the small voice that speaks to the consciousness of all mankind that reminds us what is right according to God's standards as His standards are what humanity is to live by. The Holy Spirit aids all believers in his or her witnessing Christ so the person can boldly witness Christ in obedience to the Great Commission just as He empowered the disciples on the day of Pentecost.

Being guided by the Holy Spirit is being guided by God for He is God.

Mar 23

Believers Owned As God's Property: Ephesians 1:12-14

That we should be to the praise of his glory, who first trusted in Christ.

If we were to sub-title this discussion it could be titled "Sealed by the Holy Spirit", but today's discussion will focus on being God's property.

If the question were raised, How did believers become God's property? All believers were bought with a price which is the blood of our Savior Jesus Christ and this was paid on Calvary's cross. All mankind lacked the ability to pay his sin debt because there was no one found sinless but Jesus Christ. Therefore, when God gave His Son Jesus Christ to become humanity's ransom, it was to redeem/buyback our freedom from the slavery of Satan and his demonic powers.

God's display of His unending love and the redeeming act of His Son all who believe have been reconciled back to God, thus becoming His property as all believers have been sealed with the mark of God by the Holy Spirit. This seal is visible to God, Satan and our outward actions say who we belong to-**God's children.**

It is noteworthy to say that God did what He did because man was created in the image and likeness of God to be in fellowship with Him. Man is God's only creation that has His Spirit inside of us; then we became living souls.

Man was owned by God before the fellowship was broken; therefore, man has been restored to our rightful owner-God.

Believers are owned and kept by God.

The Righteous: Proverbs 11:1-10; Romans 3:21

The righteous is delivered out of trouble, and the wicked cometh in his stead. As the righteous tendeth to life; so he that pursuits evil it to his own death. But now the righteousness of God without the law is manifested, being witnessed by the law and the prophets.

Who are the righteous? These are those who have believed God and have committed themselves to living holy lives according to God's standards. The righteous believe God's standards because according to Romans 3:23 "all have sinned and come short of the glory of God." What this means then that our righteousness comes through the redemption of Jesus Christ as we have been justified by Christ. This is to say that all who believe have been granted a pardon from the guilt of sin and the shame that it brings. This is accomplished through the atoning work of Jesus Christ all believers have been made right with God.

Taking a closer look at believer's righteousness that is achieved through justification is that it is a gift of God (Romans 3:24) and no one can make him or herself right with God by either keeping the law or doing good works. No one could keep the law accept Jesus Christ and our good works have no saving power. Our justification/righteousness is the free gift from God.

It is noteworthy to say that the righteous are believers who have received God's forgiveness of our sins which had us condemned to death, but being made right with God we now have eternal life.

The righteous are the forgiven.

Mar 25

The Word Of God: Psalm 119:105-112

Thy word is a lamp unto my feet, and a light unto my path.

The writer of this Psalm expresses his love for God's Word and what it means to him as all believers should share the same feelings. This heartfelt expression of God's Word gives the facts of the purpose of God's Word. This is because a lamp is used to light the way for a traveler and in this scenario all believers are on a heavenly journey and God's Word is our road map pointing the way.

It the question were raised, How is God's Word conveyed to His people? There is His written Word-the Bible, the spoken word that is shared by other believers through witnessing, preaching, and teaching. Then there is the divine revelation of God's Word.

The divine purpose of God's Word is that we may know God and His precepts. Also, God's Word provides spiritual principal that if adhered to will prevent us from many pitfalls, sorrows, and tragedies that come from making wrong choices for a lack of knowledge of God's Word.

Have you heard God's Word, and what is your response to His Word? Have reading and meditating on His word become a part of your daily routine? Is the Word of God shining bright in your life for others to see God's glory? Are you committed to obeying God's Word? Have you shared His word with someone today?

God's Word is our roadmap and the Holy Spirit is our compass. Follow God.

Mar 26

Truth: Psalm 25:1-5

Shew me thy ways, O Lord; teach me thy paths. Lead men in thy truth, and teach me for thou art the God of my salvation; on thee do I wait all the day.

What is truth? Truth can be defined as known facts. How do we come to know the truth? Truth can be known from different sources such as an eye witness account of an event, from recorded history and from the giver of the facts of an event.

For the focus of today's discussion we will focus on God's truth; God being the creator and sustainer of all things and cannot lie, then we know what He says is the absolute truth. This is because what God said in the beginning remains the same today and forever. Why, because He change not (Malachi 3:6).

God has proven Himself to be truthful, trustworthy, dependable and steadfast. Reflect on God's promise of rain during Noah's time, only Noah believed God and followed His instructions and begin to build the Ark. God witnessed to Christ being His beloved Son; therefore, believe it. Whatever God says it is the truth. John the Baptist and Christ's disciples witnessed the truth; Christ is the Son of God.

There are many truths in the world today, but only God's truth will stand forever regardless of what other doctrines are preached.

God's truth is the final authority.

Covenant Of Obedience: Exodus 24:7

And he took the book of the covenant, and read in the audience of the people: and they said, All that the Lord hath said will we do, and be obedient.

For the sake of our discussion, let's clarify the meaning of the two words in our subject; according to The Student Bible Dictionary (P.65) defines covenant as a mutual agreement between two or more parties. The difference between God's covenant and a regular negotiated covenant is that all parties must agree, but with God He sets the parameters of His covenant and the people must agree. This agreement is an individual commitment and begins in the heart of man.

The essential requirement of God's covenant is loyalty and obedience to Him. What God's gives in return for fulfilling those two requirements are protection, and guidance through the Holy Spirit, His assurance of His presence. It is noteworthy to say that God has made covenants with His people beginning with Adam and it extends through present day. The difference is that the covenant in the New Testament was established by Christ Himself and is known as the covenant of grace and it is written in the hearts of all men so there would be no opportunity of them being misplaced or destroyed. The new covenant is also known as the New Testament.

These questions come to mind, What does it take to enter into a covenant relationship with God? John 3:16 is the answer. We have the assurance of eternal life because all who believe have admitted to his or her sin, confessed, and believe in the risen Lord, Jesus Christ.

Therefore, in committing oneself to the Lord we are agreeing to do things God's way as opposed to man's way because the two are miles apart. So, what we are doing in essence is living in obedience to God as we have become to live like Him and to trust Him unconditionally. By doing so we can live our lives in holiness and in freedom from sin that once had us bound and destined to eternal separation from the Father.

Let's pose this question; Are we committed to living in total obedience to God and His covenant? All believers have told the world that we have embraced John 3:16 and have now committed to living according to God's holy standards and to do His will. This includes loving others because God first loved us when we didn't love Him. We have committed ourselves to telling others about Christ, His saving powers and the blessing it brings.

With that being said, we then can conclude that a covenant of obedience is submitting oneself totally to God with complete loyalty to Him.

Mar 28

Anointed To Preach The Gospel: Luke 4:18

The Spirit of the Lord is upon me, because he hath anointed me to preach the gospel to the poor; he hath sent me to heal the broken hearted, to preach deliverance to the captives, and recovering of sight to the blind, to set at liberty them that are bruised.

The word anointed means to be appointed by God for a special purpose and at a given time. Biblical history records many instances where God anointed special people for special services. Remember how King David was appointed King of Israel. An oil drip was the common method used during that time. Jesus was anointed before His Virgin birth because He is God and came to earth for a special purpose.

Our scripture verse outlines Jesus' earthly ministry's purpose. Jesus fulfilled His ministry. All believers who are filled with the Spirit have been called to share the gospel message of Christ to others. As all believers are called by God and have been sanctified for His service. The question now becomes are you and I preaching the gospel to the poor, broken hearted, healing the sick, deliverance to the captives, recovering sight to the blind, and setting at liberty they that are bruised? Unless you and I share the gospel the unsaved will remain in captivity to sin and the spiritually blind will not see.

Preach because we have been anointed by the Master.

Mar 29

Fruit Of The Spirit: Galatians 5:22-25

But the fruit of the Spirit is love, joy, longsuffering, gentleness, goodness, faith, Meekness, temperance, against there is no law. And they that are Christ's have crucified the flesh with the affections and lusts.

Our scripture verses describe the outward appearances of all believers as they have mortified the sins of the body and have taken on a new life that resembles Christ. As the Christian attributes tell the world who our Father is.

If a comparison were made comparing the fruit of the Spirit with that of the sinful nature one would see the two are contrary to each other. For example, idolatry is putting something before God our creator. God is the one true and living God and should come first in one's life. Uncleanness if unholy living whereas a believer lives in joy, peace and is slow to anger as is God. Fornication is participating in sexual activities outside of marriage and this is not God's way. It is noteworthy to say that the fruit of the Spirit causes all believers to live according to God's moral laws. As noted in our scripture text living according to the fruit of the Spirit there is no law (v. 23).

Allow me to encourage all that are in Christ let us walk in the Spirit (v. 25). We are never alone for the Holy Spirit is walking with us.

Mar 30

Blessed To Be A Blessing: 2 Kings 4:8-17

And it fell on a day, that Elisha passed to Shuman, where was a great woman; and she constrained him to eat bread, And so it was, that as oft as he passed by, he turned in thither to eat bread.

Our scripture text depicts the story of the Shunammite woman who was barren who desperately wanted a son. She was a faithful woman and trusted God would answer her prayer of giving her a son. This woman of God made a vow to God that if He would bless her with a son she would give him back to God-she kept her promise.

Our lesson text carries a deeper meaning than that of promise keeping; it depicts faithfulness in that God blessed the Shunammite woman with a son (vv. 8-1). God tested the woman's faith by taking her son from her (vv. 18-21), but God restored the son's life (vv. 22-37), because the Shunammite woman held fast to her faith in God's promise to her. What lesson can be learned form the Shunammite woman? God keeps His promise regardless of the time. God sometimes will severely test our faith by taking what we wanted so badly to see where our loyalty is. Is it Him first or to what He has blessed us with? Are we willing to sacrifice the blessing that God has given us so that it can bless others? God blesses us to be a blessing to others.

Who have you blessed today?

"Here am I, send Me": Isaiah 6:18

Also, I heard the voice of the Lord, saying, Whom shall I send, and who will go for us? Then I said Here am I; send me.

Our scripture text depicts Isaiah as man who answered God's call and was a willing servant who stood for God in the midst of an evil nation. Verses 5-7 give a prelude to Isaiah accepting the call. See, Isaiah was in the presence of a holy God and recognized his uncleanness and immediately recognized the need to separate himself from the world.

Then God proceeded to cleanse Isaiah's mouth and heart preparing him for his called service to the Lord. It is noteworthy to say that all who approach God must be forgiven of their sins. This can only be accomplished by the Holy Spirit.

What came next was God's question and Isaiah's response is the way that all believers should answer. This is because when God calls us He cleanses us so that we can serve Him in true holiness and with a willing heart.

When God required a Savior to redeem man, Christ willingly answered "Send Me I will go." Have you answered Yes to God's call? Like Isaiah and Jesus Christ both were sometimes rejected for saying "what thus saith the Lord", but both persevered so must you and I.

Here am I Lord, send me, I'll go.

Revelations From God

April 1

God Reveals Himself To Moses: Exodus 3:1-6, 13-15

And the angel of the Lord appeared unto him in a flame of fire out of the midst of a bush; and he looked, and behold, the bush burned with fire, and the bush was not consumed. And when the Lord saw that he turned aside to see, God called unto him out of the midst of the bush, and said, Moses, Moses. I am the God of thy father, the God of Abraham, the God of Isaac, and the God of Jacob...

We all know the story of the spectacular way in which God revealed Himself to Moses from a burning bush that fire could not consume the bush. This was a sight to behold and is little wonder Moses curiosity was peaked that required him to take a closer look. This was God's attention grabber.

When God appeared to Abraham, He appeared as the "angel of the Lord" (Genesis 22:11) just as He did in this scenario. In each scenario God was called His servant for a special purpose, for Abraham to walk by faith and to become the father of many nations and for Moses was to lead His people out of slave bondage.

God identified Himself as "I AM THAT I AM" and He is the same today as He was then. God is still revealing Himself to His elect to carry the gospel message of salvation to all. However God reveals Himself He is still the God of all creation.

Will you recognize Him?

April 2

The Majestic Glory And Honor Of God: Psalm 8:1-9

When I consider the heavens, the work of thy fingers, the moon and the stars, which thou hast ordained; What is man, that thou art mindful of him? And the son of man, that thou visitest him?

What is the Psalmist saying in this verse? The writer of this psalm is standing in awe of the creation process that God had made man in His likeness and image while giving man dominion over all His creations.

Consider this the beauty of all God's creations and their majesties and the wonders they perform to perfection constantly. Then consider the God who created all this majesty and how wonderfully everything is made and the love He placed on man and the order in the creation process that God created man-last and with such specialty.

With that being said God is worthy of all the praise and honor that man and all other creation can give the creator. It's no wonder the psalmist can say, "O Lord our Lord, how excellent is thy name in all the earth" (v. 9)! There is no other name worthy of such praise and the all Mighty God is the only one found worthy and with such Excellency.

Reflecting on God's majesty, glory, worship and praises is the natural order of expressions of gratitude.

Thank You God for Your creative powers as there is no other God but You. God You create and sustain all Your creations. God You hear and answer prayers of the righteous; You heal all manner of diseases. Lord Thank You in Jesus name. Amen.

God Your wonders to behold!

April 3

Ten Commandments Established: Exodus 20:1-17

Thou shalt have no other gods before me. Thou shalt not make unto the any graven image, or any likeness of any thing that is in heaven above, or that is in the earth beneath, or that is in the water under the earth. Thou shalt not bow down thyself to them, nor serve them; for I the Lord thy God am a jealous God, visiting the iniquity of the fathers upon the children unto the third and fourth generation of them that hate me; And shewing mercy unto them that love, and keep my commandments.

The Ten Commandments are considered as the Old Testament Law that was given to Moses for the children of Israel for holy living. The Ten Commandments are broken down into three categories which are (a) God's moral law that deals with His standard for holy living. (b) His civil laws as they related to Israel's legal and social life as a young nation. These laws are the foundation for today's laws and we as a nation of people are to live. (c) The third category of God's commandments deal with worship of the Lord which includes the sacrificial system that the nation of Israel observed.

Keeping God's commandments was a way for Israel to respond to God in holiness an expression of their gratitude for His deliverance from Egypt and being able to remain in the Promise Land. What do these commandments say for us today? The same principle applies for all believers and non-believers, because we are not to have any other god before the true and living God who created all that exist. The true and living God is the only God of the universe both in heaven and on earth. He is a jealous God as there are to be no graven images created or worshipped as a god. These questions come to mind, Why worship a god that you create with hands? How can an idol god provide all your needs or provide comfort in the time of trouble? Can an idol god soothe a broken heart? Can an idol god provide salvation or can an idol god provide eternal life? There is only one God that is worthy of bowing to; it is the creator of the heavens and earth; the God who holds all time in the palm of His hands--God All Mighty. A God who is worthy of all praises and honor is the one who has no beginning or end---Alpha and Omega. We are to worship the one true God who gives life and can take both life and soul.

Now that we have asked some thought provoking questions, let's look at the basics for God's commandments. They were issued as a connection with His covenant and set forth the expected loyalty to Him by His people--the nation of Israel and all believers. These laws are grounded in His saving mercy and deliverance for Israel and all who believe. The Ten Commandments reveal God's will for His people both then and now, as stipulated in the commandments are the provisions of sin atonement. Atonement foreshadowed the blood sacrifice of Jesus Christ. In both Testaments a committed trust in Him and true love for God is the guiding principle for keeping His commandments. The Ten Commandments expresses God's nature and disposition regarding His love, justice, goodness and His hatred for evil. It is important to say that salvation in the OT was never based on keeping the law, but on a covenant's faith and relationship with God. Jesus Christ brought salvation to all who believe in faith. The OT law and covenant were never intended to be permanent, but they served as a temporary guardian until the coming of Christ (Galatians 3:22-26).

To summarize the Ten Commandments they were given by God Himself and were added to the promise because of transgressions (Galatians 3:19), as they were designed to do the following (a) regulate conduct, (b) define sin, (c) show Israel and others what happens in violating God's will and doing evil, and (d) awaken ones senses to the need of His mercy, grace and redemption (Roman 3:20; 5:20; 8:2).

Ten Commandments are rules to live by.

April 4

The Works Of God: Psalm 66:1-20

All the earth shall worship thee, and shall sing unto thee; they shall sing to thy name. Come and see the works of God: he is terrible in his doing toward the children of men. He turned the sea into dry land; they went through the flood on foot; there did we rejoice in him.

What are these verses saying? First, the writer is speaking to a community of believers who must have the manifestation of the Holy Spirit in their midst in order for them to glorify God. This is because believers have experience in the convicting work of the Holy Spirit and can recognize the powerful works of God. Believers recognize the majestic beauty of God in every aspect of life as nature beholds His wonders and powers. Nature worships God in its own way and so must believers worship God as He has set forth.

When believers recognize and reverence the terrible (magnificent) works of God then they can say to other "come and see the works of God" it is then that the unsaved will believe because they too will see His mighty works. This includes believers giving personal testimony of God's saving powers through His grace and mercy at work in our lives (v. 16).

Verse 6 alludes to the mighty works of God when He made a highway through the Red Sea and the nation of Israel walked through on dry land. God will wall (partition) the trouble waters in your life if you trust in Him and cast all your cares upon Him (1 Peter 5:7).

Lastly, sharing the gospel of Christ we are never alone as Christ promised His presence, authority and power to accompany us when we witness Him to the lost souls of this world.

The mighty works of God is still being manifested today.

April 5

The Presence Of God: Psalm 46:1-7

God is our refuge and strength, a very present help in trouble. The Lord of host is with us; the God of Jacob is our refuge.

The essence of this psalm is to provide comfort in the time of trials and tribulations, because at some point in our lives we will experience stress, anxiety, and spiritual barrenness (psalm 44).

What one must do in these times is to remember these are not normal times and it is God's desire for His people to be near Him for He is there with help and comfort. We must put our complete trust in God with confidence that He will and we know that He is able to deliver us from all anxieties and or troubles. Our scripture verse provides all the encouragement needed by stating that He is our refuge. Refuge is a place of shelter which protects from all danger as it provides security during the storms of life.

Regarding "strength" it is God's might when we are battling life's storms, which also includes His power to work in us that enables us to conquer or overcome all of life's obstacles.

If the question were raised, What is the end result? The end result is God is present and available to His people, but He wants us to call on Him for help in the time of need. He answers sincere faithful prayers. We need not fear for He is sufficient.

The presence of an All Mighty God, what a blessing!

April 6

Experience God's Protection: Psalm 46:8-11

Be still and know that I am God: I will be exalted among the heathen; I will be exalted in the earth. The Lord of hosts is with us; the God Jacob is our refuge.

This entire psalm is one of courage in the time of trouble, one that reminds us of God's presence and protection for His people.

Verse 4 talks about a river in the midst of the city, which is God's presence that flows constantly with His grace, mercy, glory and power in the midst of His people. This over-flowing grace is from the Triune God as it flows from the throne of God that constantly refreshes His people. This refreshing is seen for both here on earth (John 4:13-14) and in heaven (Revelation 22:1).

It is an enormous blessing to have God's protective grace that flows like a river in the midst of His people. With such revelation there is no need to neither fear nor become anxious about the cares of this life. Verses 10 and 11 make it plain the reason to cast off all fears and doubts. This is because the God of both heaven and earth will be exalted so that everyone will know who He is and who is in control. Living in God's presence is worth more than the whole world that is against us. Biblical history records the many battles God has won for the nation of Israel while living obediently to His Will. He will do the same for you and I today.

How do we experience God's protection? We have the indwelling Holy Spirit inside each of us who aids us to live in harmony with Him and in obedience to His holy Word.

His protection is always present.

April 7

An Everlasting God: Psalm 90:1-4

Lord, thou hast been our dwelling place in all generations. Before the mountains were brought forth, or ever thou hadst formed the earth and the world, even from everlasting to everlasting, thou art God. For a thousand years in thy sight are but as yesterday when it is past, and as a watch in the night.

Many nay sayers have been trying to refute the existence of the true and living God for many years, but in their noblest effort they have failed. This is because the only justification for all of creation is the God of Abraham, Isaac and Jacob. He is the only God that has existed since the beginning of time and will exist forever. *Isn't it a blessing to know that the God of the universe lives for all the ages and has been present and will continue to be until eternity?*

There are many gods, but there is only one God, who creates, sustains, protects, provides for and saves His prized creation. Our everlasting Triune God sent His Son Jesus Christ to die for the sins of the world so that the broken fellowship is restored. *What a mighty God?*

Verse 2 gives insight into the infinite of our everlasting God, which states that God existed before the mountains, earth and the world were formed, He was in existence.

Only the Triune God can make such declaration of His existence. Which God do you acknowledge and serve? The Almighty God!

The Knowledge Of God: Psalm 139:1-9

O Lord, thou hast searched me, and known me. Thou knowest my downsitting and mine uprising, thou understandest my thought afar off. Thou compassest my path and my lying down, and art acquainted with all my ways.

This psalm gives full acknowledgment to God and His attributes while recognizing He is omnipresence, omnipotent and omniscience. God's care for His people is acknowledged by the psalmist as God is the creator of man and thoroughly knows man. The omnipresence of God means that He is everywhere regardless of where we may go. The psalmist eloquently expresses that there is no escaping God by stating that even if he went to heaven God is there or down in the pit of hell, God is there (v. 7). God also, observes everything that we do whether good or bad, and one day we will have to give an account for our actions.

God being omniscience He knows everything, which includes our thoughts, motives, desires and actions. It stands to reason that God knows our thoughts being that we are created in His likeness and image. God is actively and creatively involved in all human life from inception (v 13) and He cares for the unborn with the same love as living humankind. Therefore, all humanity both born and unborn is God's prize possession as part of Himself is instilled in each of us.

Is there anything that God doesn't know? Why would there be when He is the creator of all that exists? We serve an all-knowing, everywhere and all seeing God so there is no lack in Him.

God's knowledge surpasses all.

April 9

Security In God: Psalm 91:1-16

He that dwelleth in the secret place of the most High shall abide under the shadow of the Almighty. He shall cover thee with his feathers, and under his wings shalt thou trust; his truth shall be thy shield and buckler.

What is security? Security is a form of protection as it serves as a place of safety from harm and or danger. Regarding the security of believers as outlined in our lesson text we see that we have security in God Himself. Salvation is a form of security as it saves all believers from a life of sin destined for eternal separation from our creator to a life of spiritual protection which lasts an eternity. All believers who have come to fully trust God in faith have the security of His presence, protection, care and His righteousness. God is present with us through His Spirit--the Holy Spirit.

Verses 1-2 gives insight to the level of protection provided by God with the names used to describe His protection. The name "Most High" depicts God as being greater than all other gods and any dangerous threat we might face. "Almighty" shows God's power to confront and destroy the enemy. The name "the Lord" assures all believers of His presence as He is always with us. Lastly, the name "my God" refers to the trust all believers are to have in God as He has chosen to be intimately involved with all who trust Him.

God is your security blanket, Have you trusted Him today?

April 10

God Reveals His Faithfulness: Lamentations 3:22-26

It is of the Lord's mercies that we are not consumed, because his compassion fail not. They are new every morning; great is thy faithfulness. The Lord is my portion, saith my soul; therefore will I hope in Him. The Lord is good unto them that wait for him, to the soul that seeketh him. It is good that a man should both hope and quietly wait for the salvation of the Lord.

The prophet Jeremiah expresses both sorrow and hope for the nation of Judah as they were suffering God's chastisement for the sins they had committed and their refusal to turn back to God. Jeremiah makes a stunning revelation of God's mercies to the nation by stating that it was God's mercies they were not consumed. God has the power to bring complete destruction on any nation or evil doers if that was His will, but instead He chose to show compassion for His people because He is love and His graciousness abounds.

It is noteworthy to say that God's mercy is witnessed every morning like the fresh dew that greets His people as we awaken to a new day. Also, in this passage of scripture, the Prophet Jeremiah describes the faithfulness of God toward His people that all believers have the assurances of whatever God promises it is sure to be fulfilled. **What a faithful God!**

Reflect with me on some of God's faithful promises; God promised deliverance of Israel from slave bondage in Egypt, a promise kept. God promised Israel the promise Land, another promise kept. In spite of Israel's disobedience God led them to the Promise Land. He promised to fight their battles, yet again another promise kept. God promised a Messiah, Jesus came in God's appointed time. The promise was fulfilled exactly as prophesied. Jesus Christ is the Savior of the world as He was to reconcile man back to God. God's promise of salvation, it is provided to all who accept His Son Jesus as his or her personal Savior-promise kept. The Holy Spirit was promised and He came as a rushing mighty wind on the Day of Pentecost. Many souls were saved and the gospel message of Christ spread like wild fire. As we go into the entire world and teach Christ, His promise is that He will be with us, and He is. Promise kept. Can you name one promise that God has failed to keep? *I think not!*

As we have highlighted some of God's faithfulness, it stands to reason that God continues to display His faithfulness to His people because of His love, tender mercies, graciousness and compassion. What makes God so faithful in keeping His promises? It is because God cannot lie and His immutability (Malachi 3:6), which states in part, "ye sons of Jacob are not consumed."

Lord, thank You for Your compassion, love and tender mercies, because of Your faithfulness man is spared to see another day. In Jesus name. Amen!

God The Ruler Of All Creation: Psalm 47:1-9

For the Lord Most High is terrible; He is a great King over all the earth.

Throughout Israel's history they did not have an earthly king as the other nations, but in their quest to be like their neighbors Israel requested a king. Their request was granted by God as He knew their rejection of Him was because of human thinking. What Israel failed to realize that God was their true king because He created and sustains all that exist. Also, during their early history He placed godly leaders over them so they could walk upright in the eyesight of God. Holy living assured Israel of God's continued blessing. Most importantly, God was the source of their deliverance from Egypt and during their wilderness journey as well as during the early establishment as a young nation.

If the question were raised, What makes God the ruler of all creation? The answer lies in the fact that He is the creator of all that exist and His wonders and majesty are to behold. In God's creative process, He designed all creation to perform according to His will and purpose. He sustains all creation which includes humanity. He left His holy Word as a guide for mankind to live by and the indwelling Holy Spirit to act as our compass to keep us on the right path while we sojourn here on earth--holy living.

Would God create something and take a hands-off approach? No, because of His love He is intimately involved with all creation.

God the true ruler, abide by His standards-rules.

April 12

God And His Forgiveness: Psalm 103:1-3

Bless the Lord, O my soul, bless his holy name, Bless the Lord, O my soul and forget not all his benefits; Who forgiveth all thine iniquities; who healeth all thy diseases;

God's forgiveness is evidenced by Him giving the best that He had-His Son Jesus Christ to die on the cross for the sins of the world. Who else can make such a claim or love to the point of giving all that He has for someone else? This is because God is love and love is the very core of God's nature.

Yes God is worthy of all praises and worship that man has to offer because of what He has done and continues to do in the lives of all humanity. He loves, forgives and heals, protects, guide and supplies for all our needs. **What a mighty, but loving God!**

Answer to the question in verse 3 is God and because of His mercy that is evidenced by Him continually saying, "I forgive you and still love you in spite of your sins." Only the true and living God can and does make such a statement. The God of our salvation is the only God who has the ability to heal all manner of diseases. He does heal. God's grace and mercy is new and fresh each day because each day is another opportunity to experience His goodness, grace and mercy.

God's forgiveness paves the way for our redemption and to receive the gift of salvation which brings eternal life. He then heals us of both our physical and spiritual sickness. ***Only a forgiving God!***

April 13

His Mercy And Truth: Psalm 7:1-11

Be merciful unto me, O God, be merciful unto me: for my soul trusteth in thee; yea, in the shadow of thy wings will I make my refuge, until these calamities be over past. He shall send from heaven, and save me from the reproach of him that would swallow me up. Selah. God shall send forth his mercy and his truth.

What is mercy? According to the Student Bible Dictionary (P. 154) mercy is showing compassion, love, deep caring, sympathy and forgiveness. It is God withholding justice when it was demanded. Humanity was given a second chance because if justice had been executed then all humanity would be lost to sin as God had pronounced the whole world guilty. What did God do? He displayed His mercy by giving His Son Jesus to die on the cross for the sins of the world. God the Father and the Son willingly displayed their love and mercy for the sake of restoring a broken fellowship between God and man. **What an awesome display of mercy!**

Given the fact of what we know of God's mercy in providing salvation, it is noteworthy to say that God continues to give mercy because even in our worst situations, He is present with His mercy. He carries us through the situation on the wings of His love and protection.

What is His truth? His truth is the fact that God loves unconditionally and this fact has been proven time and again. Just as God is love so is He truth because He cannot lie.

God is worthy of all praise and honor. Praise Him! Praise Him!

April 14

His Prevailing Justice: Psalm 103:6-12

The Lord executeth righteousness and judgment for all that are oppressed. He made His ways known to Moses, his acts unto the children of Israel. The Lord is merciful and gracious, slow to anger, and plenteous in mercy. He will not always chide; neither will he keep his anger for ever. He hath not dealt with us after our sins; nor rewarded us according to our iniquities.

What is justice? Popular definitions defines justice as fairness, or a rightness, while the definition for just is righteous, fair, or right when it comes in the eyesight of God (Romans 1:17; Genesis 6:9). The common saying for justice is giving one what he or she deserves, but God applied mercy when justice/punishment was demanded for our sins. Why did He do this? Because of His love and mercy which took precedence over justice because of love for His people and His desire for an intimate relationship with mankind as well as restoring a broken fellowship.

God is just even in His punishment, because in His longsuffering He allows for repentance. This is evident by Israel's 70 year captivity in Babylon. His hand of mercy was present protecting His people. For many years His prophets preached repentance, but the people failed to listen.

It is noteworthy to say that God has promised punishment for all who fail to humbly submit to His righteousness as He has provided all the necessary means to know Him, His will and the support system to keep us in a right standing with Him.

Take heed, God's justice will prevail.

April 15

An All Compassionate God: Psalm 103:13-14

Like as a father pitieth his children, so the Lord pitieth them that fear him. For he knoweth our frame; he remembers that we are dust.

Thus far we have studied God from His forgiveness, His mercy and truth and His prevailing justice, but for today's discussion we will focus on His compassion. When we consider the term "compassion" it is to show care, concern, pity and sympathy; all of which God has put on display in His dealing with His people and humanity overall.

God's pity/mercy really shows to those who fear and love Him. This reverential fear of the Lord is a redeeming fear that causes believing humanity to turn from his or her wicked ways and turn to following Him and His percepts. In doing so the person draws near to God and His righteousness with the full knowledge that one day we will live happily in His presence.

As noted in verse 14 God knows humanity's weakness and infirmities and He is ready to shower His compassion on all who follow Him. In doing so, we become His children who share in an abundance of His mercy, loving-kindness, forgiveness, His grace and His fatherly love. God provides help according to our need (Philippians 4:19).

God is a perfect example of showing compassion as brothers and sisters in Christ, let's follow His lead.

April 16

Everlasting Love Of God: Psalm 103:17-22

But the mercy of the Lord is from everlasting to everlasting upon them that fear him, and his righteousness unto children's children; To such as keep his covenant, and to those that remember his commandments to do them.

If the question were raised, How long does God's love last? Our scripture verse provides the answer. More importantly, God Himself is from everlasting to everlasting; therefore, it is unthinkable that His love would be short lived or with time limits. There are many scriptures that discuss the long-lasting love of God, but John 3:16 stands out as it promises everlasting life to all who believe on His Son Jesus. The question now becomes, If He wants all believers to spend eternity with Him, then why wouldn't His love lasts equally as long? God and His love go together as He is love.

The writer of this psalm also points out that God's everlasting love is extended to our children's children and generations to come. God's love begins with humankind's creation-- Adam and Eve and extends forward. Why so, because God breathed--His Spirit the breath of life into mankind.

God asks all who love and fear Him to keep His covenant and commandments; given all that He has done and continues to do, is this request unreasonable? I think not, because the Holy Spirit dwells in us to aid in this request.

There is no greater love than that of God which lasts an eternity. How long does your love last?

April 17

Believers Inheritance
Hebrews 9:15; Colossians 1:12; 3:24; Ephesians 1:11

In whom also we have obtained an inheritance, being predestinated according to the purpose of him who worketh all things after the counsel of his own will (Ephesians 1:11). Knowing that of the Lord ye shall receive the reward of the inheritance; for ye receive the Lord Christ (Colossians 3:24).

What is an inheritance? Inheritance is defined as "to receive something from an ancestor" (The Student Bible Dictionary P 120). Zondervan's Pictorial Bible Dictionary P. 874) discuss as length inheritance, but for our discussion today let's begin by saying that inheritance is used in scripture to refer to property inheritance. Inheritance has a theological significance as it relates to God's promises.

In the Old Testament inheritance was used as a promise from God to Abraham and all his descendants regarding the Promise Land--Canaan. This land was theirs as long as they obeyed God's covenant; disobedience would result in the land being taken away and repentance would restore the land. The idea of inheritance expanded on two fronts; (a) the nation of Israel realized that Jehovah God Himself was their inheritance (Jeremiah 10:16), which included the individual believer. (b) God's inheritance was "His elect who was brought out of Egypt to be unto Him a people of inheritance" (Deuteronomy 4:20). The idea of believers being God's inheritance was further expanded to include the Gentiles as well (Isaiah 19:25; 47:6; 63:17; Psalm 2:8).

In the New Testament, inheritance is very prevalent and is connected to Jesus Christ who is heir to God's throne by virtue of being His Son (Mark 12:7). Therefore, believers in the NT become heirs by believing in Christ and His redemptive work on Calvary. We then become adopted sons of God and fellow-heirs with Christ (Romans 8:17; Galatians 4:7). Therefore, all believers have the guaranteed promise from God of an "eternal inheritance" for accepting His Son Jesus Christ as Savior.

Throughout this discussion we have tried to present information regarding our inheritance, so if the question is ever raised, what is the believer's inheritance? One can answer with confidence that our inheritance is "the kingdom of God with all its blessings (Matthew 25:34) which is a gift of His sovereign grace" (1 Corinthians 15:50; 1 Peter 1: 3, 4).

It can be concluded then that believers have an inheritance that is more valuable than gold and more precious than rubies. Our inheritance was bought with the blood of Jesus Christ and one day all believers will share with Him in glory.

Thanks God for His grace. We have a priceless jewel.

April 18

Created In The Image Of God: Genesis 1:26-31

And God said, Let us make man in our image, after our likeness: and let them have dominion over the fish of the sea, and over the fowl of the air, and over the cattle, and over all the earth, and over every creeping thing that creepeth upon the earth. So God created man in his own image, in the image of God created he him; male and female created he them. And God blessed them....

This month's discussion theme is God Reveals; for today's topical discussion is to refute the notion of man evolving with supporting scriptures. According to our faith we believe the Bible to be God's holy Word and is the final authority as it was written by holy inspired men of God (II Timothy 3:16).

With that being said, our scripture verses describe implicitly what God said regarding the creation of man. The "let us" phrase tells me that the Godhead was having a conversation as to who would have dominion over all God's creation. The decision was man.

First, let's notice two things, (a) the order in which man was created. He was created last. (b) God created man which includes male and female, not two males or two females. The second fact is that God blessed man after he was created. Verse 28 provides God's intention for man, which is to be fruitful and multiply by replenishing the earth. God giving man ruler ship over all His creation speaks volumes of His love and care for man.

We are God's creation, so represent Him well by holy living.

April 19

God Looks At The Heart: Matthew 6:1-8

Be not ye therefore like unto them for your Father knoweth what things ye have need of, Before ye ask.

The background from our lesson text is that it deals with piety and giving of alms, there were two men praying where one thought very highly of himself and the other was humble in his thoughts. The man listed as the hypocrite felt that if he prayed in public and with much speaking would win brownie points with God. What he failed to realize is that God looks at the heart and knew his motive as He does with each of us. This is because the heart is the center of all thoughts, actions and deeds. God knows the needs of each of us and is willing to supply all our needs if we come to Him honestly.

Another point to this discussion is to let God do the exalting, because self-exaltation is dangerous and will come to nothing. Therefore, prayer is a form of worship and should be done with sincerity, honesty and in faith.

Matthew 6:9-15 is our model prayer and the first component is to acknowledge God and His holiness. In doing so we acknowledge that He is all-knowing, all-powerful, merciful, loving and caring and has promised to supply all our needs. God keeps His promises.

Therefore, the lesson from this study is pray from the heart as God knows.

April 20

God Knows Humanity: Psalm 139: 23-24

Search me, O God, and know my heart, and know my thoughts: And see if there be any wicked way in me, and lead me in the way everlasting.

Our scripture text depicts a prayer that all believers should pray as we have been sanctified by God and taught to despise all unrighteousness. The psalmist is asking God to search him through and through and see if there is any wickedness in him and then remove it. This is because as believers we are to lead lives of righteousness for the world to see God and His holiness in us. How does God bring about perfection in believers? He does so by testing us with trials as these are designed to further His work of sanctification.

If the question is raised, Why would we need to ask God to search what He already knows? This is an acknowledgment of God being our creator and He knows each of us better than we know ourselves. It is a credit to humility because of our limited knowledge and ability to lead a life of holy living without the help of the Holy Spirit. Asking God to thoroughly search us is a commitment to doing His will so what we do and say parallels each other. Because all we do and say is to glorify God as it is done in the name of Jesus.

Submitting to God will strengthen our intimate relationship with Him and will further our witnessing power.

God knows.

April 21

Righteous Verses The Wicked: Proverbs 15:6-7

In the house of the righteous is much treasure; but in the revenue of the wicked is trouble. The lips of the wise disperse knowledge; but the heart of the foolish doeth not so. The sacrifice of the wicked is an abomination to the Lord; but the prayer of the upright is his delight.

Our above scripture text is taking a comparative look at the lives of the righteous to that of the wicked, both individually and cooperatively. Verse 6 highlights the importance of having God's presence abiding in the home as opposed to earthly wealth without God's presence. This is because the treasure of God's presence is priceless. Wherever God is present then this household has both earthly and heavenly treasures, because God is the supplier of all our needs (Philippians 4:19). The righteous recognizes this fact; one can do more with God and less earthly values than 100% earthly treasures and no God. **The absence of God equals trouble.**

Solomon describes the difference between spoken words of the righteous to that of the unrighteous. The righteous person seeks opportunities to give wise counsel as this is an opportunity to witness Jesus Christ, whereas the unrighteous is spewing hatred and evil confrontation. The unrighteous forsakes the opportunity for peaceful solutions to matters and this is not of God. The God of the heaven is one of peace, love and harmony.

Verse 8 verifies what God cherishes by stating "the prayer of the upright is his delight." How does the world see you, righteous or wicked? What are your most valuable treasures, living in the presence of God or Satan? God is the perfect choice.

April 22

God Reveals His Son: John 1:4-5, 14

In him was life; and the life was the light of men. And the light shineth in darkness; and the darkness comprehended it not.

Throughout biblical history God made many revelations of Himself and His Son Jesus Christ, but with His birth is the revelation of who Christ really is as He is considered the final revelation before He returns for His church.

The New Testament writer presented Jesus in different ways, but John presented Jesus as the Word of God authenticating His presence from the beginning of time. The most startling revelation is the presentation of Jesus life as He is the light of the world. Jesus came to shed light about everlasting life in a sin riddled world. The world failed to comprehend who Jesus really was. This is because our world both then and now is controlled by Satan and many are blinded by his masterful schemes of deception.

How do we recognize Satan for who he really is? We know that a better way is to recognize Jesus as God's Son the life giver. The following scriptures will authenticate Christ's deity. In John 14:6 Jesus is presented as the life, in 6:35, 48 He is presented as the bread and living water (4:10-11; 7:38). Christ's words give eternal life as He embodies all life (6:68; 6:33; 10:10).

Therefore, accept Jesus Christ who embodies true, genuine life and without Him there is no life. This life is made available to everyone who accepts Jesus Christ.

Accept Him and live for He is God's Son.

April 23

God Reveals His Grace And Truth: John 1: 14-18

And the Word was made flesh, and dwelt among us, (and we beheld his glory as of the only begotten of the Father,) full of grace and truth. No man hath seen God at any time; the only begotten of the Father, he hath declared him.

Today's lesson study solidifies Christ being the Son of God as He became human where deity and humanity were united together. His sole purpose was to restore the broken fellowship between God the Father and mankind. Man needed deliverance from Satan's bondage and with Christ living as man He would experience all the human limitations, pain and suffering that man would experience. He is a Savior that knows all about us as He was present during creation.

Christ being the only begotten of the Father authenticates His Sonship as He was present with God in the beginning as well as His Trinitarian being on display here. No man has ever seen God the Father only through His Son Jesus. Another note of fact on Christ being God's only begotten is His uniqueness as He is God Himself as His earthly mother was conceived by the God the Holy Spirit. Christ being the final revelation of God reveals the full extent of God's grace and truth which is His righteousness embodied in His Son Jesus. God's grace is experienced daily by all believers as it is delivered fresh daily by God the Holy Spirit.

There is no righteousness except God's--His grace.

April 24

Salvation Revealed: John 3:16-17

For God so loved the world, that he gave his only begotten Son, that whoever believeth on him should not perish, but have everlasting life. For God sent not his Son into the world to condemn the world; but that the world through him might be saved.

In today's lesson study our focus will be on salvation and how God revealed His salvation to all humanity. First, we will redefine the term "salvation" as a refresher. It is defined as deliverance or being brought safely through from harm or danger, or the one who saves. In the Old Testament God is seen as the deliverer of His people as He delivered them out of bondage in Egypt into the Promise Land. Therefore, He is seen as the one who saves His people (Psalm 27:1; 88:1). During Israel's journey to the Promise Land it was God Himself that saved, protected and guided His people. Notice if you will, how He used a pillar of cloud during the day as a covering to shield the hot desert sun and at night He used a pillar of fire to light their way for safe travels. The cloud here represented God's presence with His people. He is still present today with His people. Notice the protection God provided. The desert was full with danger both seen and unseen, such as poisonous snakes, the lack of food and water, but God provided. He fed them with manna from heaven fresh each morning and water from a rock. **Just look at God and His saving power!**

Second, the question now becomes why is it that man needs saving/salvation? The need was brought on by disobedience which began in the Garden of Eden with Adam. Every generation after was born into sin by nature. God in His grand design knew man was going to sin and need a Savior. Therefore, His Son Jesus was scheduled to be our Savior from the beginning of time. However, God provided salvation Himself until at His appointed time Christ came on the scene as Savior. With that being said, then Christ is the only way back to God to restore a broken fellowship. If the question were raised, What happened to all who died before Christ came to earth to die on the cross for the sins of the world? Faith is the key ingredient to salvation, past, present and future. The believer passes from a spiritual death to spiritual life as he or she has received forgiveness for his or her sins as this is a free gift from God. This establishes a renewed one-to-one relationship with God the Father and Jesus Christ the Son and God the Holy Spirit takes up residence in each believer. It is noteworthy to say that God did not create man in His image and likeness to have a broken fellowship with him. God's perfect plan is to have an intimate relationship with His people and He provided the means to do so--His Son Jesus Christ.

While God has made known His salvation, mankind can either choose to partake or reject God's salvation. **Which do you chose?** By choosing salvation it saves us from God's coming wrath and being eternally separated from our creator. Additional blessings for choosing salvation is that all who believe will share in Christ's glory and receive resurrected/transformed bodies and will receive a crown of life as we will be faithful over comers. Lastly, all believers will see our Savior face-to-face. *What a glorious experience!*

God has made known/revealed His salvation and the final revelation was in Jesus Christ. What are we going to with this knowledge?

April 25

Temple Of God Revealed In Christ
John 2:13-17; Luke 19:45-46

And when he had made a scourge of small cords, he drove them all out of the temple, and the sheep and the oxen; and poured out the changers' money, and overthrew the tables; And said unto them that sold doves, Take these things hence; make not my Father's house a house of merchandise.

The temple has a long and historic history as its forerunner was the tent where God instructed the nation of Israel to build in the wilderness at Mount Sinai, but after they entered the Promise Land the tent was maintained even though mobile until the reign of King Solomon who erected a permanent temple-a place of worship.

The temple symbolizes the presence and protection of God where He would be among His people. The temple also symbolizes God's redemption of His people. Two important events took place in the temple and they were, daily sacrifices for ones sins, and the Day of Atonement which was conducted by the priest yearly. In the New Testament, the temple symbolized Christ as He Himself represents the presence of God and the church is His body. Therefore, all believers are the body of Christ, and then we become temples of God through His Spirit.

Jesus cleansing the temple in our scripture text is symbolic of the holiness that both collectively and individually one must possess. When believers assemble to worship God it must be done in Spirit and in truth (John 4:24). Therefore, the church and each believer must be cleansed of all unrighteousness.

God dwells in a clean temple(s).

April 26

God Speaks: Matthew 3:17

And lo a voice from heaven, saying, This is my beloved Son, in whom I am well pleased.

Our scripture text reveals God speaking at Jesus' baptism and it also gives a vivid description of the Trinity on display as all members of the Godhead were present.

Reflect with me on other instances where God spoke; He spoke to Moses from a burning bush when Moses was called to lead God's people out of bondage in Egypt. God spoke to Joshua after he assumed leadership after Moses died. God spoke to Gideon as he prepared for battle, which he won with only three hundred men. God spoke to Elijah in a small still voice after Elijah had escaped with his life. God spoke to Mary through His angel and told her that she would give birth to the Savior of the world. God also, spoke to Joseph through His angel saying that which Mary carried was the work of the Holy Spirit (Matthew 1:20). God/Christ spoke to Paul on the Damascus Road. Paul then became a slave for Christ and His gospel message.

God has always spoken to His people through His prophets, apostle, disciples, preachers, teachers, evangelists and His holy Word-the Bible. God even speaks through nature.

God is still speaking, the question is, Do you hear God when He speaks?

April 27

God Reveals His Peace: Jeremiah 33:6

Behold, I will bring it health, and cure, and I will cure them, and will reveal unto them the abundance of peace and truth.

The prophet Jeremiah in his message to the nation of Israel promises the peace of God which surpasses all other. The reason for this hope was that false prophets were proclaiming false peace that was not going to last. The difference between God's prophets and false prophets is that they said "what thus said the Lord."

The definition of peace is the absence of conflict or stress or war. The presence of peace brings harmony, wholeness, a well-being in all areas of ones life (JKV commentary).

God's creation of man was in perfect peace and in harmony with Him, but disobedience disrupted that perfect peace and harmony. The disruption of peace began in the Garden of Eden when the first family disobeyed God's command of eating of the forbidden fruit.

When will peace be restored? The process began with redemption in Jesus Christ. At the birth of Christ the angels made the grand announcement that peace had come to earth (Luke 2:14). Jesus is the only one who is capable of destroying Satan's conflicts on human lives. Mankind has overcome the evils of this world with the death, burial and resurrection of Jesus Christ as He has overcome the world. What are we to do to have this peace now? First, we must accept Him in faith. Second, we have and know God's peace through the Holy Spirit (Galatians 5:22).

God's peace is revealed in Jesus Christ.

April 28

The Will Of God: Isaiah 53:10

Yet it pleased the Lord to bruise him; he hath put him to grief; when thou shalt make his soul an offering for sin, he shall see his seed, he shall prolong his days, and the pleasure of the Lord shall prosper in his hand.

It was the Will of God the Father to send His Son Jesus Christ to die for the sins of the world (John 3:16). Making His Son Jesus Christ the human sacrifice for humanity's sin was part of God's redemptive plan as it is His Will that all be saved. God's redemptive purpose has been accomplished as many have been saved and many more will continue to be saved by accepting Jesus Christ as his or her personal Savior. The spiritual invitation remains open as there is room for many more to come to Christ.

How does one know the Will of God? First, the Will of God is what He desires as His perfect will, and what He allows to happen is His permissive will. An example of each of His wills is His perfect Will is that all be saved. All who continue in sin and be eternally separated from Him is permitted by Him. Also, He permits evil to continue existing for the time being, but the time will come when evil will be destroyed by God. Second, we know the Will of God by establishing a close fellowship with Him through prayer and daily reading and meditating on His Word. Then we are to adhere to what His Word says. We have the indwelling Holy Spirit to aid in understanding and obeying God's Word.

Know and do the Will of God.

April 29

The Attributes Of God Revealed: Psalm 139:7-8

Whither shall I go from thy Spirit? Or wither shall I flee from thy presence? If I ascend up into heaven, thou art there: If I make my bed in hell, behold, thou art there.

The psalmist is expressing his inescapability of God due to the attributes of God our creator. Regardless of where the psalmist or all humanity may go, God is there. He extends from heaven to hell or in the depths of the sea, God is still there. This is a tribute to an all-knowing, everywhere, all seeing, and all powerful God. Other unique attributes of God is that He transcends all meaning that He is independent from all His creations as well as He is a being and His existence is far greater and higher than the created order (Isaiah 66:1-2; 1 Kings 8:27; Acts 17:2425). God is eternal meaning that He has no beginning or ending-everlasting (Psalm 90:1-2). God is unchangeable which means that He is perfect in His purposes for mankind (Numbers 23:19; Psalm 102:26-28; Isaiah 41:4; Malachi 3:6). God is holy, which means He is without sin. He is triune which is one God operating in three distinct divine persons--the Father, the Son, and the Holy Spirit.

The moral attributes of God is as follows: (a) He is good, (b) He is love, (c) He is merciful, (d) He is compassionate, (e) He is patient/longsuffering, (f) He is truth, (g) God is faithful and (h) He is just.

Most importantly, all of God's attributes were seen in God Himself and in the final revelation of Himself through His Son Jesus Christ.

Our inescapable God!

April 30

God's Glory Revealed: 1 Corinthians 2:8; John 1:14

And the Word was made flesh dwelt among us, (and we beheld his glory, the glory as of the only begotten of the Father,) full of grace and truth (John 1:14). Which none of the princes of this world knew; for had they known it, they would not have crucified the Lord of glory (1 Corinthians 2:8).

Today's lesson study focus is on the glory of God, which is glorified through His Son Jesus Christ. Our first scripture describes Jesus being the Word of God who was made of flesh as He walked the earth. His disciples traveled with Jesus and witnessed the many signs and wonders He performed authenticating His deity; yet many failed to recognize Him as the begotten Son of God the Father.

When did Jesus existence begin? Jesus was there in the beginning with His Father and upon His earthly arrival was the final revelation of God as His sole purpose was to bring salvation to the world. Therefore, Paul in our second lesson study text answers an implied question would the princes/rulers of this would have crucified our Lord? Hopefully, the answer would have been no, because after the events that occurred on that Friday, many recognized Jesus as Lord. Prophecy had to be fulfilled and His death was eminent as He had to die only to rise again on Sunday morning.

With that being said, God continues to reveal His glory in many ways; the rising and setting of the sun daily, the moon and stars performing their task on schedule, nature obeying His commands and the seasons changing without any delay. Each time we look at our self and our fellow man we see the glory of God and as each believer witness and live holy lives, His glory is manifested even more.

Look around you and see God's glory-it is everywhere.

Witnessing Christ

A Dedicated Servant: Acts 9:32-43

And it came to pass, as Peter passed throughout all quarters; he came down also to the saints which dwelt at Lydia.

Today's lesson study is focus on the dedication of a servant. Our scripture depicts the dedication of Peter and how he served until the end of his life. Peter's faith is the foundation of the Christian church and it stands to reason he would dedicate his life to following Jesus and continuing Jesus' ministry. It was Peter who stood and preached on the Day of Pentecost when the Holy Spirit manifested Himself and three thousand souls were added to the church.

It was Peter's faith and dedications that allowed him to perform the miracles noted in our scripture text. The disciples were promised powers to perform miracles, signs and wonders after the Holy Ghost had come upon them. Peter was imprisoned for preaching Christ; did he stop? No. The church prayed and Peter was released and he continued to preach Christ. The apostle Paul endured many hardships for preaching Christ; what did he do? Paul continued to preach Christ and establish churches all over the Asia Minor region. Stephens was stoned to death for preaching Christ. There are many others who remained dedicated to his or her call as many faced persecutions, but persevered. What sacrifices are you and I willing to make for preaching Christ?

The Holy Ghost's promise to give power to boldly witness Christ and perform many miracles, signs and wonders remains in effect today for all believers. Believers today must remain dedicated and committed to the call that Christ has given. Each believer is a servant of Jesus Christ and has a call to ministry if no more than simply witness. Each believer is a chosen generation, a member of a royal priesthood, a holy nation, as each is an elect of God predetermined by Him before the foundation of the world.

What greater example of a dedicated servant than that of Jesus Christ who subjected Himself to human limitations, pain and suffering, abuse and scorn for the sake of providing salvation to mankind. Jesus remained dedicated to His mission and ministry all the way to the cross and beyond as He is currently in heaven making intercessions for all who call on Him. Jesus Christ being the Son of God typifies the holiness and righteousness of God who sought no reputation for Himself only to do the will of His Father. Jesus is co-equal with God because He is God. *What an humble servant!*

Let's pray, Lord Thank You for choosing me to be Your servant. Allow me to serve You in all humility so that You will be glorified and not self-aggrandizement. In Jesus name Amen.

Know Jesus: John 14:8-11

Believe me that I am in the Father, and the Father in me: or else believe me for the very works' sake.

During Jesus' earthly ministry many witnessed His many miracles, signs and wonders authenticating His deity, but some still failed to recognize Jesus as the Christ our Savior.

If the question were raised, How do I get to know Jesus? First, one must believe there is a God the only one true living God who gave His Son Jesus Christ to become the sacrificial lamb for humanity's sins. Second, one must believe and accept Jesus as Lord and Savior (John 3:16) who died on the cross for our sins. Third, one must admit that he or she is a sinner and if saved done so by God's grace when justice demanded that mankind be eternally separated from God our creator (Romans 3:23-24). Forth, one must believe the eye witness accounts given by His disciples, apostles and the Holy Scriptures as Jesus is the center piece of the Bible. Lastly, one will come to know Jesus by adhering to the voice of the Holy Spirit as He provides divine revelation of who Jesus is.

Some of His disciples (Thomas and Phillip) had doubt as to who Jesus was and they were encouraged to believe Him for the works He had done. This encouragement applies today because who else could provide the gift of salvation for the entire human race if only one accepts this free gift.

Know Jesus for He is God's Son our Savior.

Jesus, The Way, The Truth and The Life: John 14:6-7

Jesus saith unto him, I am the way, the truth, and the life; no man cometh unto the Father, but by me. If ye had known me, ye should have known my Father also; and from henceforth ye know him, and have seen him.

Nearing the end of Jesus' earthly ministry and mission, He was having a conversation with His disciples where He promises to return and for them to "let not their hearts be troubled" (v.1). During the conversation Jesus told His disciples where He was going and they knew how to get there. Thomas refuted Jesus' statement by stating they didn't know where He was going or how to get there. Our lesson study picks up with Jesus telling them that He was "the way, truth and the life" and if anyone comes to the Father they would have to come through Him. This is a profound fact because it embodies salvation as Jesus is the way back to God, because Jesus took on humanity's sins; therefore, when God the Father looks at man He sees the righteousness of His Son.

Furthermore, Jesus is the final revelation of God the Father as He is God. Therefore, it stands to reason that Jesus expected His disciples to recognize God the Father in Him. His disciples had traveled with Jesus for three long years and had witnessed all that He had done and taught and should have concluded that He and the Father were one (vv. 7-11).

Jesus is the way, truth and life for He is God.

May 4

Promise Of The Comforter: John 14:15-16

If ye love me, keep my commandments. And I will pray the Father, and he shall give you another Comforter, that he may abide with you for ever.

As Jesus began to prepare for His return to heaven, He began preparing His disciples for what was to come, and one was the coming of the Holy Spirit. While Jesus was in the earth He was the comforter who healed many diseases, brought comfort where it was needed, preached repentance, performed many miracles and wonders, and even raised the dead.

By the mere fact that Jesus promised to send another comforter gives rise to who He was and that He would not leave His people/disciples comfortless. A comforter is one who is sent or called to aid, help or even serve as a counselor. The Holy Spirit is just such person as He resides in each believer and performs many tasks in the lives of all believers as well as the unbeliever. He convicts the unbeliever of his or her sins and gives the person a heart to live for God.

Just as Jesus provided comfort to His disciples when they would become discouraged or there was disharmony among the group, the Holy Spirit does the same thing when we as believers become discouraged or experience disharmony. The Holy Spirit brings a closer relationship with God and one another as well as giving all believers the power to rise above adversities.

The promised Comforter-God the Holy Spirit abides in each of us.

Christ The True Vine: John 15:1-2

I am the true vine, and my Father is the husbandman. Every branch in me that beareth not fruit he taketh away, and every branch beareth fruit, he purgeth it, that it may bring forth more fruit.

What is Jesus teaching in this parable? He is teaching that He is the Christ the one and only Savior (true vine) and all who come to Him in faith have life and apart from Him there is no life. The other message here is that Disciples of Christ must remain in Him to bear fruit and if and when the fruit bearing ceases then he or she is casted off. With that being said, all believers are expected to bear fruit as this builds the kingdom of God.

How do believers bear fruit? Believers bear fruit through his or her witnessing Christ as believers are the salt of the earth. The earth is to be seasoned by sharing the gospel of Christ and inviting others to believe and join the royal family of God. Fruits of our beliefs are seen by the world through the believer's lifestyle-holy living, and through the believer's fruit bearing, there is growth in the Christian community. God the Father purges/removes any and all obstacles that hinder kingdom building.

All fruit bearing is based on our love for God and others. This represents both vertical and horizontal relationships.

Fruit-bearing Christians bring glory to God and His holiness.

May 6

Abide In Christ: John 15:4-5

Abide in me, and I in you. As the branch cannot bear fruit of itself, except it abide in the vine; no more can ye, except ye abide in me. I am the vine, ye are the branches: He that abideth in me, and I in him, the same bringeth forth much fruit for without me ye can do nothing.

Jesus in His many teachings regarding all believers continued growth and walk in Christ-likeness, He is discussing the need for the believer to abide in Him as believers are the branch from the tree (vine). Branches grow from the tree and give evidence of the kind of tree they grow from-Christ. As long as each believer abides in Christ he or she has life eternally, but when the branch is separated from the vine it dies.

Believers have salvation through Jesus Christ and have the power to remain in Christ with the aid of the Holy Spirit. The question now becomes, how can we remain attached to the vine and why? Believers must remain attached to the vine to continue to live and bear fruit. This is achieved by hiding the Word of God in our hearts and living according to His word and commandments. Allowing the Word to permeate our very soul, remain in God's love and allowing the Holy Spirit to order our footsteps. Prayer must be an integral part of the believer's life.

As believers become more Christ-like the more fruit believers bear. Does the world see Christ in you?

A Spiritual Healing: Psalm 42:1-11

As the hart (heart) panteth after the water brooks, so panteth my soul after thee, O God. My soul thirsteth for God, for the living God: When shall I come and appear before God? My tears have been my meat day and night, while they continually say unto me, Where is thy God?

Our scripture text describes a vivid yearning for the presence of God; this is what happens when one recognizes his or her need for salvation and or to be in the presence of God. The absence of the Lord leaves a void in our lives that material and mortal substances cannot fill.

The writer of this psalm paints a vivid picture for the need for the presence of God through the indwelling Holy Spirit by using the body's need for water to live. On a spiritual consciousness we must have spiritual bread and water to live that only God can give (John 4:10; 6:48; 7:37).

Verse 2 drives home the point of needing the presence of the living God by: (1) Recognizing that there is only one God, (2) only the true and living God will satisfy ones needs, (3) humility by asking "When shall I come and appear before God?" God is standing by ready to forgive and receive all repentant hearts. We are never to feel forsaken by God, because He is true to His word of never leaving nor will He forsake all who call on Him. There is no need to feel cast down and without hope; God is standing by.

True repentance heals a spiritually broken heart.

May 8

"Joy Cometh in the Morning": Psalm 30:1-5

I will extol thee, O lord; for thou hast lifted me up, and hast not made my foes to rejoice over me. O Lord my God, I cried unto thee, and thou hast healed me. O lord, thou hast brought up my soul from the grave; thou hast kept me alive, that I should not go down to the pit. Sing unto the Lord, O ye saints of his, and give thanks at the remembrance of his holiness. For his anger endureth but a moment; in his favor is life; weeping may endure for a night, but joy cometh in the morning.

What are these verses saying to us? First, these verses are giving praises to the Lord for what He has done in the lives of all humanity. The phrase "for thou hast lifted me up" can be concluded to mean that God lifted humanity out of the bondage of sin when mankind was destined for eternal damnation-separation because of sin. It has a personal connation for every believer because salvation is an individual experience. All believers can rejoice because we are no longer under Satan's control where we were once slaves to his dominion.

The second meaning is like the psalmist all believers can shout I have been healed from my sinfulness and now I am free. Realizing that God has delivered all believers' souls from the very pit of hell is worthy of holy praises that can be heard from the highest mountain tops. Also, it is God through the Holy Spirit who is keeping us alive in Him. **The captives have been set free and we can shout let freedom reign. Hallelujah free at last, free at last thank God Almighty we are free at last.**

Third, because we are saved does not free us from adversities, but when adversities come and they will we have a Savior who knows all about the situation and delivers in His own time. God promised the Messiah and in His time He delivered. Whatever the situation is as a moment in God's time-night, but we can shout victory because "**joy cometh in the morning.**" Go on and shout saints, because we have a helper who is always near.

Fourth, reflecting on God's anger and seeing His hand of

mercy. He pronounced the whole world guilty before Him because of sin; What did He do? God provided a Savior. Because He is love His anger did not last a life time. When God is compelled to punish His children it is for a short while, because His mercy is too great. As love and mercy is one of His character traits.

Lesson summary is, whatever adversities we may experience, remember *"joy cometh in the morning"*, as our adversities may be to strengthen our faith in God and draw us closer to Him. The closer we are to God the better our relationship is with Him.

Remember behind every dark cloud there is a silver lining. Count it all joy (James 1:2).

May 9

A Prayer Of Mercy: Psalm 6:1-4

O Lord, rebuke me not, O Lord; anger, neither chasten me in thy hot displeasure. Have mercy upon me, O Lord; for I am weak: O Lord, heal me; for my bones are vexed. My soul is also vexed; but thou, O Lord, how long? Return, o lord, deliver my soul; O save me for thy mercy sake.

Many times when a person is experiencing pain and suffering the person will cry out saying, "O Lord have mercy on me." This phrase is a cry for God's hand of mercy on the situation, whether it is the result of self inflicted suffering or some other reason. If the pain is from a physical condition, a physical healing is being called for, or divine chastisement is being afflicted because of a spiritual condition.

Verse 2 gives insight into the extent of the psalmist pain and suffering; "my bones are vexed." The suffering extended to the soul of the psalmist, which is applicable to many today and the same cry is made to God for mercy. Just like the psalmist desired to feel the presence of the Lord so do we when situations arise and it appears as thou there is no relief is in sight. We cry to God for mercy.

It matters not if the repentant is saved or unsaved the cry for mercy is made, because the repentant realizes that he or she needs a soul restoration and to be in the presence of God (v. 4).

Mercy suits our case.

May 10

A Plea For Mercy: Psalm 41:4-13

I said, Lord be merciful unto me; heal my soul; for I have sinned against thee....O Lord, be merciful unto me, and raise me up....

Our lesson study depicts a sinner's plea when recognizing his or her sins and has a heartfelt desire for God's mercy. It also depicts that when sin is committed it is against God our Lord, the only one who has the ability to save us from our wayward situations. A plea for mercy represents humility as the repentant person has come to have a right view of God, self and others. A humble heart puts things in the right perspective such as he or she needing God the Holy Spirit to keep him or her walking upright in the sight of God as the believer is no match for Satan and his lies.

Because of God, His compassionate heart extends His hand of mercy to the repentant heart, whereas justice demands punishment. *So what is mercy?* Mercy is giving man what he does not deserve. God's mercy is seen throughout biblical history as it relates to His love for mankind to the extent that He gave His best for humanity's salvation. ***This is love at its best.***

If there is a need for mercy do like the psalmist and cry out to God for His hand of mercy for He hears the pleas of the repentant and shows compassion.

God's goodness and mercy endures for ever (Psalm 23:6).

May 11

A Compassionate God: Psalm 41:1-3

The Lord will preserve him, and keep him alive, and he shall be blessed upon the earth; and thou will not deliver him unto the will of his enemies.

The definition of compassion is to show pity, sympathy or have mercy upon someone. In our lesson study, the psalmist is making a compassionate plea for mercy. Throughout biblical history God has shown His compassion upon His people and is especially concerned for the less fortunate. All who show compassion on the less fortunate and or others in need; God has special blessings for those persons as this is an expression of God-like care and concern. It is safe to say that in our compassion for others and when we are in need we have the assurances that we can go to God in prayer and He will answer. God in His compassion heals, protects, and delivers.

Reflecting on God's compassion, one can look no further than the nation of Israel while on a typical three day journey which lasted forty years because of disobedience, but His mercy is on display because He provided for their every need. All believers have salvation because of God's pity on our lostness. **Love in action.**

God's compassion remains on display as He is still providing for man's every need because of His faithfulness. Had it not been for God's mercy man would have been swallowed up by the enemy-Satan (Psalm 56:1-2).

Praise God for His compassion for He is worthy to be praised.

May 12

Repentance And Healing: Jeremiah 3:11-12, 22

Go and proclaim these words toward the north, and say, Return thou backsliding Israel, saith the Lord; and I will not cause mine anger to fall upon you; for I am merciful, saith the Lord, and I will not keep anger for ever...Return, ye backsliding children, and I will heal your backslidings; Behold, we come unto thee; for thou art the Lord our God.

The nation of Israel had continued in its waywardness until God's punishment caused them to be led into captivity. The prophet Jeremiah was proclaiming what thus saith the Lord in an attempt to get Israel to repent and turn back to God. Verse 11 provides a glimpse of the magnitude to Israel's treacherousness as it had become worse than that of Judah. Through it all God's love remained strong and desired that Israel turn back to Him as He does with sinners today.

The main message in today's lesson is that God's love forgives each time a sinner repents of his or her sinful ways as there is spiritual healing in repentance. Only God can heal mankind of his backsliding as this is evidenced through His Son Jesus Christ. Because of God's love, He made all provisions for humanity to repent and be saved.

Repentance requires three steps, admission, confession and turning away from sin to righteousness. Just as repentance was proclaimed then, the same message is being proclaimed today. Have you heard the message?

Repent and be healed.

God's Pastors: Jeremiah 3:15

And I will give you pastors according to mine heart, which shall feed you with knowledge and understanding.

Who are pastors? According to scripture and the Student Bible Dictionary (P. 176) a pastor is referred to as a shepherd; one who feeds, leads and oversees (Ephesians 4:11). A pastor is one of the five ministerial leaders of Christ's church who has given him or herself to overseeing and caring for the spiritual needs of God's people-the local congregation and must be of sound doctrine and purity. Pastors are to guard against false teachings and doctrines that are contrary to the Word of God. Pastors are to help believers grow in the grace and knowledge of Christ. Just as Christ is the church so are pastors the head of each local congregation.

1 Timothy 3:1-8 outlines the moral qualifications of pastors/bishops, which states in parts, he must be the husband of one wife, vigilant, sober, of good behavior, given to hospitality, apt to teach, and etc. what all this means is that a pastor must be of good moral character as he or she has been called by God to watch over the souls of His people. Pastors are essential to God's purpose for His church as it is to continue growing. Pastors are not elected by some political method, but through the wisdom of God given by the body after sincere prayer.

Pastors are God's under shepherds and are given according to God's heart to exemplify His love.

May 14

Preaching The Gospel: Matthew 4:23

And Jesus went about all Galilee, teaching in their synagogues and preaching the gospel of the kingdom, and healing all manner of sickness and all manner of disease among the people.

Throughout biblical history there have been called messengers who spoke what thus saith the Lord. During the OT prophets spoke for God encouraging the people to repent and turn back to God. John the Baptist the forerunner of Jesus Christ preached repentance and encouraged his followers to be baptized with water. Water baptism is symbolic of what has taken place within the believer's heart of being baptized in the body of Christ.

In our lesson text, we see Jesus Himself preaching the gospel of repentance of the kingdom of God and salvation is in Him for He is God's Son. Christ's disciples preached the gospel of repentance for the remission of sin. The church grew as a result of preaching the gospel and the same message is to be preached today and forever as Christ left His ministerial leaders to proclaim His message to the world. Laity has a gospel message in his or her witnessing Christ.

The gospel message is to be shared as the harvest fields are great and the laborers are few. The invitation to lost souls to repent remains open as God is preparing a heavenly feast for all who will hear the gospel and repent so that the repentant heart will become members of God's royal family.

Preach the gospel!

May 15

Fishers Of Men: Matthew 4:19

And he saith unto them, Follow me, and I will make you fishers of men.

This setting for today's discussion takes place at the beginning of Jesus' earthly ministry where He had heard of John the Baptist imprisonment. John the Baptist baptized Jesus in the Jordan River. Therefore, as Jesus began His journey as well as fulfilling prophecy spoken by the prophet Esaias, Jesus took the route He did. The people along this journey were in great need of a spiritual awakening; Jesus was it and He began preaching repentance (vv 12-17).

Jesus' journey took Him by the Sea of Galilee where He saw two brothers Simon Peter and Andrew fishing (v 18) and Jesus called out to them asking them to follow Him (v.19). Their response is how all believers are to respond (v. 22). **How do you respond to Jesus' call?**

Jesus used what was relevant to these men in asking them to be His disciples so that they would be equipped to carry His message long after He returned to heaven. To be fishers of men is carrying out the Great Commission as recorded in Matthew 28:19 in bringing others to Christ. It matters not whether we are pastors, evangelists, missionaries, writers, teachers, deacons or simply laity the call is there and all believers are to answer "Yes Lord I will follow You."

The question now becomes, How will lost souls of the world know of Christ and His Saving power unless believers tell them? Unless Christ followers (true believers) tell others about Christ, His message will be lost and His church will cease to grow so will God's kingdom. What we know for certain is that Christ's church will continue to grow as will the kingdom of God, because God always has "a ram in the bush", someone who will be willing to answer "Yes Lord I will follow You" and speak to the lost souls of this world and be a beckoning light of righteousness for others to see through holy living. **The rocks will not speak for me.**

There is nothing to fear in carrying the message of the gospel of Christ to others because Christ promised that He would be with you always even unto the ends of the world (28:20). God has never failed in keeping His promises. He is with us, the presence of the Holy Spirit who resides in each believer.

It is noteworthy to say that all believers who have been baptized in the Spirit have power to do great signs and wonders just as Christ and His apostles did during His earthly ministry.

Church (collectively and individually) we are fishers of men, so preach and teach the Word of God so men will say "What must I do to be saved?"

May 16

God's People: Ephesians 1:3-14

According as he hath chosen us in him before the foundation of the world, that we should be holy and without blame before him in love; Having predestinated us unto the adoption of children by Jesus Christ to himself, according to the good pleasures of his will,

Who are God's people? God's people are all believers who accept His Son Jesus Christ as Lord and Savior and those persons before Christ's earthly birth believed in faith. Faith in the OT is counted as righteousness, as faith is essential to our beliefs.

How do we become God's people? Believe in Jesus Christ as Lord and Savior. It is noteworthy to say that God knew before the foundation of the world who would trust Him and believe in His Son as God looks at the heart and knows each of us before birth. Remember who God is and that He knows all before there was a when or where. Just as God knew that Jesus would have to be born of a woman to shed His blood in the ransoming process of mankind, God already knew who would be in union with His Son. Jesus as the elect is the foundation of our election (KJV commentary).

The KJV commentary summarizes election and predestination by stating in part that "election and predestination is a ship (the church) where Christ is the Captain and pilot and all who desire to be apart of this ship will do so in faith (believers) and our final destination is heaven which God has prepared for us from the beginning of time."

Get on board!

May 17

Spirit vs Flesh: Galatians 5:1-25

...Walk in the Spirit, and ye shall not fulfill the lust of the flesh. For the flesh lusteth against the Spirit, and the Spirit against the flesh; and these are contrary the one to the other; so that ye cannot do the things that ye would.

If the question was raised, Who is in control? God is in control as He is the essence of our being from birth to death and the more Christians develop a meaningful relationship with God and totally commits him or herself to Him through the Holy Spirit, then walking in the Spirit becomes second nature. The flesh is torn by the desires of the eye which are pleasing because of Satan's false presentations. What pleases the flesh is temporary, but what pleases the Spirit is everlasting.

Christians are constantly bombarded with Satan's attacks in his masterful scheme of derailing God's plan of kingdom building, but all believers are dressed for spiritual warfare as recorded in Ephesians 6:11-18. Notice if you will all weapons in this war are defensive except one, the Word of God (sword of the Spirit). This is what we use to attack Satan on his own turf; as Christians are to take the fight to Satan through our Bible study, meditation, prayer and witnessing Christ the world over.

If we walk in the Spirit, then we kill the desires of the flesh, because we are living in the Spirit (v. 25).

Yield to God and His Spirit and walk therein.

Sealed And Kept By The Holy Spirit: Ephesians 1:13

In whom ye also trusted, after that ye heard the word of truth, the gospel of your salvation in whom also after that ye believed, ye were sealed with that Holy Spirit of promise,

A seal is commonly looked upon as a symbol of ownership, but in NT times the seal represents the Holy Spirit and is a mark of ownership by God for His people. Why does God mark His people with the Holy Spirit? Because His Spirit provides evidence of believers being adopted children of God and we know that our redemption is real as He lives in each of us performing His many activities in the lives of all believers. He protects us, teaches us, lead us in the way of righteousness, He delivers us from the power of sin and Satan (Romans 8:1-17; Galatians 5:16-25), and He gives us the knowledge that God is our Father (v. 5; Romans 8:15; Galatians 4:6). Most importantly, the Holy Spirit gives us the power to witness (Acts 1:8; 2:4), and through our witness we build the body of Christ.

Being sealed and kept by the Holy Spirit, He enables the believer to come in full Christ-likeness (4:3; 13) as well as helping the believer in his or her prayer lives and in our spiritual warfare with Satan (Ephesians 6:11-18) as we travel this Christian journey.

He is our heavenly compass directing our heavenly paths. He is God and all believers are His property.

May 19

A Commitment To Serve: Deuteronomy 11:1

Therefore, thou shalt love the Lord thy God, and keep his charge, and his statues, and his judgments, and his commandments always.

In today's lesson study we see Moses encouraging the nation of Israel to obey and love God with all their hearts and do all that God ask of them. This plea remains in effect for all who have confessed to be followers of Christ as well as those desiring to become Christ followers.

What God wants from His followers is a heart-felt devotion to Him and not a mere outward expression through religious activities such as attending church and partaking of the Lord's Supper. A total commitment to God and service to Him begins in the heart as it is the focal point of all our actions. With that being said, we as Christians are to let our outward expression of obedience to God's commandments and holy living be of vital importance, as we may be the only Bible others are reading. Therefore, everything we do should be based on our faith in Jesus Christ and in love for Him for what He has done for us and continues to do in our lives because of who He is.

Based on the above facts of who God is, He is worthy of total obedience and a steadfast commitment to serve Him.

Blessings await our love and obedience; do as God ask and be blessed.

May 20

Empowered To Witness: Acts 1:8

But ye shall receive power after that the Holy Ghost is come upon you: and ye shall be witnesses unto me both in Jerusalem, and in all Judea, and in Samaria, and unto the uttermost part of the earth.

The background for our scripture text is after Christ's resurrection before His ascension into heaven; He gave His disciples instructions regarding the coming Holy Spirit. They were to remain in "Jerusalem and wait for the promise of the Father"(v. 4), and that shortly thereafter they would receive the Holy Ghost.

Our lesson text describes what was to happen in the promised coming of the Holy Ghost; they would receive power, this was a special power to do the works of the Lord. This power gives the ability and authority to cast out devils, heal the sick and perform many others miraculous wonders. Also, receiving Holy Ghost power causes the believer to boldly witness Christ (4:29) with great power (4:33) the world over.

After receiving the Holy Ghost, Christ followers were to begin their aggressive witnessing in Jerusalem, to Judea, Samaria and the world over. With the newly received power Christian witness is powerful and effective as many will come to Christ as they did on the day of Pentecost and continues today when Holy Ghost filled witnessing is done.

Spirit-filled believers have the power to do great things while carrying the message of Christ, hope and forgiveness of sins to the lost so they may be saved.

There is power in witnessing Christ!

May 21

Called Into Holiness: Deuteronomy 28:9

The Lord shall establish thee a holy people unto himself, as he hath sworn unto thee, if thou shalt keep the commandments of the Lord thy God, and walk in his ways.

The back drop of today's lesson study is that the Lord is expressing the blessings from being obedient to His commandment and doing things according to His will and ways. Verses 4 through 8 drives home the magnitude of God's blessing from being obedient to His commandments and ways, which was that all would be bountifully blessed. In verse 7, the Lord promises that if the enemies come against His people there is no victory because God protects His people. **What a blessing for being God's people!**

Looking at our scripture text we see that God is calling to Himself a holy nation of people who will obey His commandments and live according to His statues-ways. This is to show the rest of the world the blessings that can be enjoyed for obedience. Obedience is the basic of a covenant relationship with God in becoming His people. In obedience to God we as believers become a chose generation, a royal priesthood, a holy nation, a peculiar people (1 Peter 2:9), which means believers are set aside people doing the will of God.

Therefore, being called into holiness, all believers are to offer sacrifices of praise to God, live in holy obedience to Him, share His Word with others and shine the light of Christ in a sin darkened world.

Believers are called into holiness by holy living.

May 22

A Community Of Believers: Acts 2:37-42

Then Peter said unto them, Repent, and be baptized every one of you in the name of Jesus Christ for the remission of sins and ye shall receive the gift of the Holy Ghost....Then they that gladly received his word were baptized: and the same day there were added unto them about three thousands souls. And they continued steadfastly in the apostles" doctrine and fellowship and in breaking of bread, and in prayer.

The background of our lesson study is the promise of the Holy Spirit and what took place when He (the Holy Spirit) came as well as where the faithful followers of Christ were. The apostles were being obedient to Christ's instructions to wait in Jerusalem and not many days the Spirit would come, and as always a promise kept. The most notable is that they were on one accord in one place-**a community of believers.**

When the Holy Spirit came as promised He made His presence known in unforgettable fashion. Every nation and nationality was present in the room and when Peter and the apostles began speaking everyone could understand in his or her own language. This was such an event until Peter and the rest was accused of being drunk at mid day. Then Peter began to explain what was happening that all were witnessing the presence of the Holy Spirit and quoted Joel 2:28. Peter preached repentance to his audience and encouraged them to be baptized in the name of Jesus Christ and receive the Holy Ghost (v. 38). The results of Peter's preaching were that three thousand believed and were baptized, but the fellowship did not stop there as noted in verse 42. This verse outlines the attitude of a community of believers-a Spirit-filled church, which are (a) remain steadfast in the apostles teaching, (b) fellowship with one another as believers are to have both a vertical and horizontal relationship (God and man). (c) Continue in the breaking of bread, which means three things, (1) initial beginning of a common mea, (2) sharing of an agape meal, and (3) the institution of the Lord's Supper. (d) Prayer among the Christian Community was and is encouraged as prayer is an integrate part of Christian life. In our scripture text we see that prayers were being made and the Holy Spirit moved in a mighty way. He will do the same today when Christians pray. (e) In verse 43, we see the miraculous signs and wonders on display as a result of the presence of the Holy Spirit when we as believers are obeying the commission of witnessing to lost souls in this world. (f) Verses 44-47 talks about a sharing community as all believers are called by God to share His Word with others and live peacefully with one another. (g) Lastly, we are to make disciples as making fellow disciples grows Christ's church and God's kingdom. How is this done? We make other disciples through our righteous living and effective witnessing and in doing so we will permeate our surrounding communities.

The church and Christian community in our lesson study is a perfect example of church growth when all believers are on one accord praying, worshiping, praising and witnessing God. New believers come to Christ.

Invite an unbeliever to join the community of believers.

May 23

Hopeful Living: Acts 2:23-35

Whom God hath raised up, having loosed the pains of death: because it was not possible that he should be holden of it....therefore did my heart rejoice, and my tongue was glad; moreover also my flesh shall rest in hope.

What is hope? Hope is the expectation of receiving something. In the spiritual realm, Christians hope is in Jesus Christ and our belief that God will accomplish all that He promises (Psalm 71:5; Ephesians 2:12). Christians hope is based on biblical facts and personal testimony that God has always been faithful to His promises and will continue to do so. He promised a Savior, Christ came; He died for our sins and rose for our justifications. *A promise kept and an assured hope of salvations.* With that being said, the Christians hope is never based on wishful thinking, but with divine certainty. Christians can be assured that if we believe in Jesus Christ we will spend eternity with Him. **What an assured hope!**

Christians, as we go about our daily lives living holy unto God we can rejoice with great joy and our souls can rest in peace knowing that we are God's children and members of His heavenly kingdom as we have been made co-heirs with Christ our Savior.

What is your hope? Does it lie in Jesus Christ? Do you believe He is the Christ the promised Messiah? Do you believe He is coming back for His bride-the church?

All hope is in Jesus Christ.

May 24

Witness To The Righteousness Of God: Romans 3:21-22

But now the righteousness of God without the law is manifested, being witnessed by the law and the prophets. Even the righteousness of God which is by faith in Jesus Christ unto all and upon all them that believe: for there is no difference:

When we speak of the "righteousness of God" we are referring to the redemptive work in regards to humanity's sin. It is God's justification which puts all believers in a right relationship with God. God's redemptive activity liberates all believers from the bondage of sin and Satan. This is because mankind lacked the ability to free him or herself from sin slave bondage. The righteousness of God comes to all who believe as a free gift through His Son Jesus Christ. It is noteworthy to say that God's righteousness is continuous and will last forever.

This free gift is salvation and the only requirement from God is to believe on His Son Jesus and accept Him as our personal Savior. Remember what is free to us was costly to God and His Son, but because of a broken fellowship and God's desire for a restored relationship His redemptive activity was executed--salvation.

How can we today witness to the righteousness of God? We do so by remembering the day we were saved by God's grace through faith in Jesus Christ as we are no longer bound by sin and destined for eternal separation.

We are living testimonies to God's righteousness by our personal encounter with Jesus.

May 25

Witnessing The Incarnated Christ: John 1:12-16

And the Word was made flesh, and dwelt among us, (and we beheld his glory, the glory as of the only begotten of the Father,) full of grace and truth. John bare witness of him, and cried, saying, This was he of whom I spake, He that cometh after me is preferred before me: for he was before me. And of his fullness have all we received, and grace for grace.

John the Baptist the forerunner of Jesus Christ witnessed that Jesus was the promised Messiah in the flesh. John and all of Jesus' disciples gave eye witness accounts of Jesus being the Christ as He is the Son of God. They could testify that yes Jesus is the Christ, the eternal God who became flesh where humanity and deity were united in Jesus Christ.

Remember Peter's confessed statement, "Thou art the Christ, the Son of the living God" (Matthew 16:16). Peter's faith was on display as the Holy Spirit gave him assured knowledge that Jesus was the Christ for Peter to make such a confession. As Peter and the other disciples preached and witness Christ throughout the region was further evidence of their faith. Paul gave an eye witness account of Jesus being the Christ after His Damascus Road encounter. The question now becomes, How can you and I witness the Incarnated Christ? We see Christ through our spiritual eyes because of our faith in Him.

Christ is alive in each believer's soul because He is life.

May 26

Proclaiming Christ In The Face Of Persecution: Acts 8:1-8

...And at that time there was a great persecution against the church which was at Jerusalem: and they were all scattered abroad throughout the regions of Judea and Samaria, except the apostles.

There was a wide persecution of the church and Saul appeared to have been the leader of this persecution. This was before his Damascus Road experience because after his encounter with Jesus on the Damascus Road Paul witnessed Christ with as much vigor as he did when he was persecuting Christ's church. **What a change!**

Verse 3 describes the magnitude of persecution believers faced in this day for defending ones faith in Christ, but these devout Christians remain steadfast in their faith and were willing to die for their belief; Stephen was stoned to death for his preaching the gospel of Christ. Persecution failed in its efforts to stop the spread of the gospel; it spread even more (vv. 4 24).

These questions come to mind, How committed are we to preaching Christ in the face of persecution? If committed to prison, will we continue to preach and teach Christ? Are you willing to travel to foreign war torned nations to preach and teach Christ? True dedication is seen in proclaiming the gospel in the face of persecution. Paul, Stephens and the apostles are perfect examples who faced stiff persecution for Christ's sake.

Preach and teach Christ regardless of the situation or location for He is with you. He will never leave nor forsake His own.

May 27

Commissioned To Spread The Gospel: Matthew 28:19-20

Go ye therefore, and teach all nations, baptizing them in the name of the Father, and of the Son, and of the Holy Ghost: Teaching them to observe all things whatsoever I have commanded you: and lo, I am with you always, even unto the end of the world. Amen.

This is a powerful commission given by Christ Himself to all believers--the church as whole and individual believers as well.

If the church fails in its mission of preaching, and teaching the gospel of Christ who else will? Christ established His church for this purpose and He set an example by sending His disciples into the world to continue His gospel message. The question now becomes, How can the unsaved become saved unless he hears the Word of God from the church-believers? When the unsaved come to Christ, we are to baptize them with water through immersion in the name of the Father, Son, and Holy Ghost, and there is only one Lord, one baptism and one salvation. Obeying the Great Commission, believers are to make disciples of new converts so they too can make other disciples. New converts are to be taught holy living with the aid of the Holy Spirit as we are to be prime examples of holy living.

Christ promised to be with His followers always in spreading His gospel and He has remained true to His Word. His presence is felt through the Holy Spirit and regardless of any condition or situation He is there to solve problems, answer fears, anxieties and doubts.

Spread the gospel for He is with you.

May 28

Ingredients To Salvation: Romans 10:9-10

That is thou shalt confess with thy mouth the Lord Jesus, and shalt believe in thine heart that God hath raised him from the dead, thou shalt be saved. For with the heart man believeth unto righteousness; and with the mouth confession is made unto salvation.

What Paul is saying to us regarding our salvation is that the two essential components of salvation are confession and belief. The center of our belief is that Jesus is the Christ and the Son of God who was raised from the dead by the Spirit of God. Our belief-faith involves not only believing with our heart, but with our inner being-the heart that Jesus is the Christ and is no longer in a borrowed tomb. There were those who gave eye witness account of the empty tomb, but for us since that time must see the empty tomb with our spiritual eye. **Believe! Believe! Believe!**

The confession component is to publically tell somebody what we have admitted to ourselves, which is we (I am) are a sinner in need of a Savior--Jesus Christ. John 3:16 comes into play because of the "whosoever" meaning all. Regardless of conditions, physical, emotional and spiritual just come as you are and believe on the name of Jesus and be saved. Accepting Jesus' Lordship over our lives is giving Him authority in every aspect of our lives. Christ was the only one found worthy to die for the sins of the world and all who believe in Him died with Him and was raised to a life of righteousness with Him.

Admit, confess, believe and be saved.

May 29

The Church: Matthew 16:18

And I say also unto thee, That thou art Peter, and upon this rock I will build my church; and the gates of hell shall not prevail against it.

This verse is part of a conversation Christ had with His disciples and Peter's faith when Christ asked them who they thought He was and Peter answered, "Thou art the Christ, the Son of the living God." It is Peter like faith that Christ established the church. This leads to the nucleus of our discussion on the church.

With that being said the church is looked upon as the following:

(a) As the redeemed of God who assembles themselves together in a local congregation. Redemption was made possible by Christ's death. The people of God come together to worship Him, as believers have become citizens of His kingdom (Ephesians 2:19). This new community of believers stand firm together having a personal relationship with God.

(b) The church is a called out people separated from the world and its systems. Believers are a royal priesthood, a peculiar people living holy unto God.

(c) The church is the temple of God and the Holy Spirit as each believer is His residing place and cannot dwell in an unholy place. Therefore, believers as the individual church must separate him or herself from all unrighteousness and worldly immortality.

(d) The church is the body of Christ (1 Corinthians 6:15-16) and no true church exist apart from Him as He is the head of the church (Ephesians 1:22; 4:15; 5:23; Colossians 1:18).

(e) The church is the bride of Christ as this symbolizes a marriage of devotion and faithfulness of believers to Christ our Savior.

(f) The church is a spiritual ministry where she is to utilize the gifts given to her by the Holy Spirit to minister to a sinful world.

(g) The church is a spiritual fellowship with God and fellow believers as we come together on one accord with unity in the Spirit (Ephesians 4:4), baptism in the Spirit (Acts1:5; 2:4; 8:14-17). This fellowship demonstrates love for one another as God loves us all.

(h) The church is an army of believers who are embroiled in a spiritual conflict with Satan and his army. God has provided His holy Word to attack Satan on all fronts, and He has provided each believer with spiritual armour (Ephesians 6:11-17).

(i) The Church is the pillar of truth, which is God's Word. The truth is to be defended against all false teachers. Their mission is to pervert the gospel of Christ and deter Christians on their heavenly journey.

(j) The church is a people with a future hope which centers on Christ and His return for His bride-the church.

(k) Lastly, the church is both visible and invisible, or many refer to the church as an organism which is made up of the physical structure and the body of baptized believers. The invisible church is the body of baptized believers living in true faith in Jesus Christ, while the visible church is the local congregation made up of the physical structure where believers assemble to worship God in Spirit and truth (John 4:24).

The Church is the bride of Christ, which is comprised of all believers.

May 30

The Purpose Of The Church: Ephesians 2:10, 21-22

For we are his workmanship, created in Christ Jesus unto good works, which God hath before ordained that we should walk in them.

We determined in an earlier discussion that the church is the body of Christ which comprised of all believers who have been called by God to further the mission of the church by finding the lost and proclaiming salvation through Jesus Christ.

The purpose of the church is to worship God, both collectively and individually and to carry on the work of Christ which is sharing the truth of God's Word with all who will hear and believe on the name of Jesus. The name of Jesus is the only name by which man can be saved. This gospel is to be carried the world over.

All believers carry the church within him or her as each is commissioned to continue the gospel message of Christ and with faith set forth by the first apostles as recorded in Acts and are to live in total obedience to the inspired writings and teachings of the New Testament scriptures and eye witness accounts of Christ while obeying its truths as revealed by the Holy Spirit. The church must defend and guard any alteration of the truth of God's Word on its missionary mission. Carrying the gospel of Christ must be done faithfully and prayerfully through the power of the Holy Spirit.

Church, your mission, purpose and message will never be destroyed, because it was established by Christ to win souls for Him and to continue building God's kingdom by proclaiming salvation through Jesus Christ.

May 31

The Need For Salvation: Romans 3:23

For all have sinned, and come short of the glory of God.

Salvation has been defined numerous times, but the meaning remains the same which is being delivered from harm or danger, or bondage. For the purpose of our discussion; salvation was provided to all mankind by God's grace through faith in our Lord and Savior Jesus Christ. The need for salvation is the result of sin where God the Father pronounced the whole world guilty (vv 9-19). Salvation was first offered to the Jews and they refused, then to the Gentiles and they refused as well, which resulted in the righteous judge-God giving His ruling-guilty.

With the whole world being found guilty humanity was doomed to feel the wrath of God, but in His mercifulness God gave His only Son Jesus Christ to redeem man from the clutches of sin and Satan.

Christ's atoning work on Calvary justified man before God (v. 24); therefore, when God looks at man He sees the righteousness of His Son Jesus Christ, because Christ took on man's sins and all who believe is made right with God.

What salvation depicts are God's love, grace and mercy, because mercy replaced justice-punishment. Sin spells a broken fellowship whereas salvation is a restored fellowship. Our spiritual freedom is free to all who believe, because Christ paid our sin bill.

Thank You Lord for salvation, now I am free to live holy unto You in Jesus name Amen.

God's People In Strange Places

June 1

"If I Perish I Perish": Ester 4:16

Go, gather together all the Jews that are present in Shushan, and fast ye for me, and neither eat nor drink three days, night or day; I also and my maidens will fast likewise; and so will I go in unto the king, which is not according to the law; and if I perish, I perish.

The story of Queen Ester is well documented and her role in saving her people from planned annihilation and securing their safety in a foreign land. What's most important about Queen Ester and her act of bravery is the divine hand of God as He works through people to carry out His plan.

Ester replaced Queen Vashti because she disobeyed the King and was replaced by Ester who was a Jewish girl. This was all part of God's plan to save His people. Queen Ester never forgot her heritage and loyalty to the one true God as well as her people. When her uncle Mordecai approached her with the news, she gave him instructions for all the Jews, which was to fast for three days as she and her maidens were going to do likewise.

The lesson learned from our lesson study is giving reverence to God, preparing ones mind, body and spirit before undertaking a task and being totally committed to the task at hand.

Queen Ester's willingness to sacrifice her life for the sake of her people serves as an example for all believers as we are strategically placed to serve God in carrying out His mission.

Can we say like Ester If I perish I perish!

June 2

A Missionary In The King's Palace: Ester 4:1-3, 9-17

For is thou altogether holdest thy peace at this time, then shall there enlargement and deliverance arise to the Jews from another place; but thou and thy father's house shall be destroyed; and who knoweth whether thou art come to the kingdom for such a time as this?

Reading the preceding chapters of Ester we see the hand of God at work as well as Satan's through Haman's desire to be bowed to by people. In 3:2 we see Mordecai refusing to bow because of his loyalty to God as the Jews were devout in their beliefs. This kind of devotion was depicted in Daniel 3:1-12 when Daniel and his three companions refused to bow to the king.

What's so important about Ester becoming queen was that she could be instrumental in saving the Jews from destruction. Therefore, Queen Ester was placed in the palace by God as a missionary on behalf of God's people and worrying about saving self was not an option as it is with all believers who are committed to doing His will.

The message from the book of Ester is that God's redemptive hand is involved in the world's events to save His people and to accomplish His purpose-redemption. Therefore, we as believers are missionaries and have been commissioned to speak for God to others.

Serve God regardless of location or condition, because one day we will reign with "the King" Jesus.

June 3

Good Come From Planned Evil: Ester 7:1-8

So the king and Haman came to banquet with Esther the queen. And the king said again unto Esther on the second day at the banquet of wine. What is thy petition, Queen Esther? And it shall be granted thee; and what is thy request? And it shall be performed, even to the half of the kingdom.

The evil scheme Haman had planed for Mordecai and the Jews to be destroyed came to naught because God's divine plan of deliverance was at work for His people. Haman was so sure that his plan was fail proof that he overlooked the God of Israel, but when God's missionary Queen Esther requested and gained an audience with her husband the king, her request was granted (v 7). The king did not know that his closest ally was the one who plotted such fate of the Jewish people. Upon learning of who plotted against Mordecai and the Jews, Haman was hanged in the gallows that he had planned for Mordecai. **What a change of events!**

The lessons to be learned from our discussion is that God is true to His word in never forsaken His people, neither will He leave them. He was their deliverer just as He is for all believers today. Also, what God has for you no one can take it away nor destroy His plan of redemption.

Evil has been around since the beginning of time, but God's good is superior.

June 4

God's Hand Of Deliverance: Esther 8:1-17

...King Ahasuerus gave the house of Haman the Jews' enemy unto Esther the queen. And Mordecai came before the king; for Esther had told what he was unto her. And the king took off his ring, which he had taken from Haman, and gave it unto Mordecai. And Esther set Mordecai over the house of Haman.

Much has been written about Esther's role in saving her people from destruction as she was used by God in their deliverance. Humility displayed by both Esther and Mordecai resulted in her finding favor with the king and Mordecai being elevated to the point of being dressed by the king and the king listening to what Mordecai had to say. The revoked decree is based on Mordecai's testimony and the change of events that occurred because of divine intervention. The revoked decree was issued throughout the provinces which stretched from India to Ethiopia.

God's people had reasons to rejoice and be glad because their lives had been spared and their honour restored (vv. 16-17). This couldn't happen without God's plan for their deliverance. God's deliverance doesn't just happen; it is all by design as He is all-knowing and knows what will happen before it does. This principle applies to the plan of salvation as all believers can shout for joy because we have victory over Satan and his evil schemes.

God's hand of deliverance extends throughout the ages. Rejoice and be glad in His deliverance.

Answering When God Call: Isaiah 6:8-13

...I heard the voice of the Lord, saying, Whom shall I send, and who will go for us? Then I said, Here am I; send me. And he said, Go, and tell this people, Hear ye indeed, but understand not; and see ye indeed; but perceive not. Make the heart of this people fat, and make their ears heavy, and shut their eyes; lest they see with their eyes, and hear with their ears and understand with their heart, and convert, and be healed.

Thus far this month we have discussed God's missionaries answering the call to be instrumental in God's grand design of deliverance through saving His people. Today's discussion focus is on the prophet Isaiah in the midst of a rebellious nation where the people had turned their backs on God.

In the beginning of this chapter Isaiah was in the presence of the Lord through a vision. While in the presence of a holy God, Isaiah realized his sinfulness and uncleanness (v. 5), as well as him being unfit to see God face-to-face and Isaiah became frightened. God in His grace and mercy cleansed Isaiah's mouth and heart as he was being prepared for service. Isaiah was to preach repentance to the people, but before Isaiah could serve his sins had to be forgiven as with all of God's spokespersons. Once we have been cleansed of our sins we too can answer like Isaiah, "Send me I will go" (v. 8). It is noteworthy to say that this verse is indicative of the Great Commission recorded in Matthew 28:19-20 as all believers have been commissioned to spread the gospel of Christ.

Upon Isaiah's willingness to speak what thus said the Lord, he was given specific instructions regarding his message. Also, Isaiah was told that his message would be rejected and the people would turn even farther from God, but Isaiah was to remain faithful in his calling. Isaiah's message was one of repentance for judgment was at hand. Did the people believe him? No. Verses 11-12 speak of the judgment which history records was brought through Sennacherib in 701 B.C. as a result of this judgment Jerusalem became faithful and obedient

(Isaiah 36:21; 37:7), and from this new found obedience and faithfulness to God, Isaiah has a new ministry so to speak. This was during the reign of King Hezekiah (Isaiah 38:5).

In the midst of Isaiah's ministering to a rebellious nation God encouraged him by saying there would be a remnant of hearers that would hear and believe. This group would be preserved and a new Judah would come forth and be called holy and it was through this remnant that God's plan of salvation for the world would materialize.

Just as God had a remnant during Isaiah's time He has a remnant that will remain faithful to Him in the new covenant. So what are we to do when answering God's call? Deliver the message regardless of who hears and believe.

God's messengers are to plant the seed (Word), God will give the increase.

June 6

Why God Call?: Isaiah 5:1-30

Woe unto them that call evil good, and good evil; that put darkness for light, and light for darkness; that put bitter for sweet, and sweet for bitter! Woe unto them that are wise in their own eyes, and prudent in their own sight!

Today's topical discussion answers the question why God calls His spokespersons to speak for Him to His people. Verse 20 in a word depicts the condition of the nation of Israel then and society as a whole today. What was happening is that the nation had completely turned its back on God and His covenant regardless of His efforts to make them a righteous and fruitful nation. All manner of sin was openly practiced and wrong had become right, immorality had become the moral right and all who opposed this alternative lifestyle and accepted Biblical standards were looked upon as bigots and religious hypocrites. *What do we see in today's society?*

What we see in today's society is indicative of what was happening during Isaiah's ministry, and the sins were as follows: (a) selfish greed (v 8), (b) verses 11-12 is the conduct of drunkenness, (c) verses 18-19 depicts the mockery being made of God's power to judge sin, (d), verse 20 highlights the distortion or prevision of God's standards, (e) verse 21 displays arrogance and pride of the people, and (f) verses 22-23 is the perversion of His justice.

God calls His spokespersons to preach against sin before He pronounces judgment. Hear the preacher!

June 7

Who God Call?: Genesis 12:1-7

Now the Lord had said unto Abram, Get thee out of thy country, and from thy kindred, and from thy father's house, unto a land that I will shew thee: and I will make of thee a great nation, and I will bless thee, and make thy name great, and thou shall be a blessing (vv. 1-2): And the Lord appeared unto Abram, and said, Unto thy seed will I give this land: and there builded he an altar unto the Lord, who appeared unto him (v. 7).

God calls the faithful, obedient and devoted servants who will obey Him and then do His will, which is to reflect the moral attributes of God in the called lives.

Our scripture text is the beginning of a new chapter in the Old Testament revelation of God's plan of redemption to save His people who would know Him and serve Him. Once the called get to know God we then can teach others the ways of God thus forming a family of believers who have separated him or herself from the world.

Reflect with me on the God-like character traits of some of His called notables from the Bible. God called His Son Jesus to be man's sacrificial lamb atoning for the sins of the world. What character did Jesus have; only godly character. He was obedient to the end. Abraham was called to be the father of many nations and his faithfulness was counted as righteous. Moses walked closely with God in leading the nation of Israel out of bondage until they became friends. Paul suffered persecutions for the sake of the gospel of Christ and was willing to die for preaching Christ.

Are you one of God's called servants?

June 8

God's Messengers' Message: Judges 6:11-23

And there came and angel of the Lord, and sat under an oak which was in Ophrah, that pertained unto Joash the Abi-ezrite; and his son Gideon threshed wheat by the winepress, to hide from the Midianites. And the angel of the Lord appeared unto him, and said unto him, The Lord is with thee, thou mighty man of valor.

Israel's history is one of obedience and disobedience to the Lord God their deliverer and today's lesson study background is no different. In verse 1 we see where the nation of Israel had forsaken God and began practicing religion of their surrounding neighbors and refused to turn back to God. As a result of this behavior God allowed the Midianites, Amalekites and tribes from the east to oppress Israel. The oppression was so severe until the Israelites were forced into caves to hide their food. To f*orsake God bring oppression and punishment.*

In verse 6 the Israelites realizes that the one true God is their only salvation and cry out to Him, and as always He comes to their rescue as He does with all humanity when we cry out to Him in honesty. God sent a messenger, a prophet to remind Israel of His deliverance, but God sent one of His angels to deliver a message to Gideon because Gideon was to be God's deliverer.

His message ***"I am with thee."*** This promise is true today to God's messengers.
Deliver God's message of repentance.

June 9

Confronting The Enemy: 2 Samuel 12:1-12

The rich man had exceeding many flock and herds: but the poor man had nothing, save one little ewe lamb, which he had bought and nourished up: and it grew up together with him, and with his children; it did eat of his own meat, and drank of his own cup, and lay in his bosom, and was unto him as a daughter.

Our lesson study today focuses on repenting when confronted by the man of God. The Lord sent David's friend Nathan to him delivering the message of David's wrong doings. David's sin was that he took another man's wife for his own and sent Uriah to the front line of battle so he would be killed. David committed two sins in this scenario, adultery and murder and he would suffer punishment for his sins.

It is noteworthy to say that David had violated the commandments of the Lord through his actions. Given all that God had done for David, and David's actions declared that God was unworthy of his love, appreciation and devotion. This affected his standing with God without repentance. All who commit sin is making the same declaration. *Do like David-repent.*

We like David when we commit a sin are an enemy with God and He sends His messenger to open a blinded eye. On the other hand all believers who remain faithful to God and His commandments are commissioned to confront the enemy-the world and its systems.

Stand firm in the face of opposition.

Repentance Cleanses The Soul: Psalm 51:1-12

Have mercy upon me, O God, according to thy lovingkindness: according unto the multitude if thy tender mercies blot out my transgressions. Wash me thoroughly from mine iniquity, and cleanse me from sin. For I acknowledge my transgressions; and my sin is ever before me.

Our lesson text depicts David's confession after he had committed the sins of adultery and murder (2 Samuel 12:1-13). In yesterday's discussion it was discussed that Nathan the man of God pointed out David's sins to him and David feared that God's presence and Spirit would leave him and he would be destitute. There are several lessons to be learned from David, which are:

a) Admit our guilt and that we have sinned before God (v. 6).
b) Pray for God's hand of mercy as He is merciful to forgive the repentant heart.
c) Ask God to leave His Spirit with you (v.11).
d) Ask Him to restore the joy of your salvation (v.12), as He will not turn away a broken and contrite heart that is remorseful.
e) Lastly, commit thyself to do all that is right in God's eyesight, live according to God's standards, and commit thyself to His will.

It can be concluded then that sin separates us, but repentance restores the spiritual divide as mankind was created to have an intimate fellowship with God.

Repent and be spiritually cleansed.

June 11

A Renewed Commitment To Serve: Psalm 51:13

Then will I teach transgressors only thy ways; and sinners shall be converted unto thee.

David's actions are indicative of a person who has confessed his or her wrong doings and have asked and received forgiveness from God. This shows gratitude and thanksgiving to a worthy God.

What was David's commitment to God for giving him another chance? David committed himself to teach others the ways of God. His teaching ministry was two-fold in that it was to prevent fellow believers from backsliding as he did and convert non-believers to God. Persons like David have a renewed commitment to serve God as the person's personal testimony is a witness to the goodness of God. David understood the Great Commission as all believers are to make disciples for the kingdom of God.

The renewed commitment expressed in David's testimony is the result of having the joy of his salvation restored as both rested in God as he and all believers are kept by the Spirit of God. **Let's shout Hallelujah for the goodness of God for we serve a God of second chances.**

If when we grow weary while being bombarded with the troubles of this world, ask God for deliverance from all wickedness, then yield to the Holy Spirit as He is our protector, teacher, sealer and guide. God promised never to leave nor forsake His own and He is present always.

A renewed Spirit is growth in the Lord.

June 12

Blessed To Bless: Luke 6:32-36, 2 Kings 4:8-17

..Love your enemies, and do good, and lend, hoping for nothing again; and your reward shall be great, and ye shall be the children of the Highest: for he is kind unto the unthankful and to the evil. Be ye therefore merciful, as your Father also is merciful.

The overall focus of today's discussion is love, which begs the question, What good is it to love and or do good only to those who love or do good to you? Verses 27-36 explains that if we only love or do good to them that love and do good to us then nothing is gained. Whereas in verse 35 we are to love our enemies as this follows the love command of God because He loved us while we were enemies with Him. When we love all we emulate the Father as He is love. Our lesson text provides the answer to why we are to love our enemies; "and ye shall be the children of the Highest." Being children of God, then we are to be like Him in all ways. Being children of God is one of the most blessed honors to be received as it is a result of our salvation in Jesus Christ. Another point of view is that all believers have been blessed with the indwelling Holy Spirit who gives us the power to love our enemy.

Verse 38 brings home the point of being blessed to bless in that God blesses us so that we can bless others. The more we give to others the more God will return to us. ***You can't beat God's giving.***

In God's provisions for the poor and needy, He expressed His concern for the less fortunate, by establishing specific instructions that would eliminate poverty in our society. In the New Testament, Jesus stressed providing for the poor and especially those in the church as they are our brothers and sisters. When we give gifts to our fellowman we are giving unto God.

Acts 2:44-45 describe how the early church established a giving community of sharing their possessions to meet the needs of others and from this act the church grew steadily. **Blessed to be a blessing!** Acts 4:34 states "Neither was there any among them that lacked: for as many as were possessor of lands or houses sold them, and brought the prices of these that were sold." What these scriptures are saying is simply when God blesses then share your blessing with others.

The Old Testament it specifies that during harvest season what dropped on the ground was to be left for the less fortunate (Leviticus 19:9; Deuteronomy 24:19-21).

God blesses His people in many ways and how He blesses you then you are to bless others.

Our blessings are too numerous to count so bless others.

June 13

A Faithful Commitment To God: Numbers 6: 1-8

Speak unto the children of Israel, and say unto them, When either man or woman shall separate themselves a vow of a Nazarite, to separate themselves to the Lord (v.2). All the days of his separation he is holy unto the Lord (v. 8).

What is the meaning of the term "Nazarite? Nazarite means" to set apart", and this separation can be for a specific time or a lifetime of holy living for God. The Student Bible Dictionary (P. 162) defines Nazarite as a person dedicated to God, who vowed to abstain from certain practices such as having a haircut and drinking alcohol. Samson is the most notable Nazarite, but John is considered to be a Nazarite. These two men dedicated themselves to God in their specific service for Him.

The question now becomes, What is your vow to God? All believers have taken a vow to live holy to God and serve Him as this is a lifetime commitment. Paul gave an analogy of believers' commitment and service to God as that of a long-distant runner, whereas it is not how fast you run, but finishing the course. How do we remain faithful to God? God's Spirit (the Holy Spirit) resides in each believer to keep us on the path of righteousness so that we as believers can find the lost and bring them to Christ-the commission of the church.

Faithful commitment to God is evidenced by the believer's perseverance.

Consequences Of Disobedience: Judges 2:1-8, 11-17

And the children of Israel did evil in the sight of the Lord, and served Baalim: And they forsook the Lord God of their fathers, which brought them out of the land of Egypt, and followed other gods, of the gods of the people that were around about them, and bowed themselves unto them, and provoked the Lord to anger.

In today's topical discussion our focus is on the consequences of disobeying God's commandments, which is what our scripture text tells of Israel's actions and the consequences they suffered.

In verses 1-4 God sends one of His angels to remind the nation of Israel of His covenant and the promises He made, but the people were to worship Him only. This they did as long as Joshua was alive, but upon his death the nation of Israel forsook God's commandments forbidding them to worship other gods.

What were Israel's consequences? Israel was punished for disobeying God's command by worshipping other gods, and in His anger He allowed Israel to suffer punishment (vv. 20-23).

What does this say for believers today? God's command remains in effect and we are to refrain from worshipping other gods. Believers are to worship one true God who created us in His image and likeness breathed the breath of life into man and man became a living soul. We are to obey the God who gave His only begotten Son as a ransom for the sins of the world.

Disobedience brings severe consequences.

June 15

Seeing God In A Vision: Ezekiel 1:15-26

And there was a voice from the firmament that was over their heads, when they stood, and had let down their wings. And above the firmament that was over their heads was the likeness of a throne, as the appearance of a sapphire stone: and upon the likeness of the throne was the likeness as the appearance of a man above upon it.

The time of Ezekiel's writing was during Israel's captivity in Babylon and Ezekiel was the priest called and commissioned by God to provide hope to His people that He would restore them.

In Ezekiel's vision of God he saw the glory and holiness of God. The purpose of the vision was to prepare him for his work which was to preach repentance to God's people. The vision also revealed that God's glory had left Jerusalem (1 Kings 8:11), but was now visiting His people in exile, but at some time later God's glory would return to Canaan and Jerusalem (Ezekiel 43:2-3, 7).

The question becomes, Was the vision necessary for Ezekiel to perform his ministry? Isaiah 6 corroborates Ezekiel in visions being necessary to carry out God's mission. The vision provides clear understanding of what God wanted Ezekiel to do. The same principles apply today.

How do we receive this understanding? We receive understanding of God and His glory through His Son Jesus Christ (John 1:14), the Holy Spirit (1 Peter 4:14), and God's Word (2 Corinthians 3:7-11).

God is visible in the midst of His creations. See Him!

June 16

A New Spirit: Ezekiel 11:19-20

And I will give them one heart, and I will put a new spirit within you; and I will take the stony heart out of their flesh, and will give them a heart of flesh: That they may walk in my statues, and keep mine ordinances, and do them: and they shall be my people, and I will be their God.

The background of today's lesson study is the promise made by God to Ezekiel regarding the remnant of Israel that would adhere to God's call for repentance. They were in exile because of their disobedience to God. Even in the midst of their suffering while in exile God's hand of mercy was seen as He provided hope of their deliverance through His prophet Ezekiel as God promised to be Israel's sanctuary (v.16).

Verses 17-21 speak of Israel's physical return to their homeland, and this prophecy was partially fulfilled when they returned, but it also points to the future return in the end of this age (Revelation 12:6).

Our scripture text further looks at the promise God made with Israel promising them a new spirit and a new heart one that geared to obedience. This prophecy refers to the coming of the Holy Spirit who empowers all believers (Israel and today's) to live according to His will and law. Joel 2:28-29 speaks of the outpouring of the Spirit on all flesh, and Acts 2:4 speak of the coming Holy Spirit on Pentecost. It is noteworthy to say that this promise was fulfilled initially at Christ's resurrection.

A new spirit is available to all who believe in Jesus Christ.

Baptism In The Holy Spirit: Joel 2:28-29

And it shall come to pass afterward, that I will pour out my spirit upon all flesh; and your sons and your daughters shall prophesy, your old men shall dream dreams, and your young men shall see visions. And also upon the servants and upon the handmaids in those days will I pour out my spirit.

What is the meaning of the Prophet Joel's prediction? This means that one day God will pour out His spirit on all who "call on the name of the Lord" (v. 32), and accept Jesus as Lord and Savior. This ongoing promise is for believers both then and now. This out pour will cause a great manifestation among God's people.

It is noteworthy to say that the Holy Spirit was active in the Old Testament as He was active in creation (Genesis 1:2), He communicated God's message to His people (Nehemiah (9:20), and He energized God's leaders in the OT (Exodus 33:11).

Being that the Holy Spirit has always been active since creation begs the question what does it mean to be baptized in the Holy Spirit? Baptism in the Holy Spirit brings personal power and boldness in the life of believers to do mighty works in the body of Christ. Baptism in the Holy Spirit enhances ones sensitivity to sin and gives the believer a greater desire to seek righteousness and a deeper awareness of God's judgment of sin and all ungodliness (John 16:8; Acts 1:8). Lastly, baptism in the Holy Spirit brings the believers into a renewed relationship with Him (Acts 4:31) and one which is maintained by Him-the Holy Spirit (Ephesians 5:18).

Be baptized!

June 18

Serving Under The Influence-Holy Spirit: Acts 2:4

And they were filled with the Holy Ghost, and begun to speak with other tongues, as the Spirit gave them utterance.

What does the phrase "under the influence" mean? It means under the control of something or someone other than yourself. We have often heard of others being under the influence of alcohol or drugs, but being under the influence of the Holy Spirit means to be endued with power from on high-God (Acts 1:8). The influential powers of the Holy Spirit enables all believers to boldly witness Christ the world over without fear and reservations. Serving under the influence of the Holy Spirit causes believers to answer God's call, do His will, live holy, and aid in His kingdom building. In the believer's servant work, the believer will not only bring others to Christ, but will make converts as well.

It is noteworthy to say that serving under the influence, the believer has yielded his or her will to that of God's and the Holy Spirit imparts gifts according to God's desire to continue His works for the kingdom. If you have the gift of prophecy, then prophesy to the glory of God. If you have the gift of speaking in tongue, then speak to edify the body of Christ. Whatever gift that God has gifted you with use it to glorify God, because the greatest gift all believers have is the gift of salvation through Jesus Christ.

Thank God for the gift!

June 19

A Call For Repentance: Joel 2:12-17

Therefore also now, saith the Lord, turn ye even to me with all your heart, and with fasting, and with weeping, and with mourning: And rent your heart, and not your garments, and turn unto the Lord your God: for he is gracious and merciful, slow to anger, and of great kindness, and repenteth him of the evil.

In today's' lesson study we see a genuine call for repentance one that begins with the renting of the person's heart. What God was asking His people to do was to rent/tear their hearts and turn back to Him. It is not enough just to say I repent and the heart is omitted from the process.

What is true repentance? True repentance begins in the heart as the heart is the epicenter of all of our actions. Repentance is a three step process. Step 1 is to admit that you are a sinner. Step 2 is to confess your sins, and lastly, turn from your sinful ways and back to God as He is merciful to forgive sin.

Verse 13, God asked the nation of Israel to rent their hearts, not just their clothes; this is because our all-knowing God looks at the heart. The heart is where the truth lies. Therefore, if the people would turn from their sins and back to God He promised to pity/have mercy on them. This is because it is in God's nature to have compassion as His grace and mercy is ever present. God is still calling for true repentance today as many are failing to serve God with his or her whole being.

The prophet Joel was dedicated in his ministry of preaching repentance to God's people. Verse 17 explains how God expects His ministers to intercede to Him on the behalf of the people. Moses interceded many times for the young nation of Israel as well as many other OT prophets. In the age of grace God has pastors, and other leaders of His church to intercede for His people.

These questions come to mind, What is the message of God's preachers in the age of grace? Repent and be saved. How must one be saved? All are saved by grace through faith in Jesus Christ. What is the work of the Holy Spirit in the saving process? The Holy Spirit is the agent of salvation; He convicts us of our guilt; He reveals to us the truth about Jesus Christ as He is the Son of God; He is the agent of sanctification; He incorporates all believers into the body of Christ and He lives in each believer.

With that being said, there are blessings in God's preachers calling sinners to repentance as each is obeying his or her call and there are blessings for all who hear the call and ahead to the call for repentance.

Hear the call for repentance, it's open. Heaven is waiting!

June 20

An Obedient Heart Repents: Joel 2:18-27; Deuteronomy 5:28-33

Ye shall observe to do therefore as the Lord your God hath commanded you: ye shall not turn aside to the right hand or to the left. You shall walk in all the ways which the Lord your God hath commanded you, that ye may live, and that it may be well with you, and that ye may prolong your days in the land which ye shall possess(5:32-33). And ye shall know that I am in the midst of Israel, and that I am the Lord your God, and none else: and my people shall never be ashamed (2:27).

Verses 7-21 is a repeat of the Ten Commandments that God had given the nation of Israel as recorded in Exodus 20 as a reminder of what He expects from His children.

Every so often we have to be reminded of what God expects His children to do and act as all believers are born into the family of God and we are to display His character traits. Our lesson study today is just such reminder as all God's children are to walk in His ways and we shall a live a long life; here on earth and eternity through our salvation in Jesus Christ.

When a person obeys the Word of God, he repents and then will be willing to adhere to all God's commands as His commands have promises and God's promises are sure. Our scripture text has just such promises and His assurances that He would reside in the midst of His people. He alone is our God and no one else and all His children will never be ashamed or His gospel message.

What a blessing!

Willing Servants Of God: Ezra 5:5; Job 36:7

But the eyes of their God was upon the elders of the Jews, that they could not cause them to cease, till the matter came to Darius: and then they returned answer by letter concerning this matter.

Today's lesson study focus is on willing servants of God who have committed themselves to serve God regardless of the situation or conditions. A bit is historical background on this scripture is that the temple rebuilding had begun some eighteen years earlier and ceased (Nehemiah 1:3) because of opposition. This opposition was strong enough to stop the rebuilding process, but God's plan will be completed regardless to any and all opposition.

In verse 2 we see God's prophets getting involved in God's plan for His place of worship. God always has some willing servant who will stand for Him in the face of opposition to see the completion of what God has revealed to him. The prophets provided inspiration, and influence while reminding the people of God's presence in this matter as it is with whatever God has planned for His servants to do.

It is noteworthy to say that all who have dedicated/committed their lives to God and His cause are special in God's eyes. Job 36:7 sums up the assurance God servants have, which states in part *"He withdraweth not His eye from the righteous."* The question is With God watching who can harm us? No one, not even Satan.

God's eyes are upon His servants.

Sanctified To Serve: 1 Peter 1:2

Elect accord to the foreknowledge of God the Father, through sanctification of the Spirit, unto obedience and sprinkling of the blood of Jesus Christ: Grace unto you, and peace, be multiplied.

Much has been written about sanctification and how one receives sanctification, but for today's discussion we will focus on being sanctified to serve God and His purposes.

God knew from the beginning of time who would hear His Word and obey the call to serve Him as these persons are the "elect" of God. being the elect of God, puts all believers in elite company as we are the true believers, chosen in harmony with God's perfect plan of redemption for His church-believers through the blood of Jesus Christ as believers are sanctified by the Holy Spirit (KJV Commentary). God's elect-believers must respond to God's call through faith to make his or her calling and election sure (2 Peter 1:5-10).

With that being said, believers are set apart to serve God in true holiness, have a willingness to obey His Word, share His Word with others-witness, and remain and maintain a harmonious relationship with God the Father and His Son Jesus Christ.

What sanctification does for the believer is it separates us from this world's sinful practices and gives us a new nature in-line with that of God, which produces the fruit of the Spirit that will enable us to live holy and victorious lives dedicated to Him as Christ won the victory for all believers.

Serve as we have been set apart for this purpose.

June 23

Servants Of God: 1 Peter 2: 16-18

As free, and note using your liberty for a cloke of maliciousness, but as the servants of God. Honour all men, Love the brotherhood, Fear God, Honour the king. Servant, be subject to your masters with all fear; not only to the good and gentle, but also to the forward.

What Peter is saying to his audience is that believers have been set free from the bondage of sin to love and honor all men as we emulate God who is love and loves all. Also, Peter was encouraging his readers to do away with all hateful thoughts and deeds that would cause believers to mistreat our fellowman. This begs the question, How can one say he or she is a believer and mistreat his or her fellowman? Malicious acts toward another are difficult to phantom stemming from a child of God. This is because all malicious acts and or sinful deeds are not works of the Spirit.

Also, Peter was providing instructions on Christian submission to God as all believers are a concentrated people who have been called by God and are to separate themselves from the world and its systems. This is because God's ways/system is different from that of man-the world.

To be a servant of God one must be willing to separate him or herself from the world. Abraham had to separate himself from his family, and there are many others who did likewise to serve God.

Jesus Christ our perfect example of a servant.

June 24

Christ The Perfect Servant: 1 Peter 2:21-25

For even hereunto were ye called: because Christ also suffered for us, leaving us an example, that ye should follow his steps.

For the past several days we have discussed some form of servant hood, but today we will focus on the perfect servant hood of Jesus Christ. After accepting the call to serve God and the "called" is experiencing doubt as how and what we have been called to do, look no further than Jesus Christ our Savior. Jesus Christ provided an example of every situation believers will encounter in his or her service to God. Christ remained faithful in His service to the end of His earthly life. While in heaven He continues His servant work as He is seated at the right hand of the Father making intercession for mankind.

During Christ's earthly ministry He explained the true meaning of servant, which is to serve and not to be served; then Christ demonstrated this meaning by washing His disciples' feet. In our service to God if washing of feet is required then do so, if suffering is required then do so. Many missionaries have performed what the world considers menial tasks/services to aid others.

The question now becomes, Will we have to suffer for Christ's sake? Yes we will; Christ suffered greatly for our sins. Christ also stated that we would suffer for His sake because as the world hated Him we likewise will be hated.

Servants, our perfect example is Christ follow His lead.

June 25

Servants Kept By God: Revelation 7:3

Saying, Hurt not the earth, neither the sea, not the trees, till we have sealed the servants of God in their foreheads.

To set the tone of today's discussion, in chapter 6 the sixth seal being opened and the events that were occurring during this time. In verses 12-17 speaks of the signs in heaven that John saw, verse 12 speaks of the great earthquake that appears to shake the earth to its very core. The great earthquake is viewed as God's judgment on the earth and is a preview of the events that is described in chapter 8.

There is such upheaval in the earth until the ungodly that are left here on earth cry for the mountains and rocks to fall on them for protection. This reflects the cry of the ungodly during Noah's day when the people refused to repent and ahead to God's Word.

Chapter 7 expresses God's desire that no hurt, harm or danger come to the earth, trees, nor the sea until He has put His seal of protection upon His people. This chapter is viewed as an interlude between the opening of the sixth and seventh seals, which talks about God's protection on all the faithful believers during the tribulation. Those included are both Jews and non-Jews. What does this say about faithful believers before the tribulation? Just as God declared His protection on those faithful believers He protects us today who will stand firm on His Word in delivering His gospel.

Believers, we are God's servants and we are kept by Him.

June 26

God Saves His People Through Joseph
Genesis 37:12-36; 41:37-40

And pharaoh said unto Joseph, Forasmuch as God hath shewed thee all this; there is none so discreet and wise as thou art. Thou shalt be over my house and according unto thy word shall all my people be ruled only in the throne will I be greater than thou.

What do we know about Joseph? Joseph was a dreamer and the youngest of his father Jacob. Joseph's father Jacob made him a coat of many colors and showed other favoritism toward his young son. This brings on sibling rivalry among the older children when one child appears to be the favorite of the parent.

Joseph being a dreamer and one of his dreams God showed him his future where he would be ruler over the land of Egypt and rule over his brothers. Joseph shared his dream with his brothers which further fueled the flame of discontent so much so that when the opportunity presented itself to get rid of Joseph they seized the opportunity. For Joseph sharing his dream one could argue that he showed insensitivity and immaturity, regardless the dream was providing insight into Joseph's future where his faith would be tested as God was preparing him to save His people from the oncoming famine. During the time when Joseph was sold into slavery, and even during his stay at the Pharaoh's house where he suffered imprisonment as the results of a lie by the king's wife he remained faithful to God.

We see God's hand of protection on Joseph and deliverance for His people (Israel) as promised because He allowed the events to occur in Joseph's life as he had been called by God for this purpose- deliverance of Israel. Joseph was later elevated to be the governor of Egypt and through God's divine intervention Egypt was well prepared for the oncoming famine. It was through the famine that Joseph and his brother were united and the nation of Israel delivered.

Even in the midst of suffering God is present and have given each of us a gift to be used to His glory, just as with Joseph's ability to interpret dreams. Every believer has been given a gift to be used to the glory of God and His kingdom building. As believers we are to be obedient to our call and grateful for our gift and be willing to serve in strange lands. God has predestined each of us a place of service according to His will and purpose.

If the question were raised, What is my calling and purpose in life according to God's will? God makes known His call to us in several ways, as discussed in several of this month's discussion; there have been visions, dreams, and revelations through His Word and the Holy Spirit. Our purpose is to live holy lives to him and witness His gospel to the lost.

God has a divine perfect plan to save His people as He is their deliverer. Through Jesus Christ God saved the whole human race.

God saves!

June 27

Daniel Serves Through Dreams and Prayers
Daniel 4:19-27; 9:1-19

This is the interpretation, O king, and this is the decree of the most High, which is come upon my lord the king (4:24). To the Lord our God belong mercies and forgiveness, though we have rebelled against him. Now, therefore, O our God, hear the prayer of thy servant, and his supplications, and cause thy face to shine upon thy sanctuary that is desolate, for the Lord's sake.

Much has been written about Daniel and his ability to interpret dreams as well as his faithfulness to God. However, as a bit of background, King Nebuchadnezzar was a powerful king during his reign. He was the same king that wanted Daniel and his friends to bow to him and his god. They refused the kings request and risked death, but God saved them so that He would be glorified.

A new found respect was gained from Daniel's and his three friends commitment to God, and when God spoke to the king through dreams and his magicians failed to provide the correct interpretation, King Nebuchadnezzar called on Daniel. The message that God was trying to get over to the king was for him to repent and turn to righteousness and His judgment would be averted (v. 27). The dream was fulfilled as promised (vv. 28-33).

Daniel would always spend time alone in prayer with God before as he prayed for his people he asked for forgiveness of their sins (vv. 18-19).

Use your gifts for God as Daniel did.

June 28

Joshua And The Israelites: Joshua 1:2, 5

Moses my servant is dead; now therefore arise, go over this Jordan, thou, and all this people, unto the land which I do give to them, even to the children of Israel....as I was with Moses, so I will be with thee: I will not fail thee, nor forsake thee.

Our lesson study is one set in time where Joshua is taking over the leadership role of God's people to lead them into the Promise Land. God gave Joshua a promise of His presence just as He was with Moses. Therefore, Joshua and the Israelites had nothing to fear under Joshua's leadership for two reasons, (a) Joshua walked closely with Moses all those years and had learned from him, and (b) Joshua was a God-fearing man even though he needed reassurance from God. The promise made to Joshua applies to all believers today as we have His abiding presence through the Holy Spirit.

It is noteworthy to say that the Promise Land typifies God's spiritual inheritance and salvation in Jesus Christ, but all believers must fight the good fight of faith to enter into God's eternal rest (1 Timothy 1:18-20). Just as Joshua and the Israelites entering into the Promised Land was predicated on their faith and obedience so it is with NT believers. With that being said possession of the land (God's inheritance) rests in His presence, power, and faith in His promises.

Faithful believers have a blessed promise from God.

June 29

Elijah In The Midst of A Rebellious Nation: 1 Kings 18:17-46

And it came to pass, when Ahab saw Elijah, that Ahab said unto him, Art thou he that troubleth Israel? And he answered, I have not troubled Israel; but thou, and thy father's house, in that ye have forsaken the commandments of the Lord, and thou hast followed Baalim.

Elijah was the man of God who stood in the face of a rebellious nation and preached what thus said the Lord. Therefore, it is no wonder that Ahab knew who Elijah was and questioned him preaching repentance. Ahab represented the face of the sinful Israel and they were comfortable in worshipping Baalim and not live according to God's commandments. God wants His people to live holy lives unto Him as He is the one true God. He is the creator and sustainer of all life. If any man says he is a believer then the person must separate himself from worldly ways, because sin is a powerful tool used by Satan.

Elijah being a devout man of God could confront the people with sinful life styles by giving them a choice of gods to worship, "If the Lord be God, then follow him, but if Baal, then follow him"? This principle is true of all believers today; we must choose who we are going to follow, God or Baal?

Believers, we are in the midst of a rebellious nation, therefore, stand for the true God, because when we call on Him He answers.

God's Promise To His Servants: Isaiah 41:10-11

Fear thou not; for I am with thee: be not dismayed; for I am thy God: I will strengthen thee: yea I will help thee; yea I will uphold thee with the right hand of my righteousness.

In an earlier writing we have the promise of God being with His servants (Joshua 1: 2, 5), and in today's lesson discussion is another of God's promises. There are many other scripture verses of God being with His servants, as noted in the Great Commission (Matthew 28:19-20). God has proven to be true to His promises. This is because God is immutable and cannot lie. God promised to be with His disciples as they carried the gospel message and He was; He promised to be with all who believe and He is.

The lesson to be learned from today's discussion is that whom God has chosen to carry out His message has nothing to fear and or doubt (v. 8). God chose Israel as His nation by which His plan of redemption would come and He has chosen His servants to carry forth the message of redemption into the entire world. The other lesson is that Israel was to be an example to the world of God's love and blessings.

Who is Israel in spiritual terms? Israel is all believers who have accepted Jesus Christ through faith. This applies to all before Christ's birth, during His earthly ministry and beyond.

"Fear not, I am with thee."

Follow God

July 1

Fishing For Lost Souls: Luke 5:1-11

And He entered into one of the ships, which was Simon's, and prayed him that he would thrust out a little from the land. And He sat down, and taught the people out of the ship. Now when He had left speaking, He said unto Simon, Launch out into the deep, and let down your nets for a draught.

Today's lesson study is on lost souls as Jesus was teaching a crowd of people and He came to the Lake of Gennesaret He saw two ships standing idle without their fishermen as these men had toiled all night and had caught no fish (vv.1-2). Jesus entered Simon Peter's boat and instructed him to move farther away from the bank because He knew where the fish were. In obedience the catch was so great until both ships were filled to the brink of sinking (vv. 4-7). **O! What a catch?**

Peter's response was one of humility, worship and confession of his sins, but Jesus had bigger plans for Peter and his partners. Just as Peter and his partners caught multitude of fish likewise they would bring lost souls to Christ. This is the result of preaching the gospel of Christ.

Just as Christ's first disciples became fishers of men so must believers today win souls for Christ as this is part of Christ's great commission. All believers' should respond without hesitation as the early disciples did when hearing the call "Follow Me and I will make you fishers of men."

Soul winning is preaching Christ to a lost world.

July 2

A Spiritual Healing: Luke 4:40

Now when the sun was setting, all they that had any sick with divers diseases brought them unto him; and he laid his hands on everyone of them, and healed them.

Today's scripture text depicts Jesus healing the many sick people of their different diseases that were brought to Him in this particular setting. Also, in the gospel writings of the New Testament talks about the driving out of demons, performing miracles and healing the many diseases that Jesus encountered while many physical healings led to spiritual healing of the person's soul. The fact being that all unsaved are in need of a spiritual healing from Jesus as only He can give.

How must one be spiritually healed? Spiritual healing comes through accepting Jesus Christ as one's personal Savior as He came to earth by way of a virgin birth to die for the sins of the world (John 3:16). To be spiritually healed one must admit that he or she is a sinner, confess his or her sins and then turn away from the sin and to God through faith in Jesus Christ.

It is noteworthy to say that unless the unsaved is spiritually healed the person will die a spiritual death which is eternal separation from God. Who wants to be separated from our creator and sustainer? Hopefully no one. Just as physical healing continues so does spiritual healing for all who come to Jesus.

Jesus is healing!

July 3

The Model Prayer: Matthew 6:9-13; Luke 11:2-4

....When ye pray, say Our Father which art in heaven, Hallowed be thy name. Thy kingdom come. Thy will be done, as in heaven, so in earth. Give us day by day our daily bread. And forgive us our sins, for we also forgive every one that is indebted to us. And lead us not into temptation; but deliver us from evil.

If you read the two scriptures you will see slight differences in the wording, but for the most part they are the same as this is our model prayer that Jesus gave His disciples and all who pray should follow this model.

What Jesus indicated in this model prayer is six areas of concern that all believers should address when praying. The first three are the holiness of God and the Will of God and the second three are ones personal needs.

The order in which these concerns are expressed is giving reverence to God who is in heaven, because God the Father is the creator of all things which includes both heaven and earth. God the Father resides in heaven while His Spirit resides in each believer. Next, we are to hallow God's name because of His holiness and righteousness and there is no other beside the holy God. God is worthy of all praises and worship and when we give reverence to Him we worship Him. God is the only one worthy of exaltation, because of who He is. It is noteworthy to say that it is a privilege and honor to come into the presence of a holy God, the one who supplies all our needs, the one who cares for all our problems and concerns. He is the only one who is able to handle all situations.

The third area of concern is that we must pray for our wills to align with the Will of God, because we know for certain that God's Will is going to be done. Why should we desire that God's Will be done in our lives? Because He has a purpose for our lives as we were created to have an intimate relationship with God and live holy unto Him. This cannot happen if we are out of the perfect will of God.

The personal concerns for us are that we are to ask God to

supply our daily needs as He promised (Philippians 4:19). If the question were raised, Why must we ask God when He knows everything? Asking represents a spirit of humility. As a child would you go in the refrigerator without asking? No.

There is also a need for God to deliver us from evil, because we lack the ability to fight sin in our own strength. As believers we are bombarded by Satan and his attacks daily. Next, we are to ask for forgiveness; therefore, we as believers/Christians must be willing to forgive others. This is because our loving Father forgave us and continues to do so. If we are unwilling to forgive others, then our Father is unwilling to forgive us (Matthew 6:15).

Pray, give God His due.

July 4

Purposeful Prayer: Matthew 7:7-8

Ask, and it shall be given you, seek, and ye shall find, knock, and it shall be opened unto you. For everyone that asketh receive, and he that seeketh findeth, and to him that knocketh it shall be opened.

What is our scripture text saying to us? We know that God knows our needs before we ask, but as stated earlier we are to ask in humility with faith knowing that God in His compassionate care will give what we ask for in the name of His Son Jesus Christ. Also, when we go to God we are exercising our faith in Him while knowing that God hears and believing without a doubt that He will answer our prayers.

Daily communication with God in prayer we (a) become more like Him, (b) get to know His will for our lives, (c) we learn to align our prayer requests with His Will as outlined in our model prayer, and (d) we get to experience His love, goodness, grace and mercy.

We have looked at why we should pray, now allow me to say that according to scripture we are commanded by Jesus to pray (Matthew 26:41, Luke 18:1; John 16:24), and it is God's desire to have a fellowship with us. This is obtained through prayer, Bible reading and meditating on His Word. Lastly, prayers are necessary to receive God's blessings.

Prayers have a purpose-Pray.

July 5

The Pattern Of Love: John 3:16

For God so loved the world, that he gave His begotten Son, that whosoever believeth on Him should not perish, but have everlasting life.

Why would we call this scripture the pattern of love? It is because it expresses the magnitude of all love. God's love is inescapable. His love extends to the pit of hell and to the far reaches of the heavens, God's love is there. His love includes all mankind. Regardless of our sinful conditions God's love is still present.

God's love is unconditional because while man was an enemy with God He still loved us to the point of sending His only begotten Son into the world to die for the sins of the world. God loves us whether we love Him in return, whereas we love those who love us. What does God say? We are to love all as He loved friends and enemies alike.

We have looked at the inescapable love of God, the question now becomes, Are we required to love to the point of death for another? No, because we cannot die for our own sins, but we are commanded to love all as God does. When we love all we emulate the love of God; therefore, the world will see Christ in us.

This question begs an answer, What kind of love do you have God's (agape) or man's (filo) love?

Love as God loves-unconditionally.

July 6

Do All We Do In Love: 1 Corinthians 13:1-3

Though I speak with the tongues of men and of angels, and have not charity, I am become as sounding brass, or a tinkling cymbal. And though I have the gift of prophesy, and understand all mysteries, and all knowledge, and though I have all faith, so that I could remove mountains, and have no charity, I am nothing.

What is Paul saying to his readers? Paul is saying that although he has all the above described gifts and love/charity is omitted, then he is nothing more than a noise maker-tinkling cymbal.

With that being said, then love is the epicenter of all we do because we emulate the love of God in our actions. This is true when we use our God-given gifts in ministry. Another point is that when exercising our God-given gifts it is for God's glory instead of self-aggrandizement.

Paul and God's other spokespersons diligently carried out their called gifts of ministry in pure love and sought no glorified reputation for themselves. Look at God's Son Jesus Christ and all that He has did for mankind-all in pure love, humility and obedience to the Father.

The question now becomes, Are you serving God in love or for show? Doing all we do in love, then God will reward, but if for show there is no reward only what man gives, which is temporal.

The triune God working on the behalf of man's good out of love.

The Supremacy Of Love: 1 Corinthians 13:4-13

Charity suffereth long, and is kind: charity envieth not: charity vaunteth not itself, is not puffed up, Do not behave itself unseemly, seeketh not her own, is not easily provoked, thinketh no evil. Rejoice not in iniquity, but rejoice in the truth: beareth all things, believeth all things, hopeth all things, endureth all things.

Yesterday we talked about doing what we do in love, but today's discussion will focus on the behavior and activity of love compared to love that is motivated by selfish love desires or feelings.

Verses 4-7 depicts the love characteristics of God, the Father, God the Son and God the Holy Spirit and is the same characteristics that all believers are to have and display at all times. This is because we are children of God and are to show resemblance of our heavenly Father. Verse 8 tells of love/charity lasting forever as prophesy, speaking in tongues and other gifts will cease, but not love. Another school of thought on everlasting love is that God is love who is eternal, then so is love.

Verse 13 authenticates our discussion topic title by stating that love/charity is the greatest of the three (faith, hope, and charity). If the question were raised, What's love got to do with it (Tina Turner)? Short answer everything. God values and exalts character that is motivated by love. The more believers love God and others, His love overflows the believer's heart through the indwelling Holy Spirit.

Love conqueror's all.

July 8

Neighborly Guidance: Leviticus 19:17-18

Thy shalt not hate thy brother in thine heart: thou shalt in any wise rebuke thy neighbor, and not suffer sin upon him. Thou shalt not avenge, nor bear any grudge against the children of they people, but thou shalt love thy neighbor as thyself: I am the Lord.

Today's topical discussion focuses on how to treat our neighbors, which begs the question, Who are our neighbors? Are our neighbors the persons living next door, or on our block, our neighborhoods, or are our neighbors anyone we meet? Our neighbors are anyone we come in contact with regardless of surroundings.

Jesus Christ addressed this issue in Matthew 22:39 so did Paul in Romans 13:9 and James 2:8 as well. These cited scriptures reference the second of the Ten Commandments as it relates to loving thy neighbor as thy self. Every person has a built in nature to love thyself and will do self no harm, and if we love our neighbor likewise then there is neither hatred nor harm directed to others.

The question now becomes, Why was this practical principal necessary? This principal was necessary because we are commanded to love all even our enemies as God loves all. God loved mankind when we were at odds with God. Therefore, our love for others must first be preceded by our genuine love for God. This is because without a virtual love relationship it is impossible to have a horizontal love relationship with our fellowman.

Loving God equals neighborly love.

July 9

Believers Beloved Sons Of God: 1 John 3:1

Behold, what manner of love the Father hath bestowed upon us, that we should be called the sons of God: therefore the world knoweth us not, because it knew him not.

This month's theme is Follow God and what better way to follow God than in love, because we know the love of God which He shed on His beloved children so much to that all who believe on His Son Jesus He has made all believers Sons of God/His children.

God's ultimate goal in making us His beloved sons is to save us forever and conform us to the likeness of His Son Jesus. With that being said there are beneficial privileges from being Sons of God such as (a) believers receive a high honor and salvation, (b) believers have a future hope and will share in the glory of God when we get to heaven, (c) believers are heirs of God and co-heirs with Christ, and (d) believers have a reason to live to please God.

It is noteworthy to say that believers are looked upon as strange in that we are a peculiar people to the world as we see things differently from the world. This is because believers have been consecrated to live holy lives before God. Believers are a holy nation and of the royal priesthood of God (1 Peter 2:9).

Blessings abound from being sons of God believe and join the family of God.

Christian Witness: Acts 13:31

And He was seen many days of them which came up with Him form Galilee to Jerusalem, who are His witnesses unto the people.

If the question were raised, Who is a witness? Popular definition defines witness as one who testifies to an act or word of truth. This is telling what you know to be the truth either by an eye witness account or documented factual evidence.

In a court of law witnesses are called to provide truthful evidence to the case in question, but in Christian witness are those persons who can give factual evidence as to Christ, His deity and His saving works. The Bible records several eye witnesses to Jesus Christ, His works, deity and His saving grace. The question now becomes, How do believers become witnesses for Christ? All believers who have accepted Jesus Christ after His earthly stay must witness Him in faith as we see Him with our spiritual eye. Paul can witness Christ from his Damascus Road encounter as well as many others who preached Christ. All who believe have an encounter with Jesus; it may not be as dramatic as Paul's encounter, nevertheless it is an encounter that makes the believers want to tell everyone he or she meets what Jesus has done in his or her life. *He saved my soul from a burning hell.*

Let's segway to Christian witness by looking at the guiding principals of Christian witness, which are:

(a) Christian witnesses must be willing to obey the Great Commission (Matthew 28:19-20) by going into all nations sharing the good news of the gospel of Christ.

(b) Christian Witnesses must preach, teach and witness Christ's death, burial, resurrection, His saving power and the indwelling Holy Spirit.

(c) Christian witnesses must have a strong conviction regarding sin, the righteousness' of God and His judgment, and how they were saved by grace through faith.

(d) Christian witnesses must separate him or herself form a world to one of righteous living.

(e) Christian witnesses are prophetic ministers empowered by the Holy Ghost (Acts 1:8).

If the question were raised, Why is Christian witness so important? First, Christian witness is a mandate by Christ Himself and in obedience to Christ we as believers are to witness Christ the world over. Second, Christian witness is important because it spreads the gospel of Christ and aid in kingdom building. In biblical times we see the spread of the gospel from witnessing Him. Third, Christian witness is important because believers are the salt of the earth and we are to season, witness Christ to a dying world. Lastly, believers are the light of God in a sin darkened world and we are to let our light so shine before men that they may see Christ in us.

Therefore, Christian witness is vital to the spread of the gospel as all believers are to witness Christ as mandated by Him.

Witness, witness, witness Christ for He is worthy.

July 11

Preaching The Gospel Of Christ World Over: Acts 14:1-2, 7-10

And it came to pass in Iconium, that they went both together unto the synagogue of the Jews, and so spake, that a great multitude both of the Jews and also of the Greeks believed... And there they preached the gospel.

In our lesson study we see how Paul and his companion Barnabas traveled to different cities preaching Christ and the results were that many both Jews and Greeks believed on the name of Jesus.

However, when the unbelieving Jews saw the effects from Paul's preaching Christ, they caused trouble which resulted in Paul and Barnabas leaving and going to another city where Christ was preached. What we see from this incident is that controversy caused the gospel to be preached in another place where people heard and believed.

Studying the life of Paul we learned that he traveled to many places preaching Christ and establishing many churches throughout the Asia Minor region. In many instances the church grew out of controversy; however this did not deter Paul from preaching Christ wherever he went. Paul preached Christ while prison bound; the jailer and his household were saved.

In obedience to his calling Paul was steadfast and committed to preaching Christ so that the entire world would hear the gospel of Christ. The command to witness and preach Christ worldwide remains in effect so carry God's message of the good news of salvation to a dying world.

God's word is good news so share it.

July 12

Effectively Preaching Christ: 2 Corinthians 4:5-6

For we preached not ourselves, but Christ Jesus the Lord; and ourselves your servants for Jesus' sake. For God, who commanded the light to shine out of darkness, hath shined in our hearts, to give the light of the knowledge of the glory of God in the face of Jesus Christ.

If the question were raised, **What makes for effective preaching?** Our scripture text provides the answer of effective preaching as we are to only preach Christ as Paul did during his ministry. We are to preach Christ because He is the only one who has the power to save. Man has no saving power, therefore, self should not be preached. It is noteworthy to say that when we preach Christ He will draw men unto Him.

All believers are saved by God's grace through faith in Jesus Christ, therefore, we are His servants called to spread the good news of Christ. In doing so we are a shining light for Him in a sin darkened world.

Where does this burning desire to share God's Word begin? It begins in the hearts of all believers as it is like fire shut up in our bones where true believers just can't keep still--*you just have to tell somebody.*

Preaching Christ the Lord always opens doors to the hearts of many (v 12); it is effective and God gets the glory for His message is to being shared in every place (v.14).

Preach Christ!

July 13

Christ Followers Face Trials: 2 Corinthians 4:8-15; 5:1

We are troubled on every side, yet not distressed: we are perplexed, but not in despair; Persecuted, but not forsaken; cast down, but not destroyed; always bearing about in the body the dying of the Lord Jesus, that the life also of Jesus might be made manifested in our body.

Why must Christ followers suffer? Believers suffer for Christ's sake because He Himself suffered and the world hated Him; therefore, being a follower of Christ we can expect to suffer trials and tribulations simply because the world hates us as it did Christ.

Romans 8:35 asks the question, Who shall separate me from the love of Christ? This scripture goes on to list some trails that we as followers of Christ will encounter, but because of His love for us and our love for Him there is nothing that can separate us from Christ. Therefore, we can say like Paul who was troubled on every side, but he never became distressed, nor was Paul in despair. Throughout the many persecutions Paul faced he was never forsaken and his persecutor could not break his spirit simply because Paul was ready to die for Christ.

What does this say for you and me today? The same principal that applied to Paul applies to you and me today. We are never forsaken, nor forgotten by the Lord, because as promised He is always beside us.

Christ followers will face persecution, but the love of God shall never separate us. Christ suffered so must we as it is never in vain.

July 14

Standing For God The End Results: 2 Corinthians 4:16-18

For which cause we faint not; but though our outward man perish, yet the inward man is renewed day by day. For our light affliction, which is but for a moment, worketh for us a far more exceeding and eternal weight of glory; While we look not at the things which are seen, but at the things which are not seen for the things which are seen are temporal, but the things which are not seen are eternal.

In yesterday's discussion we focused on suffering for Christ and why we face the trials and tribulations we do, but today's focus is on the end results of standing for God. Our scripture text provides the profound answer of spending eternity with the Master.

It is through our perseverance we have the endurance to finish the race of living for God in spite of what we may encounter daily. The Holy Spirit renews us each day from within. Paul calls our afflictions light and momentary this is because the Jesus in us is bigger than he who is in the world. We are more than conquerors through Christ Jesus who conquered all. Also, Paul encourages us to focus on unseen things rather than on what we see.

It can be concluded then that standing for God is a blessing in that when "this earthly house (body) is dissolved; we have another house not made with hand, eternal in the heavens (2 Corinthians 5:1-2).

Our heavenly home awaits, stand for God!

July 15

Preserved In Jesus Christ: Jude 1:1-3

...To them that are sanctified by God the Father, and preserved in Jesus Christ, and called. Mercy unto you, and peace, and love, be multiplied....exhort you that ye should earnestly contend for the faith which was once delivered unto the saints.

I remember my mother preserving/canning fruits and vegetables in season for use in the winter. This process assured the family of having fresh fruits and vegetables in the winter. Some of the fruits canned/preserved were peaches and pears. In her canning process she would select the freshest fruit and or vegetables, cook them and add the necessary preservants and then place the fruits and or vegetables in a special container until ready for eating in the winter.

What does this analogy say for Christians being preserved in Christ? It says that God has called each of us for His special purpose and during our canning process we are sanctified, justified, and kept by God through the Holy Spirit. This analogy also states that just as my mother's preserved fruits/food was for a good use God called believers for His use. He called us; sanctified and purified us through trials and tribulations and we have been justified by Christ. The blessed part of being preserved in Christ is that all saints of God get to spend eternity with Him. ***What a blessing!*** Lastly, all believers are kept by the Holy Spirit as He is our sealer.

Believers are preserved in Christ for God's use as we are His property.

July 16

Precious In God's Eyesight: Psalm 116:15

Precious in the sight of the Lord is the death of his saints.

Our focus in today's discussion is all humanity being precious in the sight of God and death as it relates to both non-believers and believers. The question that comes to mind is, Why is mankind so precious in the sight of God? This is because man was created in the likeness and image of God. When God created man He breathed the breath of life into man and he became a living soul; therefore, man has God's spirit living within. Also, we can reflect on the order of creation and note that man was created last and God gave man the task of overseeing all of His creations. It is noteworthy to say that man was a planned creation not an afterthought; this renders him precious in the sight of God. Most importantly, man was created to have fellowship with God; sin broke this fellowship, but love restored the fellowship.

The magnitude of man's preciousness to God is evidenced by His Son's death on the cross for man's sins and now we have a living Savior who intercedes for us to the Father.

Death to believers is precious in that physical death is not the end, but the beginning of eternal life where the believer will see Jesus face-to-face. Whereas the non-believer will spend eternity separated from the creator.

Which do you choose heaven or hell? Hell was created for Satan not God's precious creation-man.

July 17

Believers Kept In Perfect Peace: Isaiah 26:2-6

Open ye the gates, that the righteous nations which keepeth the truth may enter in. Thou will keep him in perfect peace, whose mind is stayed on thee: because he trusted in thee. Trust ye in the Lord, for ever; for in the Lord Jehovah is everlasting strength.

The prophet Isaiah is offering words of encouragement to all who believe in the Lord as He is our keeper at all times. He is our high tower, our rock of salvation, and our refuge in the time of storm (Psalm 62:2; 46:1; 61:3). Isaiah's encouraging words also states that only the righteous will enter into the gates (heaven) because these are the ones who have remained faithful and truthful to God and His righteousness. The righteous nations in this scenario are all believers who have remained focused on the Lord and His saving powers and developed the mind of Christ as believers are unified with Christ. These nations/believers have trusted in God to provide for all their needs even in the times of troubles. The righteous of God has come to know God for who He is and what He can and will do in the lives of all believers. He is the source of our being.

Psalm 62:1-2 explicitly states that God is the source of our salvation as this is the truth by which all believers come to God, because it is His grace and our faith in Jesus Christ that saves. The other truth is that God is our keeper and sustainer as He is able to sustain all creations-man included. In the time of trouble we are to turn to God in complete trust knowing that He will deliver in due time. This speaks to the believer's faithfulness in trusting the one true God for deliverance. Also, during trouble times it is comforting to know that God provides perfect peace and all believers can rest safely in the arms of God; this is because His protection is everlasting. God's peace surpasses all understanding simply because the world's peace is temporal while God's peace is everlasting.

Reflecting on the perfect peace (shalom) that God created was disturbed by sin and His perfect peace will be re-established when Christ returns and all the righteous of God will once again enjoy that perfect peace. However, while we as believers wait Christ's return we can enjoy peace by totally submerging ourselves in God. Believers are not controlled by the events of this world nor its systems. Believers are in this world, but not of this world and it is God's love that we can presently enjoy His peace and be in harmony with Him.

How does one stay in perfect harmony with God? This is achieved by daily communicating with God through prayer, reading and meditating on His Word. The more we talk to God the closer our relationship becomes with Him.

Closing this dialogue on being kept in perfect peace by God is that believers/the righteous nations are focused on God and His righteousness and has committed his or herself to do things God's way.

Perfect peace is God's peace, live for Him and enjoy it.

July 18

Man's Way VS God's: Exodus 2:11-25

And it came to pass in those days, when Moses was grown, that he went out unto his brethren, and looked on their burdens; and he spied an Egyptian smiting a Hebrew, one of his brethren. And he looked this way and that way, and when he saw that there was no man, he slew the Egyptian and hid him in the sand.

The focus of today's discussion is an implied question of which is best God's or man's way? From our scripture text we see Moses taking matters into his own hand as it relates to relieving the oppression of his fellow countrymen. Moses failed to consult with God as how to best handle the situation. This scenario is played in our society daily.

In hind sight of Moses' actions, one could easily say that his actions were by divine plan and the beginning of his training by God to lead His people out of bondage. This is because Moses had to flee the country where he remained for forty years as he was in a strange land-Midian herding sheep. Moses' curiosity got the best of him when he went to investigate a burning bush.

During Moses' training period he learned humility, patience, and to always consult God before acting. Consulting God eliminates confusion, second guessing, and negative consequences. This principle applies to all today in that God's way is perfect.

Ask God first He has the better plan.

July 19

God A More Excellent Way: Exodus 3:1-22

And the angel of the Lord appeared unto him in a flame of fire out of the midst of a bush; and he looked, and behold the bush burned with fire, and the bush was not consumed....God called unto him out of the midst of the bush, and said, Moses, Moses, And he said Here am I....He said, I am the God of thy father, the God of Abraham, the God of Isaac, and the God of Jacob....And the Lord said, I have surely seen the affliction of my people which are in Egypt, and have heard their cry by reason of their task masters, for I know their sorrows; And I have come down to deliver them....

Previously we discussed Moses taking matters into his own hands which was neither God's way nor time for deliverance of the Israelites from bondage.

There are several lessons to be learned from this passage of scripture, one of which is that God moves in His own time and His way of doing things is far better than man's. Another lesson is that God sees all as nothing escapes His all-seeing eye; therefore He knew the pain and suffering His people were going through as He does with believers today. Still another lesson is that in every situation God already has a deliverer in place to deliver His people, but what we must do is patiently wait on God.

On the other hand if you have been called to service by God then we are to respond without hesitation, because God has made the way for His called servants to perform the specified task.

Do it as Moses did, God's way is best.

Made Perfect In God: Genesis 17:1

And when Abram was ninety years old and nine, the Lord appeared to Abram, and said unto him, I am the Almighty God; walk before me, and be thou perfect.

What is the meaning of our scripture text? To be perfect in the Lord is to wholly dedicate ones self to the Lord and thus performing the will of God as He planned, but one must humbly submit him or herself to God. Also, to walk in perfect submission before the Lord encompasses faith, trust and obedience just as Abraham exhibited in his faith walk with God.

We know that God had promised Abraham a son, but faith and patience were at work in this scenario as it is with all believers. Abraham and Sarah became impatient and interfered with God's plan so they thought, but God delivered on His promised in His time, instead of Abraham's. He does so in the lives of believers today.

The phrase "I am the Almighty God" says it all that God alone can do what and when He is ready. There is no need for man's interference. Often times we loose our blessings by being impatient and trying to interfere in God's business. With that being said, **How do we receive God's blessing?** By living faithful lives before God and keeping our hearts and minds focused on Him. 2 Corinthians 5:7 speak of the righteous faith walk journey; therefore, we are made perfect in God by faith.

Faith is the key to our perfection in God.

Unified In Christ: Ephesians 4:13

Till we all come in the unity of the faith, and of the knowledge of the Son of God, unto a perfect man, unto the measure of the stature of the fullness of Christ.

Chapter 4 of Ephesians, Paul teaches about unity of the Spirit (v. 3) and unity of the faith and how this unified body of Christ is accomplished and maintained, which is through our faith walk with Christ and adhering to the gospel message of Christ that is being preached by His spirit-filled leaders of His church.

The Godhead operates in perfect unity and harmony so must the body of Christ as it is comprised of different members performing each specified function.

It is noteworthy to say that unity of the spirit is not created by man or came into existence by man, but has been in existence from the beginning of time for all believers who have believed the truth and received Christ as his or her personal Savior. Also, unity in the spirit is maintained by being in union with God's Spirit (vv.1-3, 14-15; Galatians 5:22-26). We are unified in Christ because there is one Lord, one faith, one baptism, one God and Father of all, who is above all, and through all, and in you all (vv. 5-6).

A unified people make a unified church because we are unified in Christ!

July 22

Guided By The Holy Spirit: Romans 5:5

And hope maketh not ashamed; because the love of God is shed abroad in our hearts by the Holy Ghost which is given unto us.

If we were to sub-title today's discussion it would be *The Results of Justification by Faith.* Because once the believer is justified or rendered not guilty because of his or her faith then the Holy Spirit dwells in each believer.

The presence of the Holy Spirit residing in each believer He then begins to perform His functions of guiding, teaching, protecting and showering His love on the believer. We as believers must follow the leading of the Holy Spirit as He will guide us into all truth because He is truth-God.

Who is the Holy Spirit? The Holy Spirit is the third person in the Godhead and has been involved in humanity's life since creation. He was active in creation and He is pictured as the "moving" (Genesis 1:2) over creation, preserving and preparing it for God's further creative work" (KJV Bible commentary).

The Holy Spirit was active during Jesus' time in the wilderness just as He was active in the church on the day of Pentecost and growing Christ's church and He gives power to each believer to boldly witness Christ. The Holy Spirit imparts spiritual gifts to each believer as we each function in our spiritual gifts edifying the body of Christ-the church.

The church-individually combined believers are guided by the Holy Spirit who is God-Follow Him.

July 23

Abiding In God's Strength: Ephesians 3:16-19

That Christ may dwell in your hearts by faith, that ye being rooted and grounded in love, May be able to comprehend with all saints what is the breath, and length, and depth, and height: And to know the love of Christ, which passeth knowledge, that ye might be filled with all the fullness of God.

What these verses are saying to us today is that we can do nothing within ourselves. Our existence from birth to death depends on God and His strength. Christians have come to recognize this fact while many unsaved have yet to acknowledge such truth. Whether saved or unsaved God's love surrounds and abounds in us as there is no escaping God's love.

The believer's inner man what abides in God's strength as he- the believer is energized by God's spirit to an even greater works for Christ. The more we as believers draw closer to God we come in the full knowledge of Christ and His love.

Paul placed great emphasis on the inability to escape God's love by using the metaphor "rooted and grounded", because considering roots of a tree there is one root called the tap root which extends deep into the ground which gives strong support to the other roots and the tree. The term grounded signifies something with a solid foundation that is not easily moved. God's love and strength provide just such anchor.

Abide in Christ as He is in you and is greater than he that is in the world.

Rejoice In The Wisdom Of God: Proverbs 4:5

Get wisdom, get understanding: forget it not; neither decline from the words of my mouth.

What does the phrase "get wisdom, get understanding" mean? Let's define wisdom, which according to The Student Bible Dictionary P. 248 defines wisdom as "understanding, knowledge gained by experience, a gift of God. Wisdom is a characteristic of God." I like to refer to wisdom as the wise use of knowledge. If the question were raised as to why I define wisdom as the wise use of knowledge is because a person can have knowledge and use it foolishly; meaning making bad or ungodly decisions.

James 1:5 suggests that if you lack wisdom then we are to ask God for wisdom. I can think of two reasons for asking God for wisdom, (1) God's wisdom will aid in our decision making so the right decision will be made according to His will, which aids in us living holy lives before Him. (2) We know that God answers prayers of the heart and He does so liberally. Also, persons with a fervent prayer life have a close relationship with God.

We have defined wisdom, where and how to get wisdom; let's look at its importance by asking this question, **Why is godly wisdom essential to the believer's life?** Godly wisdom is essential because it provides God's instructions for our lives in that godly instructions are designed to transform our lives from one of sin to one of godliness. It is noteworthy to say that above all asking God for wisdom should be of high priority. Therefore, we gain wisdom by asking and diligently seeking it from God. Sometimes we gain wisdom from being disciplined by God and at others times by readily accepting His commandments. We can also gain wisdom from listening to our godly parent and other godly persons.

Let us discuss "get understanding" by defining understand (ing); according to Merriam-Webster Dictionary P. 1003) it is defined as having the "ability to grasp the meaning of, to comprehend." With that being said, we gain the ability to comprehend the meaning of

God's Word and His discipline. God's Word provides instructions for our lives and when it is not adhered to then discipline occurs. This too is instructional because we learn from our mistakes and or experiences. Disciplinary actions are out of love for us from the Father. Just as our earthly parents discipline us for bad behavior so does God.

Closing this discussion on rejoice in God's Wisdom is that there is joy in having wisdom and the proper use of knowledge as it prevents consequences from making unwise choices. Also, there is joy in understanding God's Word and how it applies to our daily lives. Then there is joy in knowing that God gives wisdom and gives it freely and above all else ask God for wisdom. Solomon asked God for wisdom and became the wisest man to ever live.

Wisdom and understanding go together get both they are godly.

July 25

Know The Will Of God: Isaiah 53:10

Yet it pleased the Lord to bruise Him; He hath put Him to grief: when thou shalt make His soul an offering for sin, He shall see His seed, He shall prolong His days, and the pleasure of the Lord shall prosper in His hand.

The Will of God is sometimes defined as the law of God, sometimes referred to as His perfect will and sometimes referred to what God permits or allows to happen, which is often time referred to as His permissive will (KJV commentary P. 1066).

Let us look at the Will of God and His law as it relates to His instructions for man's godly living. Theses instructions can be found in His Word-the Bible. The Ten Commandments are perfect examples of God's law as they are designed for us to live by.

The perfect Will of God is what He desires for His people. His perfect will is that all mankind be saved (1 Timothy 2:4; 2 Peter 3:9); although He knew that many were not going to be saved as they will refuse to hear and adhere to His word.

Lastly, the permissive will of God is what He allows to happen as He made man a free will agent; meaning man has the right to choose salvation and spend eternity with God or refuse salvation and spend eternity separated from Him. The continuance of sin is God's permissive will and He will eradicate sin at His appointed time.

We know God's will through studying His Word and responding to His Word.

July 26

Doing The Will Of God: Ephesians 5:17; Mark 3; 35

Wherefore be ye not unwise, but understanding what the will of the Lord is. For whosoever shall do the will of God, the same is my brother, and my sister, and mother (Mark 3:35).

In yesterday's discussion we held a lengthy discussion on defining the Will of God, today our focus is on doing His will after knowing it. We have determined that to know God's Will is obtained from daily Bible reading, meditating on scripture and daily prayer. While praying we must ask God to align our will with His.

Earlier we discussed getting wisdom and understanding and concluded that wisdom comes from God with the ability to comprehend His instructions. With this knowledge in hand the question now becomes, What is our response to God in doing His Will? Once we have the understanding of what God's Will is for our lives we then are to respond by committing ourselves to doing His will. Help is available through the Holy Spirit-just ask (Psalm 143:10). Help will be needed to do God's Will because Satan is an active foe. Believers must aggressively take the fight to Satan by aggressively preaching Christ to a sinful world.

We do the Will of God by living according to His laws, accepting Jesus Christ as our personal Savior and then standing firm against all manner of evil.

Do His will it is profitable to all.

July 27

Believers, Christ's Church: Matthew 16:18

And I say also unto thee, That thou art Peter, and upon this rock I will build my church; and the gates of hell shall not prevail against it.

What was Jesus saying to Peter? Was Christ saying I will build my church upon you Peter or on your knowledge that I am the Christ? Christ was saying to Peter that His church would be built on the solid foundation of Him as He is the head of all and it was Peter's confession, faith and knowledge as revealed by the Holy Spirit that Jesus was the "Christ", the Son of the living God. Peter's true confession that Jesus was the Christ is the foundational truth which Christ's church is built.

1 Peter 2:4; 6-7 referrers to Jesus as the "living stone…a chief corner stone…the stone that was disallowed by men", but thanks be to God that Jesus was "chosen by God." Therefore, all believers are living stones part of Christ's church.

The church is comprised of two parts the visible and invisible. The visible church is the local congregation where the baptized body of believers assembles to worship the Lord. The invisible church is the spirit part of Christ's church where the Spirit of God resides in each believer. Christ's church is believers who have developed an intimate relationship with Him as He is the head and the church is His bride. Lastly, believers as members of Christ's church have become temples of God.

Christ's church the solid rock I stand.

July 28

The Bride Of Christ: Ephesians 5:27

That he might present it to himself a glorious church, not having a spot, or wrinkle, or any such thing; but that it should be holy and without blemish.

Growing up in the south I often heard my mother speak of the church as the bride of Christ and the church is to be without spot or wrinkle. I lacked the full understanding of what she meant. I learned the meaning of this phrase as I grew in the knowledge of Christ. The phrase means to be without sin as sin defiles the believer who makes up the church. Christ is the head of the church so she becomes His wife/bride. Also, being that Christ is God in the second person who is holy so must the church be holy.

Christ requiring the church to be holy and without blemish means she is to be separated from sin and we know that sin remain present in this world. Another thought is that Christ cannot present His bride to His heavenly Father riddled with sin.

Therefore, all believers who make up the church must be separated from the world and its sins. 1 John 2:15-16 provides insight on believers gaining spiritual separation from the world by loving not the world. In 2 Corinthians 6:17-18 also encourages believers to separate themselves from the world and its wickedness. Believers have the indwelling Holy Spirit to aid in this effort.

Believers we are the bride of Christ washed in His blood.

July 29

Jesus The Life Giver: John 6:35

...Jesus said unto them I am the bread of life: he that cometh to me shall never hunger; and he that believeth on me shall never thirst.

This must have been a profound statement for Jesus' audience, but what Jesus was saying is that He is the only one who can give life as He is God who can do all things including providing salvation. Jesus was explaining to His audience is that He was the one who would give everlasting life.

Another school of thought is that Jesus was using the bread and water metaphor to express the necessities for spiritual life. Just as one needs bread and water to sustain physical life the same apply for one spiritual life. Jesus used this metaphor to get His message of salvation over to His audience. Jesus reminded the people of their forefathers being fed with manna that fell from heaven and they were now dead, but He was the everlasting bread from heaven (vv 48-49).

In the book of John there are seven "I am statements" used by Jesus solidifying the need for salvation, and who He is. Some of those statements are: "the light of the world" (8:12), "the door" (10:9), "the good shepherd" (10:11, 14), "the resurrection and the life" (11:25), "the truth, the way, and the life" (14:6), and "the true vine" (15:15). All above statements tell who Jesus is in providing for humanity's needs.

Jesus is life.

July 30

Believer Have Eternal Life: 1 John 5:1, 11-12

Whosoever believeth that Jesus is the Christ is born of God: and every one that loveth him that begat loveth him also that is begotten of him...And this is the record, that God hath given to us eternal life, and this life is in his Son. He that hath the Son hath life; and he that hat not the Son of God hath not life.

Our scripture text makes it very plain the reward for believing in Jesus Christ as our Savior, which is eternal life. Eternal life carries the benefit of living forever in the presence of God. To have this eternal life one must first come to Christ by genuine faith that He is God's Son who came to earth to die for the sins of the world. The other connotation is love for God as all believers are begotten (born) of the Father-God. Love is a necessary commodity in this relationship because God first loved us when we didn't love Him. With that said, then faith and love are inseparable commodities in being born of God. The question now becomes, How does one get this love? Romans 5:5 provide the answer by stating that believers receive God's love from the Holy Spirit who is God.

Allow me to say that eternal life has an intertwined relationship as the believer abides in Christ He abides in the believer (John 15:4).

Eternal life is in Jesus Christ abide in Him.

July 31

A Crown Of Righteousness: 2 Timothy 4:8

Henceforth there is laid up for me a crown of righteousness, which the Lord, the righteous judge shall give me at that day; and not to me only, but unto all them also that love his appearing.

What does a crown signifies? First, a crown is a wreath or band worn on ones head. Second, it signifies honor or victory. In today's society we have crowns being worn by kings, queens and others in a position of honor. In regards to believers we are all in a position of honor and are victorious because we are God's children who have remained faithful to Him and His righteousness to the end. All believers' reward for doing so is a crown of righteousness. Believers have been made right through the shed blood of Jesus Christ on Calvary's cross. It was Jesus atoning work on Calvary that gave us the right standing with God the Father. We were given the right standing with God to live holy lives before Him and to bring others to Christ through our witnessing so the world will see Christ in us.

If the question were raised, How do we remain steadfast in Christ? All believers have the indwelling Holy Spirit to help us remain committed to Christ and His gospel. Remaining faithful to the Lord we can say like Paul that we have as a reward a crown of righteousness and life waiting for us. It is noteworthy to say that God rewards His faithful followers as He is not short on His blessing. Believers can rejoice in the fact of knowing that we have rewards waiting for us in heaven. Our rewards begins here on earth in that we have God's assured promise of living forever with Him, and then He has provided for us golden slippers, a royal white robe that was washed in the blood of Jesus our Savior, the removal of all heartaches and pains, and lastly, the crowns signifying our honored status in God's eyesight.

Paul likened believers' steadfastness to that of a long distance runner who has the faith to endure the race to the finish line. Believers on this spiritual journey/race to heaven must be spiritually fit to endure to the end. Believers remain spiritually fit through reading God's Word and yielding to the voice of the Holy Spirit as He is our heavenly compass. *Follow your compass, because there are rewards waiting.*

Given the outlined blessed rewards waiting for all believers what more to be said for a loving God whose love is immeasurable, inescapable, unconditional and everlasting. I like many other believers can and will shout for joy giving praises to God for who He is and what He has and continues to do in the lives of all believers. Most of He rewards us for our faithfulness.

He is worthy! He is worthy! All praises to a holy God!

Follow God

Aug 1

God Call Moses: Exodus 3:4-6, 10

And when the Lord saw that he turned aside to see, God called unto him out of the midst of the bush, and said, Moses, Moses, And he said, Here am I...Come now therefore, and I will send thee unto Pharaoh, that thou mayest bring forth my people the children of Israel out of Egypt.

Today's topical discussion is a familiar one in that it deals with the call of Moses as the first leader of Israel. The main focus today is to highlight God's chosen leaders that will carry out His plan of service whether in leadership, speaking for Him to His people or simply witnessing the good news of salvation.

See, Moses had been in God's training university for a long time before Moses encountered the burning bush as he was tending his father-in-law's sheep where he learned patience, humility, and dependence on God. Another school of thought is that God sees years ahead of man. God knew the date, time and hour when He and Moses would meet and what would be Moses' response when called. **What is your response to God's call?**

God's called people/leaders are predestine by Him from the beginning of time and are strategically placed at His appointed time and place to carry out His mission. Also, God never call His people to do anything unprepared and they are never alone.

God's calls leaders for His people!

Aug 2

"Joshua Lead My People": Joshua 1:1-11

Now after the death of Moses the servant of the Lord it came to pass, that the Lord spake unto Joshua the son of Nun, Moses' minister, saying, Moses my servant is dead; now therefore arise, go over this Jordan, thou, and all this people, unto the land which I do give to them, even to the children of Israel.

What we see from today's lesson text is the death of Moses and Joshua succeeding him as Israel's leader. Joshua was a minister under Moses; therefore, he was prepared to assume leadership of God's people on their journey to the Promise Land.

A noteworthy point in this discussion is that Joshua was called by God as He knew the heart of Joshua and his ability to lead the nation of Israel to the Promise Land as well as what challenges lay ahead for the nation.

History records the success of Joshua and the nation of Israel conquering Canaan, but there is a spiritual side to this story, which is Joshua and Israel's faith in God was expressed in their obedience to His Word and laws (vv. 7-9). **What does this say for believers today?** Believers today are to remain obedient to God's Word and obey His laws just as the nation of Israel were commanded to do. Our Jericho walls are the many sins and worldly challenges we face today. Leaders and laity are well equipped (Ephesians 6:10-18) for the challenges we will encounter.

God is still calling leaders to lead His people.

Israel Demands A King: 1 Samuel 8:1-22

....Behold, thou are old, and thy sons walk not in thy ways; now make us a king to judge us like all the nations...And the Lord said unto Samuel, Hearken unto the voice of the people in all that they say unto thee; for they have not rejected thee, but they have rejected me, that I should not reign over them...Now therefore, hearken unto their voice; howbeit yet protest solemnly unto them, and shew them the manner of the king that shall reign over them.

If we were to sub-title this discussion it would be Man's Called Leaders, because in the history of Israel when God was their leader through His appointed called leaders Israel prospered. However, in her prosperity, Israel desired to be like other nations with a human king. This was prophesied by Moses many years earlier (Deuteronomy 17:14-15; 28:36).

There are several lessons from this demands by Israel, some are (a) we are prone not to leave well enough alone, (b) God sees the heart of all mankind and His called leaders are after His own heart, (c) man has a tendency to change whereas God does not, (d) God is all-knowing whereas man isn't, (e) man is limited in his wisdom whereas God isn't, (f) God loves unconditionally while man's love is conditional, and (g) lastly, God is sovereign whereas man isn't.

What happens when man calls its leaders? The history of Israel paints a vivid picture of what happens when man call its leaders. When God is omitted from calling a nation's leaders corruption, confusion, chaos, greed, oppression and all manner of wickedness follows.

When God calls a leader both church and nation blessing follow.

Aug 4

David Anointed King: 1 Samuel 16:1-13

And the Lord said unto Samuel, How long wilt thou mourn for Saul seeing I have rejected him from reigning over Israel? Fill thine horn with oil, and go, I will send thee to Jesse the Beth-lehemite; for I have provided me a king among his sons....Arise, anoint him; for this is he (v. 12).

Today's discussion is a continuance of our monthly theme of God's called leaders. Today's lesson takes a leap ahead in history from yesterday's discussion where a human king was demanded and the transitioning from Samuel to Saul as Israel's first king to God anointing David as king. David was a man after God's own heart. He committed sin, but he would always repent and ask God for forgiveness.

Saul's disobedience to God's laws resulted in him being rejected as Israel's king by God (15:23), and God instructing Samuel to anoint David as king of Israel. An important lesson to be learned from this scenario is that when God allow you to be place in leadership it is for His glory instead of self. Most importantly, leaders are to follow God and walk closely with Him and lean not unto his or her own understanding (Proverbs 3:5b). The danger in leaning on individual understanding is that leaders are failing to fully trust God. Leaders are to lead God's people according to His will and ways and when that fails to happen then God will punish leaders with many stripes.

Leaders, you are chosen by Go so follow Him.

Aug 5

God Call Special People For A Specific Service: Judges 17:6

In those days there was no king in Israel, but every man did that which was right in his own eyes.

The spiritually depraved conditions that existed during the time of this scripture writing is a direct result of what happens when Israel and man as a whole turn from God.

The book of Judges records Israel's history when there were no king and "the cycles of apostasy, foreign oppression, servitude, their crying out to God in their distress and His deliverance through leaders anointed by His Spirit" (KJV Commentary). This is the period of the judges where God anointed special judges to lead His people. God chose judges who were spirit-filled and would obey His commands.

God in His compassionated mercy is ready to forgive and deliver them from adverse situations and conditions. The need for deliverance is the result of men doing what they perceive as right which is normally wrong in God's eyes (2:11; 4:1; 6:1; 10:6).

The spiritual apostasy that existed during this period in Israel's history is prevalent in today's society. This is because man is doing what he thinks is right according to his understanding and is overlooking God's laws.

It is noteworthy to say just as God called special people to speak a word for Him in biblical times He still has special people preaching His Word to heal our land.

Believers, be a leader of one and tell a dying world about a risen Savior.

Aug 6

Gideon A Chosen Deliverer: Judges 6:1-39; 7:1-4

And the angel of Lord appeared unto him, and said unto him, The Lord is with thee, thou mighty man of valor....And the Lord looked upon him, and said, Go in this thy might, and thou shalt save Israel from the hand of the Midianites, have not I sent thee?

The story of Gideon is well documented and how God used him to deliver the children of Israel out of the hands of the Midianites as Israel was allowed to suffer because of their evil ways. Each time the nation of Israel would turn away from God and cry out to Him for deliverance, He would have compassion on them. God's love remains on display today for all who come to Him in humble repentance.

What does this say for God and His mercy? God's action shows His love, grace and mercy toward true repentance. All God asks is to obey His commands and worship Him in truth (John 4:24) with ones whole heart. Also, mankind is to have no other gods before the one true living God, and when this occurs then punishment occurs. This is what happened to Israel as well as mankind today.

It is noteworthy to say that regardless of mankind's sins God always has a deliverer chosen to lead His people back to Him. History has shown God repeating just such acts. *What a loving God!*

God has chosen godly leaders who will stand in the face of the enemy and say "what thus saith the Lord."

Ezra Leads God's People To Reform: Ezra 9:3-15

And when I heard this thing, I rent my garment and my mantle, and pluck off the hair of my head and of my beard, and sat down astonished....Should we again break thy commandments, and join in affinity with the people of these abominations? Wouldest thou not be angry with us till thou hadst consumed us, so that there should be no remnant nor escaping? O Lord God of Israel, thou art righteous; for we remain yet escaped, as it is this day: behold, we are before thee in our trespasses; for we cannot stand before thee because of this.

From our scripture text we see the prophet Ezra's grief over the condition of Israel and his repentant heart for their spiritual condition. Israel's spiritual waywardness is what caused them to be exile in Babylon for seventy years, but through it all God's hand of mercy was with them and He kept His promise to restore the nation. After about two years after the Babylonian empire was destroyed the Jewish restoration began. God always keeps His promises to His people. Just as God kept His promise to Israel He does so today. *Just trust Him!*

What does this say for God and His called leaders who are called to serve at God's appointed time? Regardless of the situation God always has a chosen leader and or person who remain steadfast in his or her commitment to God and His righteousness. Ezra is just such a person as he was a God-fearing man. Ezra was greatly concerned and saddened by the spiritual condition of Israel so much so that he began plucking the hairs from his head and beard and just sat down in astonishment. *What great concerns?*

Lacking the ability or desire to accept the spiritual conditions, Ezra went to God in prayer and humility in his attempt to bring about a restoration of the nation. Ezra prayed for the entire nation its iniquities and trespasses as he realized the mercies of God were at work in restoring the Jewish remnant to their homeland. The returned remnant was on the verge of jeopardizing God's grace, love and His compassionate promise by their wayward living. *To God be the glory,* because God always has a chosen leader who is willing to stand in the gap and declare the Word of God and to remind His people of His righteousness, which is what all mankind will be judged.

It is important to remember the blessings God has and continues to give His people, but dire consequences are sure to follow for disobeying His commands. Ezra depicts the character of God's chosen leaders as they understand it is God's righteousness by which all will be judged and all will be held accountable for his or her actions. There are many noted God-chosen leaders who stood in the face of corruption and preached the Word of God. Today's leaders must do likewise in the midst of a wayward generation; some will hear and turn to the Lord while others will refuse.

Preach the Word!

Nehemiah A Praying Leader: Nehemiah 1:1-11

And it came to pass, when I heard these words, that I sat down and wept, and mourned certain days, and fasted, and prayed before the God of heaven.

Today's discussion is a continuation of looking at God's chosen leaders who displayed a genuine concern for the condition of Israel as well as their return to their homeland-Jerusalem. Yesterday's focus was on Ezra and his display of his saddened emotions over the conditions, and through Ezra's prayers a restoration began, but today's focus is on Nehemiah and his concerns for the nation which led him to act. He was deeply sorrowful for the people and God's work while God's house lay in ruins.

God answers prayers because Nehemiah went in prayer to God about the condition and God moved on the heart of the governor who willingly gave Nehemiah permission to go and rebuild God's house. *Prayer change things!*

The lesson here is that always go to God in prayer before beginning a project/calling and God will supply all you need and all doors will be open unto you for your success. Also, God will increase ones courage, faith and will remove all emotional fears when doing His works (2:1).

It is noteworthy to close by saying, when answering God's call we must always pray and then walk on in faith as God will never leave nor forsake His children and especially His called leaders.

Pray then go in faith God is with you.

Aug 9

Isaiah The Prophesying Prophet: Isaiah 1:1-25

The vision of Isaiah, the son of Amoz, which he saw concerning Judah and Jerusalem in the days of Uzziah, Jotham, Ahaz, and Hezekiah, kings of Judah. Hear, O heaven, and give ear, O, earth; for the Lord hath spoken, I have nourished and brought up children, and they have rebelled against me.

If the question were raised, Why is Isaiah referred to as the prophesying prophet? It is because Isaiah was shown visions by God through the Holy Spirit of coming events that would affect Judah and Jerusalem. Notice the kings that reigned during Isaiah's prophecy and the spiritual conditions during these times were rebellious in nature. God showed Isaiah the coming events in His plan of salvation. In spite of God's love, mercy, and grace in that He brought the nation of Israel out of bondage, fed, provided water and protected them yet they disobeyed His laws, commands and totally disregarded His covenant. *What an ungrateful spirit? Show gratitude for God's blessing.*

God used Isaiah to warn the people of what lay ahead for their worshipping other gods and the rewards for obeying His commands. This command remains in effect today as God's spokespersons are called to preach repentance and spend eternity with God and if no repentance eternal separation from God waits. In spite of these warnings, both then and now rebellion still exists. This question begs and answer, Do you believe there is a heaven and a hell? Both exist.

Hear the preacher.

Aug 10

Solomon A Man Of Wisdom: Proverbs 2:1-7

To know wisdom and instruction; to perceive the words of understanding. To receive the instruction of wisdom, justice, and judgment, and equity; A wise man will hear, and will increase learning; and a man of understanding shall attain unto wise counsels.

In an earlier writing I defined wisdom as the wise use of knowledge and from our scripture text we have the implied definition as such with understanding. It is prudent for man to gain wisdom and understanding by asking God for wisdom as King Solomon did. God granted King Solomon's request and he is recognized as the wisest man that ever lived.

King Solomon used his wisdom to teach mankind about wisdom and understanding in many of his writings. Proverbs 3:5-6, King Solomon encourages all to trust in the Lord and lean not unto our own understand, because there is danger in doing so because God's understanding is far superior to that of man's. Also, a wise man recognizes who God is His sovereign powers and is worthy of our honor and reverence. Therefore, it is prudent to hear and adhere to wisdom as there is increased learning and the person that seeks godly wisdom is counted as wise.

We can conclude that it is wise to seek wisdom and understanding from an all-wise God. Just as God gave Solomon wisdom He will do the same for you and me.

Get wisdom, get understanding; be wise.

Aug 11

Jeremiah Weeps For A Sinful Nation: Jeremiah 9:1-29; 13:17

O that my head were waters, and mine eyes a foundation of tears, that I might weep day and night for the slain of the daughters of my people. O that I had in the wilderness a lodging place of wayfaring men; that I might leave my people, and go from them for they be all adulterers, and assembly of treacherous men.

Our scripture text gives some insight to the depth of Israel's sins when the man of God wept for his sinful nation both day and night and wanted to run and hide in the wilderness.

This text tells me two things, which are (a) that God's prophet honestly and steadfast preached God's Word to a hardhearted nation who refused to repent. Was this because the unbelievers felt God's judgment would somehow escape them? Was the nation relying on God's compassionate heart for deliverance? Is this the problem with today's society? Did the nation of Israel feel as though the preacher was just an annoying noise maker? Was the nation of Israel practicing self-authority in their failing to repent? Failing to repent is being displayed in today's society, so what are our beliefs? God will punish sin and His punishments are sure to come.

(b) The second thought from our text is that it depicts the depth of Jeremiah's love for God, His message and Jeremiah's commitment to delivering God's message to a rebellious people in spite of their waywardness. Jeremiah wanted the people to know that even though he may be weeping today, but tomorrow when judgment comes you will weep for God's mercy.

Preachers and laity cry if you must over spiritual apostasy, but stand fast and deliver God's Word.

Aug 12

Can These Bones Live?: Ezekiel 37:1-14

The hand of the Lord was upon me, and carried me out in the spirit of the Lord, and set me down in the midst of the valley, which was full of bones.

Our topical discussion today is focus on Ezekiel's vision where God used an analogy of dry bones to show the depth of the nation's sins. Ezekiel was to preach God's Word to a sinful nation who had become so sinful until they were likened to dry bones in the valley. God asks Ezekiel "can these bones live?" God knew the answer because He knows all and His prophet would obey His command to preach even if the people were as dry bones.

The vision continues to the conversation between God and Ezekiel with instructions been given to preach and God would cause the bones-people to hear and repent (v. 5). In verse 6 we see Ezekiel preaching and the results is flesh coming on these bones-people coming alive by hearing God's Word and repenting.

This scenario brings these questions to mind, given the magnitude of today's sins can our nation be considered a valley of dry bones? Are we listening to God's preachers? There is power in the Word of God; it brings a spiritual healing from ones sin sickness. There is salvation in His word. There is joy in His word; there is peace in His word.

Preachers preach because these bones can live and the valley of dry bones becomes a valley of living souls.

Aug 13

God Promises A New Heart: Ezekiel 36:26; Romans 11:26

A new heart also will I give you, and a new spirit will I put within you, and I will take away the stony heart out of your flesh, and I will give you a heart of flesh.

Yesterday we answered the question Can these bones live, and today we will look at God's promise to Israel of a new heart one that will become soft as flesh and one that will cause a change in direction that is focused on Him. The promise of a new heart depicts both a physical and spiritual restoration for the nation of Israel and believers under the new covenant, which was established by Christ (Jeremiah 31:31-34).

A new heart was necessary because God's people had turned their backs on Him forgetting all that He had done for them. Their hearts had become waxed cold as they were doing all manner of evil in God's eyesight so much so God referred to them as dry bones (yesterday's discussion).

However, we see God getting ready to make a change in the people's condition as His prophet were to preach His Word and He would do the rest, which was a heart transplant one which obeys His Word and walk according to His statues.

With this new heart and God's spirit living within people will be saved, both then and now "all Israel/believers." Why? Because when God's Word is preach it has a positive effect on the hearer.

A new heart one that is obedient to God

Aug 14

God's Spirit Within Us: Ezekiel 36:27; Acts 1:5

And I will put my spirit within you, and cause you to walk in my statues, and ye shall keep my judgments, and do them.

What do we know about God's Spirit? God's Spirit is the Holy Spirit who is God in the third person who resides in each believer. God's Spirit the Holy Spirit has been active in all God's works because without the Holy Spirit there would be no Bible to read (2 Peter 1:21), there would be no New Testament (John 14:26; 15:26-27; 1 Corinthians 2:10-14), there would be no power to proclaim the gospel message of Christ (Acts 1:8). Lastly without the Holy Spirit there would be no faith to accept God's Word, no new birth, no holiness as we lack the ability to live holy. It is by God's Spirit that the human heart become softens to receive His Spirit that enables each believer to obey God's commands.

God's Spirit-the Holy Spirit is the one who convicts all believers of his or her sins and is the sanctifying agent that sets apart all believers to receive this new heart God promised. It is the Holy Spirit that moved on Old Testament prophets who stood in the face of a rebellious nation and proclaimed God's Word while calling for repentance. It was His Spirit who enabled His chosen leaders to obey the call. It was God's Spirit who enabled the hearers during the Old Testament days to spiritually hear God's Word.

It was God's Spirit-the Holy Spirit who fell upon all who were present on the day of Pentecost and three thousand souls were saved. It is God's Spirit-the Holy Spirit who baptizes all believers into the corporate body of Christ. God-the Holy Spirit within causes us to do great and mighty things for His kingdom building for He is bigger than the "god" of this world. It is by God's Spirit that God calls leaders and spokespersons to stand in the face of a perverted generation both then and now and say *"what thus saith the Lord."*

It is God's Spirit-the Holy Spirit that enables each believer to boldly witness Christ the world over to make other disciples. It is God's Spirit that enables each believer to continue to walk in true holiness and refrain from reverting back to his or her old self as the believer has become new creatures in Christ.

Why must God's Spirit live in each of us? God's Spirit must live in each of us as we were created in His likeness and imagine as He breathed the breath of life in all humanity. Therefore, we represent God and He cannot dwell in a filthy place.

Believers are temples of God as His Spirit dwells within.

Aug 15

God's New Covenant: Jeremiah 31:31-34

Behold, the days come, saith the Lord, that I will make a new covenant with the house of Israel, and with the house of Judah: Not according to the covenant that I made with their fathers in the day that I took them by the hand, to bring them out of the land of Egypt; which my covenant they brake, although I was a husband unto them, saith the Lord.

On many occasions the term "covenant" has been defined as a mutual agreement between two or more parties. However, in regards to the covenant agreement between God and the nation of Israel is that God sets the terms of His covenant while the people of Israel agreed and were expected to follow what was agreed upon.

History records that God has made covenant beginning with Adam and Eve and His covenants extends to the present. Genesis 15 records God's most far reaching covenant that was made to Abraham which included the Hebrew nation. History records God's covenant being broken and a new covenant was required.

The old covenant were written on stones and or tables which gave way for misplacement and or just forgetting to learn and or study God's covenant with a desire for obedience. God's new covenant would be written in the hearts of men (v. 33) as this removed the requirement of men teaching men (v. 34). The new covenant was far better because every man who believes in Christ will know God for him or herself and will have direct access to God.

God's new covenant is of grace through Jesus Christ (Jeremiah 30:22).

Aug 16

What God Requires From His People?: Deuteronomy 5:1

And Moses called all Israel, and said unto them, Hear, O Israel, the statues and judgments which I speak in your ears this day, that ye may learn them, and keep, and do them.

Answering our title question in a simple answer is to simply obey God's commands and do what He asks. Loyalty and faithful living is found in God's covenants both then and now. What God gives in return for obeying His covenant are His presence, His protection, His care, His guidance, and His assurance of whatever He promised.

The Old Testament/covenant was based on grace, the law, and obedience. Under the law man found it difficult to keep the law, but God removed this barrier with the new covenant/testament which came through His Son Jesus Christ. In the age of the new covenant every person will come to know God and have a personal relationship with Him. All believers have direct access to God and His presence through the Holy Spirit; this encompasses John 3:16. It is noteworthy to say that all Christians/believers have a covenant agreement with God and know what He expects from each believer. All non-Christians can enter into a covenant agreement by accepting His Son Jesus as Lord and Savior (John 3:16; Romans 10:9-10).

To summarize our title question is to say God requires obedience and loyalty to Him and He will be their God and they His people.

Keep His covenant.

Aug 17

Live In Holiness: 1 Kings 2:4; Psalm 119:33-40

...If thy children take heed to their way, to walk before me in truth with all their heart and all their soul, there shall not fail thee (said he) a man on the throne of Israel.

Our overall theme for this month is God's chosen leaders where we have looked at several of His leaders and their character which is to say they walked closely with God.

If the question were raised, How do one live in holiness? The writer of 1 Kings, David encourages all to take a careful look at your lifestyle and stake heed to it and then walk in true holiness by obeying God's commands. David learned this painful but valuable lesson of walking closely with God as it opened the door to God's blessing and His truth. When David failed to walk according to God's commands he suffered, but David would go to God in sincere prayer and with a repentant heart asking for forgiveness.

You and I today can live in holiness by living according to God's Word as we have God's Word the Bible and the indwelling Holy Spirit as our guide. It is noteworthy to say that holy living requires a willing heart and a humble spirit; in doing so we give honor and glory to a Sovereign God.

The world will see God in you through your holy living. Live holy!

Aug 18

Promise Of God: 1 John 2:24-25

Let that therefore abide in you, which ye have heard from the beginning. If that which ye have heard from the beginning shall remain in you, ye also shall continue in the Son, and in the Father. And this is the promise that he hath promised us, even eternal life.

What did God promise? God promised that if all believers abide in Christ they will experience salvation. What does this mean? All believers must accept Jesus Christ as his or her personal Savior (John 3:16). Just as the Son and the Father abides in each other so must believers remain in Christ Jesus. How must believers remain in Christ? This is achieved by adhering to Christ and the New Testament apostles doctrines, where Christ is the foundation for the true church. The apostles doctrine is the infallible truths as revealed to them by the Holy Spirit (Ephesians 2:20). Believers also remain in Christ by reading and studying God's Word-the Bible and then yielding to the guidance of the Holy Spirit. This enables believers to live holy lives before God so the world will see Christ manifested in us.

It is noteworthy to say that God always keep His promises; He promised a Savior, Jesus came. He promised the indwelling Holy Spirit for all who believe God the Holy Spirit lives in each believer. God promised never to leave nor forsake His own, we are never alone.

Promises made promises kept; God the promise keeper!

Aug 18

Promise Of God: 1 John 2:24-25

Let that therefore abide in you, which ye have heard from the beginning. If that which ye have heard from the beginning shall remain in you, ye also shall continue in the Son, and in the Father. And this is the promise that he hath promised us, even eternal life.

What did God promise? God promised that if all believers abide in Christ they will experience salvation. What does this mean? All believers must accept Jesus Christ as his or her personal Savior (John 3:16). Just as the Son and the Father abides in each other so must believers remain in Christ Jesus. How must believers remain in Christ? This is achieved by adhering to Christ and the New Testament apostles doctrines, where Christ is the foundation for the true church. The apostles doctrine is the infallible truths as revealed to them by the Holy Spirit (Ephesians 2:20). Believers also remain in Christ by reading and studying God's Word-the Bible and then yielding to the guidance of the Holy Spirit. This enables believers to live holy lives before God so the world will see Christ manifested in us.

It is noteworthy to say that God always keep His promises; He promised a Savior, Jesus came. He promised the indwelling Holy Spirit for all who believe God the Holy Spirit lives in each believer. God promised never to leave nor forsake His own, we are never alone.
**Pro*mises made promises kept; God the promise keeper!*

Aug 20

Christ Chosen Of God: Luke 23:35

And the people stood beholding, And the rulers also with them derided him, saying, He saved others; let him save himself, if he be Christ, the chosen of God.

The setting for today's discussion is Jesus hanging on the cross dying for humanity's sins while His mockers wondered why He did not save Himself as He had done so much for others. The most important point is that Jesus was the Christ chosen by God the Father to do what He did. It weren't the matter of Christ's ability but the mission for which He came to complete. It is worth noting that had Jesus came down from the cross there would be not salvation and no hope for tomorrow.

Let's look at a hypothetical scenario; let just say that Christ changed His mind and told the Father "let me not die for ungrateful man. Let man die for himself." We know this wouldn't have occurred because Jesus is God who changes not. Also, God the Father found His Son as the only one worthy who met all the requirements to atone sin. What does this mean? It means that Christ was chosen by God from the foundation of the world that He would be born of a woman and shed His precious blood for the sins of the world.

First, thank God for Jesus and I am glad Christ was the chosen sacrificial lamb. Second, my blood is too tainted with sin for me to save myself.

Thank You God for choosing Your Son Jesus as the spotless lamb.

Aug 21

Christ's Church: Matthew 16:13-18

...Whom do men say that I the Son of man am? And they said, Some say that thou art John the Baptist; some Elisa; and others Jeremias, or one of the prophets. He saith unto them, But whom say ye that I am? And Simon Peter answered and said, Thou art the Christ, the Son of the living God.

The scene of our scripture text take place on the cost of Caesarea Philippi where Jesus was having one of His many conversation with His disciples. There were many speculations as to who Jesus really was other than who He really was. From the conversation some of His disciples didn't recognized Jesus as the Christ; only Peter believed Jesus to be the promised Messiah-Christ. This revelation came through the Holy Spirit.

It was Peter's faith that Jesus was the Christ the Son of God and it is this foundational fact that Christ built His church. He is the solid rock the sure foundation for which the church is built. 1 Peter 2:4, 6-7 talks about Christ as the "living stone, the chief corner stone that the builders rejected." All who believe that Jesus is the Christ and accept Him as his or her personal Savior become living stones as part of Christ's spiritual church.

Christ is the head of His church and any church that is not built on Christ is not of Christ. Christ's church will prevail against Satan's attacks. Just as all believers are outfitted for spiritual warfare so is Christ's church. Christ's church will rise up in faith, power and authority over all evil that exist in this present world because Satan is a defeated foe.

If the question were raised, **Who is the church?** The church is comprised of a body of baptized believers who assemble themselves together typically on Sunday mornings to worship and praise God thanking Him for all His goodness, grace and mercy. Then believers depart the four walls of the physical church to serve God in the community. **How so?** If there is a need in the community believers are to address that need as each believers makes up the Christian

Community of faith. When believers do God's work in the community by serving others we are emulating Christ because while He was in the earth He met both physical and spiritual needs of those He encountered. Another point to believers serving in his or her respective communities is that we are letting our light shine for Christ so the all saved and unsaved will see Christ in us.

Serving in our respective communities there is an opportunity to witness Christ and in other communities when the opportunity presents itself. Others will come and join the Community of Faith; this is *Growing Christ's church.*

Let me remind you that wherever we go we carry the church with us because the true church lives inside of us and we are to live in such a manner that the world will see Christ and His church in us.

Let me close this discussion by saying that Christ's church will never be defeated, it operates in power, authority and in holiness as Christ is its head and believers are its body. Christ's church is the beaconing light that is set upon a hill shinning the light of spiritual freedom to all who approach it celestial shores.

Come join Christ's church.

Aug 22

Ministry Gifts In Christ's Church: Ephesians 4: 7-12

But unto every on of us is given grace according to the measure of the gift of Christ. And he gave some, apostles; and some, prophets, and some evangelists; and some, pastors and teachers. For the perfecting of the saints for the work of the ministry, for the edifying of the body of Christ.

The focus of today's topical discussion is the different ministry gifts given to the church by Christ as all ministerial gifts are given for the edifying the body of Christ-the church.

With that being said, Christ as the head of the church and its members is the body. Each ministry member serves the body in its own capacity and is built on the same principle as the physical body. For example, the eyes serve its purpose, the ears serves their purpose, and the feet do likewise. With this knowledge in hand each member of Christ's body the church has a special calling as God saw fit and each member is to use his or her gift to the glory of God.

Another school of thought is that each member of Christ's church-His body is to operate in perfect harmony as the Godhead does. What brings this unified harmony is a unified faith in Christ Jesus our Lord. Ephesians 4:4-5 solidifies the oneness in the body; One Spirit, one Lord, one faith and baptism.

Believers, we are members of Christ's church with different gifts to be used to His glory and honor.
Use your gifts.

Aug 23

Pastors God's Under Shepherds: Acts 20:28; Philippians 1:1

Take heed therefore, unto yourselves, and to all the flock, over which the Holy Ghost hath made you overseers, to feed the church of God, which he hath purchased with his own blood.

Being that pastors are God's under shepherds they are to be very careful how they minister to God's people-the church. Christ is the head of the church as it is His bride who will be presented to His heavenly Father.

Pastors are called to a local congregation by the Holy Spirit and not by some political election method. There are certain qualifications that all pastors must possess (1 Timothy 3:1-13), and there are specific duties each pastor is to carry out and they are (a) promote true faith in God and in doing so pastors are to feed God's people His word through teaching and preaching. (b) Pastors are to guard the faith of the congregation by diligently protecting his or her congregation as to who stands and proclaim the gospel. Pastors are to warn his or her congregation against false teachers and or leaders who are spreading false doctrines. Then too pastors are to be mindful of the many sins that can infiltrate the church. Lastly, pastors themselves must live in holiness before the congregation and be careful not to scatter God's sheep (Jeremiah 23:1).

Pastors as God's under shepherds you are to emulate the good shepherd-Christ (John 10:11).

Pastors your local congregation-the church go as you go, Pastors feed God's sheep.

Aug 24

Teaching A Leadership Gift In The Church
Ephesians 4:11; 1 Corinthians 12:28

And God hath set some in the church, first apostles, secondarily prophets, thirdly teachers; after that miracles, then gifts of healing, helps, governments, diversities of tongues.

Our scripture texts outline the ministerial leadership gifts Christ left for His church, but today's focus discussion is teaching and the importance of teachers in the role of ministry and church growth.

Let's begin by saying that teaching is expounding, clarifying and proclaiming God's Word with effectiveness and power that through teaching the church will grow as souls are added to the body of Christ. With that being said then teachers are an important ministry in the church as these called leaders are gifted by God with the gift of explaining God's Word. In other words, teaching is an anointed gift by God to His called teachers to carry His message to the world as teachers come along side of apostles, prophets and pastors/preachers.

Therefore, teaching is essential to any church growth as called teachers "rightly divide the word of truth" (2 Timothy 2:15). Church growth is evidenced by teaching where there is a structured teaching ministry in addition to Sunday Church School and mid-week Bible study. Teaching is not just proclaiming God's Word, but living His Word for all to see Christ in you.

Lastly, teaching God's truths prevents congregants from being swept away by false doctrines that man deems to be the truth.

Teachers teach God's Word as you have been called by God for such a ministry.

Aug 25

Believers' Role In Ministry: Matthew 28:19-20

Go ye therefore, and teach all nations, baptizing them in the name of the Father, and of the Son, and of the Holy Ghost: Teaching them to observe all things whatsoever I have commanded you; and lo, I am with you always, even unto the end of the world.

For the past several days our discussions has been focused on Christ, His church and leaders in the church, but today's focus discussion is on the believer's role in ministry as mandated by Christ Himself. This mandate is known as the Great Commission given to Christ's followers as all believers are part of Christ's church that is to spread His gospel throughout the world.

The question now becomes, If believers don't witness Christ, then who will? Non believers certainly can't witness Christ because they do not know the Lord neither have they accepted Him as his or her personal Savior. Therefore, the task is left to all believers in obedience to Christ.

Most importantly, in obeying Christ's command, believers are never to feel alone nor forsaken because Christ is present through the Holy Spirit. All believers have been given power by the Holy Spirit to boldly witness Christ the world over. Another important point to believers' witnessing is to make other disciples not just converts. As others become Disciples of Christ another has been freed from the bondage of sin, the church grows and Satan is angry.

Believers, Witness! Witness! Witness Christ!

Aug 26

Spiritual Separation: 2 Corinthians 6:16-18

And what agreement hath the temple of God with idols? For ye are the temple of the living God; as God hast said, I will dwell in them, and walk in them; and I will be their God, and they shall be my people. Wherefore come out from among them, and be ye separate, saith the Lord, and touch not the unclean thing; and I will receive you. And will be a Father unto you, and ye shall be my sons and daughters, saith the Lord Almighty.

If the question were raised, **Why must Christians separate themselves from the world?** The answer is simply as stated in our scripture text that we are the "temple of the living God" and God has no dealing with idols. Also, believers are the dwelling place of God-the Holy Spirit who cannot and will not dwell in an unholy place. Most importantly, this is a requirement of God as He is holy and all believers are to be likewise-holy.

With that being said, then separation is required because righteousness and unrighteousness cannot co-exist in the believer. Man is no match for sin in his own strength, but with the aid of the Holy Spirit believers have the power to live righteous lives before God and refute worldliness. On the other hand all believers who refuse to separate him or herself from sin loses fellowship with God (2 Corinthians 6:16).

Believers separate yourselves; God lives in you.

Aug 27

Spiritual Accountability: 2 Corinthians 5:10

For we must all appear before the judgment seat of Christ; that every one may receive the things done in his body, according to that he hath done, whether it be good or bad.

What is accountability? Accountability is being held responsible for something, to someone, or an act. With that be said then spiritual accountability is that all believers is held responsible by God to Him for his or her actions in this life. Our record is being kept in heaven and one day all will appear before God where our service record will be read and each will have to answer.

If the question were raised, Why must believers stand in judgment when I am a Christian? According to scripture (Romans 14:12; 1 Corinthians 3:12-15) states that all is subject to judgment and there is no exceptions. Believers have no worries concerning judgment if they have lived holy lives before God and according to His commandments. I say this because Christians must be mindful of coming judgment day and will be required to give an account of their faithfulness or unfaithfulness. Christians good deeds and love is remembered by God and is rewarded (Ephesians 6:8) whereas unrepentant bad deeds are punishable by God.

Judgment will occur when Christ returns for His church as He is the righteous judge. Therefore, believers get your house in order if you want to hear the Master say "good and faithful servant job well-done come on higher there is a crown of life waiting for you."

Every Christian is held accountable for his or her deeds.

Aug 28

Qualities Of God's Leaders: 1 Timothy 3:1-7

...If a man desires the office of a bishop, he desireth a good work. A bishop then must be blameless, the husband of one wife, vigilant, sober, of good behavior, given to hospitality, apt to teach; Not given to wine, no striker, not greedy of filthy lucre; but patient, not a brawler, not covetous; One that ruleth well his own house, having his children in subjection with all gravity.

Our scripture text outlines the qualities of God's leaders and discusses what they mean in terms of leadership. The first quality of a called leader is to be blameless which means in Greek terms "not to be laid hold of" which is to say the leader must have a proven observable conduct as it relates to his or her marriage, social, family and business life. In other words the leader must be of good moral conduct in every aspect of his or her life.

Another quality is that the leader must be the husband of one wife; in my mind/understanding is that the leader must be married for life to one spouse. Then he or she must be vigilant, which is being attentive to the needs, care and concerns of the household whether it is the church or family. A leader who is sober is of sound judgment and decision-making in all that he or she does. Also, a godly leader who posses and displays God-like qualities is one that refrains from greed's temptation that Satan may bring his or her way while knowing what blessing God has for them is only for that person.

Out lesson text outlines the other godly qualities that are expected of God's leaders as they are to be an example for his or her congregation as well as the community. God's leaders may be the only Bible others are reading and with these qualities on display the unsaved with come to Christ and the saved will continue to grow in Christ. It is important to point out that God's leaders have a genuine love for Him and doing His will as each has been called by God for a special service to and for Him. It is noteworthy to say that God's leaders understand the importance of obeying God's command for spiritual separation because in our strength we are no match for Satan and his tactics.

Allow me to close this discussion by saying God's leaders' posses the outlined qualities and have dedicated his or herself to maintaining such qualities as this person have answered the call of God and realizes what an honored position it is to serve as a ministerial leader in His church. Therefore, his or her conduct is beyond reproach and the leader relies on the help of the Holy Spirit to maintain such character and dignity.

God's leaders possess godly qualities.

Aug 29

Baptism In The Holy Spirit: Acts 1:5; 10:44-45

For John truly baptized you with water, but ye shall be baptized with the Holy Ghost not many days hence.

It is well documented as well as an established fact that the Holy Ghost is God in the third-person. However, the setting for this lesson is Jesus addressing His disciples and giving them final instructions regarding the promise of His Father which is the coming of the Holy Ghost (v 4) and what would happen after He come.
    It is important to point out that baptizing in the Holy Ghost and being filled with the Holy Spirit is used interchangeably in Acts, but receiving the Holy Spirit what believers receive at regeneration. Also, Jesus Himself baptizes believers in the Holy Spirit (John 1:33).
    Two things occur when believers are baptized in the Holy Spirit; (a) believers receive power, and (b) believers have the ability to boldly witness Christ. Each carries a profound manifestation of the work of the indwelling Holy Spirit. Let's look at each briefly; this new power is the ability to boldly witness Christ to a lost world so they too may be saved. In our witnessing Christ we are brave enough to travel to the far reaches of the universe preaching Christ without fear of and from anyone or thing. Believers have the promise of God that He would be with us unto the ends of the world (Matthew 28:20).
Baptism in the Holy Spirit brings God's saving power.

Aug 30

Believers' Spiritual Warfare: Ephesians 6:11-18

Put on the whole armour of God, that ye may be able to stand against the wiles of the devil. For we wrestle not against flesh and blood, but against principalities, against powers, against the rulers of the darkness of this world, against spiritual wickedness in high places.

Christians are in a spiritual warfare against Satan and his army as this spiritual conflict is known as the warfare of faith (v. 12). God knew that whom He called to be His servants that the battle lines were drawn in the sand-earth and He prepared His warriors for battle.

If the question were raised, What is the believer's battle armour? God dressed His warriors with the helmet of salvation, He girded our loins with truth-His truth as this is the only truth that will stand against Satan and his attacks. God covered His warriors with the breastplate of righteousness as this is His righteousness by which all mankind will judge. Believers' feet are shod with the gospel of peace as believers are to carry the gospel of Christ to a lost world. Believers are outfitted with the shield of faith so that we can withstand all Satan's fiery darts of wickedness that is designed to shake our faith. The last piece of body armour given by God is His sword-the Bible which is His word and with this offensive weapon we take the fight to Satan and his demonic schemes.

In the believer's warfare we remain in constant communication with our Commander-in-Chief-God through constant prayer.

Believers, fight on because we have victory.

Aug 31

Believers Disciples Of Christ: John 8:31-32

Then said Jesus to those Jews which believed on him, If ye continue in my word, then are ye my disciples indeed: And ye shall know the truth, and the truth shall make you free.

By popular definition a disciple is a student or learner of something; however for our discussion purposes we will focus on believers as Disciples of Christ who have accepted the teaching of one Lord, one Baptism and one salvation as it is given by God's grace through faith in Jesus Christ.

Jesus' earthly ministry consisted of the twelve original Disciples of Christ who immediately left their vocations to follow Jesus. However there were many others who became Disciples of Christ during Christ's earthly ministry though unnamed. With that being saith all followers of Christ both then and now are Disciples of Christ (Luke 14:26-27; Acts 9:36).

Believers being Disciples of Christ are sent on the mission of carrying the gospel message into the entire world so that all who hear God's word have the opportunity to be saved. Salvation is a free gift to all humanity, but one must accept Jesus Christ as Lord and Savior.

Believers as Disciples of Christ have accepted the commitment of discipleship which is life changing to Bible study, applying its truths, sharing its truths with others, fulfilling God designed goal and becoming more Christ-like.

Believers as disciples are Christ-focused and Christ-centered. What a focus!

Christian Growth and Maturity

Temples Of God Through Spiritual Growth: Ephesians 2:21

In whom all the building fitly framed together growth unto a holy temple in the Lord.

The term "temple" has two known meanings, and they are (a) house or place of worship (Psalm 11:4; Matthew 21:12), (b) temple as it refers to Christians or a group of believers (1 Corinthians 3:16-17; 6:19) (The Student Bible Dictionary P. 222). With this being said, then believers are the dwelling place of God through His Spirit-the Holy Spirit. God cannot live in an unholy place; therefore, through spiritual growth believers become the dwelling place of God. Also, believers are members of Christ's body-the church as it is commonly referred to as the bride of Christ who is holy, righteous and without spot or blemish.

If the question were raised, How do we as believers grow to the point of being holy temples of God? This is achieved by daily reading, studying and meditating on God's Word, and then yielding to the Holy Spirit who will guide and teach you all truths concerning the Father and His righteousness. It is noteworthy to say that the more we commune with God through prayer and daily scripture reading the greater our desire become to please Him and become more like Him. Believers are to be separated from this world and its sinful systems as they are contrary to God and His standards. This too is accomplished with the aid of the Holy Spirit.

It can be concluded then that as believers grow in the knowledge of Christ and become like Him we become temples of God; who is holy and righteous.

Believers, God dwell in you; therefore be holy!

Sept 2

Godly Truth Equals Growth: Ephesians 4:15

But speaking the truth in love, may grow up into him in all things, which is the head, even Christ.

What is the meaning of our scripture verse? Verse 13 talks about unity of the faith among the brothers, but truth in love supersedes all differences whether it is in the physical church, institutions, or among people as God's truth is the ultimate authority. Another point is that as we seek and speak the truth we as believers will grow in Christ as He is the head of all things and this includes His church. Also, God's Word does not compromise the truth; this is because God is unchangeable.

How do we as believers grow in godly truths? Our growth comes through standing firm on God's Word and failing to compromise on any part of His Word. Believers who remain faithful to God's Word will not be tossed to and fro by every wind of doctrine that we are sure to encounter (v.14). Several mandates are necessary for believers' spiritual growth and they are worldly separation, daily Bible reading and meditation and yielding our will to that of the Holy Spirit. Worldly separation is necessary for the believer because in our own strength we are no match for Satan and his masterful schemes. Believers must rely on the Holy Spirit to fight our battles as this is a spiritual warfare. On many occasions we as believers may feel that we are standing alone on God's truth, but stand firm as God is with you. His truth is ever lasting.

Learning more of God's truth increases our knowledge of Him and His ways.

Sept 3

Babes In Christ: 1 Peter 2:2

As newborn babies, desire the sincere milk of the word, that ye may grow thereby.

Peter is using the analogy of a new born baby to explain how new believers are when we first come to Christ. A newborn cries for milk when he or she is hungry so it is with the new convert. As the newborn grows; then the baby can take some soft solid foods; as we grow in Christ we began to increase our food intake with sold food that is thoroughly explained to our understanding. This growth process continues as the child grows (both physically and spiritually) until the believer reach the age of majority and can decipher right from wrong.

Another point to this analogy is that as the child desires more and more milk likewise do the new convert. What this shows is a sign of spiritual growth and a desire to continue feeding on God's Word. The new convert/believer has an unquenchable thirst and hunger for the nourishing Word of God, which is pleasing to the palate. Yielding to the indwelling Holy Spirit will prevent the new convert/believer and older believers as well from becoming choked with the worldly weeds that can and will infiltrate our daily lives.

Let me close this discussion by saying all believers were babes in Christ and we grew by feeding on God's Word and our spiritual growth mimics our physical lives. As we become old in age spiritually we are seasoned believers/Christians.

Grow in Christ.

Grow In Grace: 2 Peter 3:18

But grow in grace, and in the knowledge of our Lord and Savior Jesus Christ. To him be glory both now and forever.

Let's begins today's discussion by looking at grace and what it mean to each believer and what inspired God's grace on all who believe on His Son Jesus Christ. First, grace is God's unmerited favor, getting what we do not deserve-God's grace. Man did not deserve God's free and loving gift of grace, but God in His divine justice system granted His grace to all humanity only if you believe in His Son Jesus Christ. Grace can be viewed as God's deferring justice when it was demanded because it is God's will that all be saved.

Second, God's grace comes with salvation through Jesus Christ, because all have sinned and come short of the glory of God (Romans 3:23) and all humanity was destine for death because of our sins (Romans 6:23), but God mercy is at work here through His grace.

Third, God's grace means that all humanity has been given another chance at eternal life and all believers has acknowledged that God is a God of second chances while accepting the free gift of salvation which spells grace. This means that it is God's righteousness at the expense of His Son Jesus Christ who shed His precious blood in the atonement process of humanity's sins.

Fourth, God gives His grace to bring us into a right standing with Him as all who believe has been pardoned of his or her sins. It is God's righteousness that all humanity is judged. With His grace, believers do His will, live in holiness, and grow in Christ (3:18), and as we grow in Christ we have the ability and power to witness to others about the goodness of our Lord Jesus Christ (Acts 4:33; 11:23).

Fifth, we grow in grace by humbling ourselves before the Lord, diligently seeking Him and His knowledge, praying daily, worshiping Christ and being continually filled with the Holy Spirit who aids in our holy living. It is noteworthy to say that the more we live in God's holiness we grow more like Christ.

To answer the implied question on what inspired God's grace is love as He is love as depicted so eloquently in John 3:16. In addition to God being love is that He created man to be in fellowship with Him and this fellowship was broken by sin. Death was the punishment for sin, but again because of God's love nature He could not nor would He neither did He allow His prize creation to remain separated from Him. Therefore, His grace brings us unto a right standing with Him.

Believers, grow in His righteousness and live holy.

Sept 5

Growing In True Knowledge: 2 Peter 1:3-5

According to His divine power hath given unto us all things that pertain unto life and godliness, through the knowledge of him that hath called us to glory and virtue. Whereby are given unto us exceeding great and precious promises; that by these you might be partakers of the divine nature, having escaped the corruption that is in the world through lust. And besides this, giving all diligence, add to you faith virtue; and to virtue knowledge.

The long and short of today's discussion is that without the true knowledge that God provides we have nothing. Why do I make such profound statement, it is God's knowledge that will stand forever as man's knowledge is temporal and lacks divinity. More importantly, no human wisdom, intellect, or technique is complete without the knowledge of God. All biblical doctrines that is preached or shared that lack the true teachings from the Word of God are in error and should be casted aside. These teachings are riddled with corruption designed to hinder believers' growth in the true knowledge of God. Another point is that any gospel that leaves the believer wanting something extra is not of the gospel of Christ. This is because the true gospel of Christ is filling each time it is proclaimed and leaves no room for something else. The Holy Spirit overflows our cup.

We gain true knowledge of God through daily Bible reading and meditating while asking the Holy Spirit for divine revelation and interpretation of His Word.

God reveals His truth; know the truth and grow therein.

Sept 6

God Our Lordship: 1 Corinthians 11:3

But I would have you know, that the head of every man is Christ and the head of every woman is the man; and the head of Christ is God.

From the relationship outlined by Paul to the Corinthian church states that God is the supreme ruler of both man and woman, as man is the head of his wife while Christ is the head of the man as God is the head of all. The term "head" in this discussion is authority and divine order (cf 3:23; 11:8, 10; 15:28; Judges 10:18; Ephesians 1:21-22; 5:23-24; Colossians 1:18; 2:10).

Let me be perfectly clear this is in the order of submission as Christ submitted to the will of His Father to become a human sacrifice redeeming man back to God. Also consider the order of creation of man and woman, man was created first in the human chain while woman was taken from the side of man. This order is not demeaning, but expresses the worth God places on woman as she is the helpmate to the man. The man's responsibilities involve leading the woman in such a manner as to fulfill the will of God in both the church and home.

Our virtual order is about servanthood and obedience as Christ in obedience to His Father became the suffering servant for mankind. In obedience to Christ serve as He is Lord.

God is Lord of my life; Jesus Christ makes it complete and I will serve Him in total obedience.

Sept 7

Discipling For Christ: Acts 18:22-23; 19:1-3

And after he had spent some time there, he departed, and went over all the country of Galatia and Phrygia in order, strengthening all the disciples...And it came to pass that, while Apollos was at Corinth, Paul having passed through the upper costs came to Ephesus: and finding certain disciples, He said unto them, Have ye receive the Holy Ghost since ye believed? And they said unto him, We have not so much as heard whether there be any Holy Ghost.

Our scripture text explains the definition of discipling for Christ in that is means to make other disciples for Christ. The Apostle Paul lived the life of true discipleship in that he was a student of Christ and traveled throughout Asia Minor making other disciples. During the Apostle Paul's missionary journeys he preached Christ to all who would hear; he established churches throughout the Asia Minor region and nurtured these churches/new believers in the Word of God so they too would make other Disciples of Christ.

It is imperative that believers/Disciples of Christ today follow Paul's example of discipling for Christ because when we make new converts they are to be nurtured/strengthened with a follow-up ministry giving them the necessary support needed to remain in the body of Christ.

If the question were raised, What is a follow-up ministry? A follow-up ministry consists of praying with, providing instructions and nurturing new converts in the Christian way which is the true doctrine of Christ, meeting with other Christians/believers for worship, ministering the Word of God and letting the manifestation of the Holy Spirit have His way.

Discipling for Christ is discipleship in action.

Cost Of Discipleship: Luke 14:26-28

If any man come to me, and hate not his father, and mother, and wife, and children, and brethren, and sisters, yea, and his own life also, he cannot be my disciple. And whosoever doth not bear his cross, and come after me, cannot be my disciple.

Allow me to clarify the word "hate" in this text as it means to love less, which in essence Christ was saying that to be a Disciple of Christ calls for self-denial and all other attachments are meaningless.

The cost of Discipleship demands loyalty and love to God as disciples have made a commitment to follow Christ as He is our Lord and Savior. With that being said, disciples must sacrificially follow Christ. Christ's twelve disciples provide examples of following Christ as His disciples. They walked away from occupation, family and friends to make other disciples for Christ.

Another cost of discipleship is daily making a choice of self-denial as oppose to living out our selfish desires. The choice we make determines our eternal destination as one day we will give an account for our service record. *How will it read?*

Luke 9:57-62 records Jesus teaching on the cost of discipleship as this scripture text correlates with our lesson text. Therefore, discipleship is a commitment to Christ and the Bible truths while applying these truths daily to our lives and sharing the good news of the gospel of Christ with others.

Discipleship may be costly to us (self-denial), but that's nothing compared to what Christ did for us.

Grow In Compassion: John 11:33

When Jesus therefore saw her weeping, and the Jews also weeping which came with her, he groaned in the spirit, and was troubled.

The setting for our lesson text was the death of Lazarus and his sisters Mary and Martha wept mightily as did the Jewish mourners. This family was friends of Jesus and as their brother lay sick, the sisters sent for Jesus, but Jesus chose to tarry where He was until Lazarus died.

Jesus' action was to authenticate His deity, because verses 25-26 where Jesus states that He is the resurrection and the glory of God were on display (v. 40). How did Jesus show compassion in our lesson text? First, He groaned in the spirit (v. 33), second He wept (v. 35). What these verses reveal is the heart and feeling of Jesus that He witnessed during His earthly ministry. Jesus was heartbroken by the pain and suffering caused by the sins of the world. Verse 35 also reveals the sorrow God feels for His people and He moved with compassion on mankind's behalf.

Believers must posses and move with Christ-like compassion for the pain and suffering caused by sin as we are to pray daily for others to repent of their evil ways. Also, when there is a need believers are compelled to address the need to the best of our ability. *Whatever we do for the least of God's people we do unto Him.*

Compassion is a moral attribute of God; grow in compassion.

Church Discipline: Matthew 18:15-35

....If thy brother shall trespass against thee, go and tell him his fault between thee and him alone; if he shall hear thee, thou hast gained thy brother. But if he will not hear thee, then take with thee one or two more, that in the mouth of two or three witnesses every word may be established.

Our scripture text outlines the proper procedures for disciplining one another in the Christian Community. These outlined instructions are godly and designed to restore a broken fellowship between the two parties and to continue to walk in the unity of the faith. If these instructions are neglected then spiritual compromise and eternal consequences are sure to follow.

If the question were raised, Why are church discipline necessary? Several reasons come to mind and they are (a) to protect God's reputation (Matthew 6:9; Romans 2:23-23) as He is not the author of confusion, (b) to guard the moral purity and integrity of the church (1 Corinthian 5:6-7; 2 John 7-11), (c) these instructions are designed to save errant members and restore them to Christ-likeness (1 Corinthians 5:5; James 5:19-20), and lastly (d) Church discipline must be administered in the spirit of love, humility, regret, and self-examination (Matthew 22:37; 2 Corinthians 2:6-7; Galatians 6:1).

Church discipline is a necessary tool so that all members of Christ's church remain in harmony with each other and Christ.

There is growth and maturity in church discipline and even more in self-discipline.

Sept 11

Christians Christ Followers: Acts 11:26

And when he had found him, he brought him unto Antioch; And it came to pass, that a whole year they assembled themselves with the church, and taught much people, and the disciples were called Christians first in Antioch.

The term "Christians" is defined as followers of Christ, or one who belongs to Christ. With that being said then all believers who have confessed his or her faith in Jesus Christ becomes a Christ follower/Christian. Another attribute of being a Christian is that the person has committed his or herself to the teachings of the NT apostles about Christ as well as having made a conscious decision to be guided by the actions and attitude of Christ. Christ followers-Christians become more like Christ in character as we grow in the knowledge of God.

The history of the term "Christians" were once used derogatory by pagans or non-believers, but the term took on a different meaning in that it became identified with all who follows Christ and the label Christians were worn proudly as Christians became known world-wide as Christ followers. Given the fact of what Christ done for all who believe on His name should be proud to tell the world "yes I am a Christ follower/Christian."

Romans 2:24 talks about the redemption of Christ for all who believe in Him; therefore, the term "Christian" identifies our relationship with Christ for all who have received Him as Lord and Savior (Romans 5:1). Hebrews 5:9 states that Christians' eternal salvation is in Christ. What this means is that when Christians die it is not the end of life, but the beginning of a new life that has no end. Therefore, being a Christian means that Christ and His word as revealed in scripture is the final authority and the source of our hope for tomorrow-eternity (Colossians 1:5,27).

Christians has a mandate by Christ Himself to go into the entire world and make other Christians/disciples so that they too may become Christ-followers. In sharing the gospel of Christ we build the kingdom of God as it is God's desire that all be saved. It is God's permissive will that all who fail to hear and obey His Word will be lost and will spend eternity separated from our creator.

There are benefits from being a Christian and some are, we have been redeemed from the bondage of sin and now have a spiritual freedom, peace, joy, love and holiness that were once unavailable. Through Christ's shed blood Christians now has been declared righteous and our sins pardoned. Christians are members of the royal family of God a set aside peculiar people and has been made co-heirs with Christ. Therefore, Christians are blessed beyond measure and have an inheritance that the world cannot give.

Christians, you are of royalty so wear your label proudly.

Sept 12

Faithfulness: Hosea 2:20

I will even betroth thee unto me in faithfulness; and thou shalt know the Lord.

The book of Hosea serves as an illustration of a faithful husband to an unfaithful wife, which is God's faithfulness to an unfaithful people. Even though written to the Israelites the principle applies to all believers today because it depicts God's faithfulness to His people.

The term betroth used in our scripture illustrates God's covenant commitment to His people and desires the same commitment from His people given all that He has done for all mankind. He loved us while we were enemy toward Him, He protects us from all hurt harm or danger some known and unknowns, He provided salvation and the only requirement is to accept His Son Jesus Christ as Lord and Savior in faith. He provides the indwelling Holy Spirit to keep us in faithfulness to Him as we walk this faith journey. *What a loving God?*

Given the pledged commitment from God what is our commitment to Him in return? Are we reciprocating God's love back to Him in our dedicated service? Are we showing God's love to Him first, and then others as ourselves? Have we dedicated ourselves to holy living so that we manifest the glory of God and His righteousness in our lives? How do we express our gratitude to God for all that He has done in our lives?

Remain faithful to God as He is faithful to you. He is a God of faithfulness do likewise.

Sept 13

Holy Living Brings Growth: Jude 1:20-21

But ye, beloved, building up yourselves on your most holy faith, praying in the Holy Ghost, Keep yourselves in the love of Good, looking for the mercy of our Lord Jesus Christ unto eternal life.

If the question were raised, **What is holy living?** Let's answer the question by saying holy living is living according to God's standards and His righteousness. This is because it is by God's standards by which all humanity will be judged. Isaiah 64:6 states in part that "all our righteousness is as filthy rags."

However, our righteousness is in Jesus Christ who shed His blood to give all believers the right standing with God the Father. Another point to holy living is that believers can live holy in that we have been sanctified by God as a called out people to live in holiness to Him. Holy living is achieved by daily Bible reading, mediating on His Word and with the aid of the Holy Spirit believers has the ability to refrain from conforming to this world and its standards. The world's standards are contrary to those of God. Therefore, all believers are mandated by God to live in holiness.

Living in holiness the world will see Christ manifested in each believer as we are lights shinning in a sin darkened world. As we submit ourselves to God's ways we grow in our faith walk with Christ.

Holy living requires a willing heart and a humble spirit.

Sept 14

The Holiness Of God: 2 Corinthians 7:1

Having therefore these promises, dearly beloved, let us cleanse ourselves from all filthiness of the flesh and spirit, perfecting holiness in the fear of God.

Zondervan's Pictorial Bible Dictionary (P. 358) summarizes holiness as "the idea of holiness which originates in the revealed character of God, and is communicated to things, places, times and persons engaged in His service." God's holiness is interwoven with righteousness and purity and all believers are to have such characteristics.

If the question were raised, **What makes up the holiness of God?** God is holy because He is the creator and supreme ruler of all that exist both seen and unseen. He is just, righteous, merciful, love, gracious and above all He has no beginning nor ending-He is alpha and omega. God is holy in that His righteousness and purity as there is no evilness in Him and His righteousness is the standards for all and is above all. Attributes that transcends the holiness of God is that He is omniscient, omnipotent, and omnipresent. He is eternal, He is unchangeable and He is triune-God the Father, God the Son and God the Holy Spirit.

Christ's church is holy both collectively and individually in that it is comprised of holy people-Christians who have the indwelling Holy Spirit who is God and He cannot live in an unholy place.

Believers grow in the holiness of God as we are sons of a holy God.

Sept 15

Love: John 3:16-17

For God so loved the world that He gave His only begotten Son, that whosoever believeth in him should not perish, but have everlasting live. For God sent not His Son into the world to condemn the world; but that the world through Him might be saved.

Our lesson text give insight into pure love as it depicts the heart of God and displaying His love for mankind. God's love is so wide until it encompasses the entire world "the whosoever". God's love is unconditional and He desires that man return His love by accepting His Son as our redeemer-Savior. *Only God could love with such depth and devotion.*

Understanding the magnitude of God's love stand to reason that He commands us to love one another as He first loved us. This begs the question, How can we say that we believe in God and love Him and do not love our fellowman that we see daily? 1 John 4:7-12 talks about man and God's love and we have not the love of God in us if we fail to love as commanded by God. God has proven His love by giving His Son as our propitiator. Love is the very nature of God (vv. 7-9) and believers are born of Him because of His love. If we continue loving one another, then God continues to live within each of us and His love is made perfect in each believer (v. 12).

Love conquerors all. It saved us.

Sept 16

Unity Among The Brethrens: Ephesians 4:3

Endeavoring to keep the unity of the Spirit in the bond of peace

The focus of today's discussion is unity among believers as this unity is patterned after the unity of the Spirit-God's Spirit. Unity among the brethrens is made possible through the indwelling Spirit of God. Just as the Godhead operates in perfect togetherness so must the body of Christ-the church. There is unity among the brethrens because of the oneness of God; one faith, and one body. Each member has his or her distinct calling for the edification of the body of Christ (vv. 4-5, 12).

It is noteworthy to say that God in His divine wisdom made provisions for any disharmony that may arise by instilling His Spirit in each believer to bring peace. God is a God of peace, love and harmony not confusion. Therefore, each believer is to operate in the Spirit of God thus assuring unity as we witness Christ to a dying world. Allow me to say that neither human efforts nor organizations can bring unity among the brethrens without the Spirit of God. With that being said, all churches operating in harmony has God as its head and His Spirit as its guide.

Church, we have our example for unity-the Godhead.

Sept 17

Patience Brings Growth: James 1:3-4

Knowing this, that the trying of your faith worketh patience. But let patience have her perfect work, that ye may be perfect and entire, wanting nothing.

In our scripture text the term perfect in this scenario means maturity as it relates to the right relationship with God that will bear fruit in love, devotion, obedience, blameless and service to him.

If the question were raised, Why is it necessary to strive for perfection in Christ? Believers are to strive for perfection because we are members of Christ's body. Being that we are His representatives we are to resemble Christ. In the perfecting process believers will experience trials that are designed to test our faith in God and the results of these trials are patience (Romans 5:3) as God is our deliverer. Consider this, God as the potter and we are the clay and as we experience trails God is removing every weight of hindrances that will impede our growth. It is noteworthy to say that believers are a sanctified people and they are to be perfect in Christ.

Patience teaches the believer to operate in God's time instead of man as the two are vastly different; patience prevents dire consequences. How do we gain patience? This is accomplished by asking God for strength to endure the situation. God is sure to answer heartfelt prayers.

The cliché "patience is a virtue" has some truth in it because a necessary character for God's people as it teaches that all things operate in God's time.

Be patient everything is in divine order.

Sept 18

Joy In Jesus: John 15:11; 1 Peter 1:8

These things have I spoken unto you, that my joy might remain in you, and that your joy might be fill. Whom having not seen, ye love; in whom, though now ye see him not, yet believing, ye rejoice with joy unspeakable and full of glory (1 Peter1:8).

The setting for today's lesson is that Jesus was teaching on Him being the true vine and all who believe and remain in Him remains connected to Him and the Father as well as receiving eternal life and the power to remain therein through the Holy Spirit (vv 1-4). Consider this, just as a branch cannot sustain itself absent from the tree so is it with the believer who cannot sustain his or herself absent from Christ through the Holy Spirit.

As believers remain connected to Jesus and His love we experience His presence, love and the joy that the world cannot give nor understand. Joy in Jesus brings a gladness that supersedes all others and it makes the believer tell everybody what the Lord has done in his or her life. This joy is like fire shut up in the bones of the believer; it gives a new energy to live in holy obedience to the Lord. Joy in Jesus makes the believer ask *"What is this?* It makes the believer tell the world *"I am not ashamed of my new found joy."* **Have you found your joy in Jesus?** *It's like none other.*

It is noteworthy to say that joy in Jesus is evidence of the residing Holy Spirit who refreshes our cups with love, happiness, obedience, loyalty daily. Joy in Jesus come forth as a ray of sunshine each day and cause the believers to boldly witness Christ and His goodness.

If the question were raise, What do this say for today's believers' faith in Jesus Christ? Does it say that we have greater faith than those who saw Christ in the flesh during His earthly stay? My interpretation of 1 Peter 1:8 is that believers after Christ's resurrection and ascension must see Him with spiritual eyes through faith in the New Apostles doctrines and as believers live this faith they are blessed with the gift of joy given by God Himself (Galatians 5:22; Romans

15:13; John 16:24). Although, I must say that those who saw Christ in the flesh some recognized Him as the promised Messiah and some did not. The Holy Spirit was at work making revelations even during those times. Peter's confession that Jesus was "the Christ" (Matthew 16:16) is an example of some who witnessed Christ in the flesh and recognized Him for who He was. What does this say for believers today as well as then? It says that yes Christ is alive and giving unspeakable joy as we abide in Him and He in us.

There is no joy like the joy of Jesus. What a joy to have?

Sept 19

Worship The Lord: Psalm 96:1:12

O sing unto the Lord a new song; sing unto the Lord, all the earth. Sing unto the Lord, bless his name; shew forth His salvation from day to day...O worship the Lord in the beauty of holiness; fear before Him, all the earth.

The Psalmist is encouraging us to worship the Lord because He is worthy of all praises, honor and songs as we are to bless His holy name daily for what He has done and continues to do in the lives of all believers. Unbelievers are encouraged to recognize the Lord for who He is as He blesses the unbeliever in providing the necessities of life. The Lord blesses all humanity daily with His air, sunshine and a reasonable portion of health and strength.

We worship the Lord in giving reverence to Him, in adoration, obedience, love, prayer and giving of our time, talents and tithes as well as being in His presence. We can worship God both publicly and privately. We worship the Lord by aiding others in need as He cares for the needy as well. *Just simply worship the Lord.*

As all nature worship the Lord by obeying His commands and performing each assigned task on schedule so must man. The sun shines on some parts of His majestic creations at all times, and when the sun's daily task has ended, then the moon and stars bring forth light. When the wind blows the trees bow to His majesty and will.

If nature can worship the Lord what about you and I?

Sept 20

The Grace Of God: Psalm 84:11

For the Lord God is a sun and shield; the Lord will give grace and glory; no good thing will he withhold from them that walk uprightly.

In an earlier writing, we discussed "Growing In God's Grace" and determined that God's grace is His unmerited favor that we didn't deserve. However, in His grace we share in His holiness, we experience His love and compassion, protection and He provides salvation through His Son Jesus Christ.

Today's lesson text support the findings of God's grace as it can be expressed as love in action. The Lord being a "sun and shield" is saying that God's glory shine brightly in all and through all who have decided to live in obedience to His righteousness. All believers have a right standing with God through the atoning works of Jesus Christ. The Lord protects "shield" His obedient children from all evil and wickedness that we will encounter.

The last phrase of our lesson text is directed to believers who have decided to live godly and righteous lives before Him. This allows His purposes to be fulfilled in our lives. If the question were raised, What is our responsibility in receiving God's grace? Believers' task is to walk upright before the Lord, then trust God to provide for all our needs, physically, spiritually, temporarily and eternally. God is faithful to His promises and His mercy endureth forever (Psalm 23:6).

God's grace is sufficient.

Sept 21

Reverence God: Hebrews 12:28

Wherefore we receiving a kingdom which cannot be moved, let us have grace, whereby we may serve God acceptably with reverence and godly fear.

Verses 18-29 issues a dire warning against turning away form God as He is sure to pronounce judgment so strong that the world as we know it today will cease to exist and the only survivors will be His kingdom and those who are His children-believers.

Man should not take God's longsuffering as His tolerance of sin because it is not and what God is saying by His actions is that He is giving mankind time to repent. It is noteworthy to say that many in today's society feel that the many natural disasters are God's warning signs of His impending judgment as He is angry because of the world's sins and wickedness. With that being said, What are we to do? We are to turn from wickedness and sin and turn to God with sincerity and reverence as He is worthy of all praises, honor and glory. What we can expect with assurance is Christ's return to rule the world with justice and peace as all manner of sin will be wiped away. God's kingdom will last forever and all who is in Christ will live forever with Him in His kingdom.

Let's honor God with reverence for He is worthy.

Sept 22

Hope For The Future: Galatians 5:5; Romans 8:24-25

For we through the Spirit wait for the hope of righteousness by faith...Fore we are saved by hope: but hope that is seen is not hope: for what a man seeth, why doth he yet hope for? But if we hope for that we see not, then do we with patience wait for it (vv24-25)?

If we were to define hope as it relates to believers it is defined as our beliefs that God will accomplish all that He has promised (Psalm 71:5; Ephesians 2:21). As Christians our hope is based on the fact that God is faithful to His promise. 1 Corinthians 15 talks about resurrection and all believers have an assured hope that if we die in Christ we will be raised again and will reign with Him when He establishes His earthly kingdom.

Another point on the believer's hope is that through God's Spirit we have righteousness by our faith in Christ Jesus and we are saved by this hope. Also, believers have the assurance that we died to sin with Christ and rose with Him into a life of righteousness. With that being said, believers hope is never wishful thinking, but something that we can count on--salvation through Jesus Christ. I agree with Paul in his question of why hope for what you can see as there would be no faith in hoping for what is seen. We are to walk by faith not by sight as our spiritual eyes make the invisible visible.

Jesus Christ is our hope for tomorrow.

Sept 23

Witnessing Power: Acts 1:8

But ye shall receive power after that the Holy Ghost is come upon you; and ye shall be witnesses unto me both in Jerusalem, and in all Judea, and in Samaria, and unto the uttermost part of the world.

The writer, Luke explains what happens after receiving the Holy Ghost (Spirit) and the power in which believers will perform this task and where. Believers will be baptized in the Holy Spirit to effectively witness Christ to the entire world as they will witness with such boldness as never before.

The Holy Spirit gives believers the power to witness about the righteousness and truth of Christ in both words and deeds. Additionally, the believer has a personal testimony of the saving power of Christ and the convicting work of the indwelling Holy Spirit. Believers can testify of the personal presence of Jesus and the intimate relationship with Him. Through this personal relationship with Christ, believers can also testify of the love for and of God and the desire to live holy unto Him and honor Him as the believer become more Christ-like.

The reason for witnessing is to carry the message of Christ to a lost world so that the unsaved can be saved. Being saved is the result of witnessing the good news of Christ. What is the good news? Christ's death, burial and resurrection. Just look at what God done for us; therefore, stand up and be a witness for the Lord.

Witness! Witness! There is power in witnessing Christ.

Sept 24

Service To God: Romans 12:1

I beseech you therefore, brethren, by the mercies of God, that ye present your bodies a living sacrifice, holy, acceptable unto God, which is your reasonable service.

Let's begin today's discussion by posing a personal answerable question, What can I give in return for what God has done in my live? Our scripture text provides an answer that every believer can give which is a reasonable service to God by presenting your bodies a living sacrifice unto Him. Given all that God has done in our lives the least we can do is to live holy unto Him, praise Him, honor Him, worship Him and witness to others about His goodness.

To accomplish the above stated task of being a living sacrifice to a holy God requires spiritual separation from this world as we are a consecrated people that have been called out by God to do His will. Consecrating our bodies to God for worship and service is a lifetime commitment and we have the Holy Spirit aiding us in this commitment. Also, we are to offer our bodies dead to sin and instruments of righteousness because we died with Christ to sin and rose with Him to a life of righteousness. Being instruments of righteousness our bodies become temples of God-the dwelling place of the Holy Spirit.

Let's close this discussion with this question, Is Sunday worship considered reasonable given all that God has done and continues to do in our lives?

Let's serve the Lord daily.

Seasoned Speech: Colossian 4:6

Let your speech be always with grace, seasoned with salt, that you may know how ye ought to answer every man.

What is Paul saying to his audience? Even though Paul was writing to the church as Colossae his wisdom applies to all believers today in that we are to speak with words of wisdom being pleasant both in tone, verbiage, kind and gracious in what and how we say. What Paul is really saying, the language used by believers must be generated by the Holy Spirit because we operate in the grace of God in love which begins in the hearts of all believers. Allow me to state it another way, when a believer talk to someone it should not be street language or worldly in nature.

To speak to another in a "seasoned with salt" tone is to use words that is appropriate for the conversation, but with purity as oppose to corruption (Ephesians 4:29). To speak with a seasoning of salt does not mean that a stern warning is out of order if necessary, because it is to correct the person not tear down the person. Allow me to reflect on my childhood when mothers of the church and community adults would correct the wrong doer with such kind but stern words that were very humbling but with motherly love. The corrected person never lost respect for the corrector. This question begs an answer, Where have our seasoned speakers gone?

Let's look at season in the context of maturity which is to say that seasoned speakers are salting the earth with godly wisdom whether they are correcting another or providing encouragement. The term salt is used as an analogy to drive home the point of adding flavor or palatable taste to food; with regards to speech it too is palatable to the hearer. The same analogy can be used in our witness when witnessing Christ as we are the salt of the earth seasoning it with words of wisdom and encouragement while proclaiming the goodness of the Lord.

As members of the body of Christ grow in His knowledge we become seasoned in our speech and actions realizing that we are an open book manifesting Christ in our walk. As we become mature Christians we are to continue teaching the younger Christians as this grows Christ's church and God's kingdom. Christian seasoning in our speech begins at conversion and continues during our earthly stay.

These questions come to mind, When speaking are you glorifying God with your speech? Does your speech reflect love, care and concern?

A seasoned speech glorifies God.

Sept 26

Gained Knowledge Through Study: 2 Timothy 2:15

Study to show thyself approved unto God, a workman that needeth not to be ashamed, rightly dividing the word of truth.

If the question were raised, Why must Christians study God's Word? First, Christians are to study God's Word to know the truth as we hold His Word-the Bible to be the final authority on what's right and wrong. Second, Christians are to study to prevent being swayed by false teachers as they are sure to come our way. This is because Satan is at work trying to impede God's kingdom building. Never mind the fact that he is a defeated foe, but he is relentless in his efforts of destroying souls. Third, Christians are to study God's Word for continued growth in the knowledge and wisdom of God so that we might do His Will. Fourth, Christians are to study God's Word as we are His workmanship created in Christ Jesus (Ephesians 2:10), and part of our workmanship is witnessing to lost souls of this world. Fifth, Christians are to study God's Word because it is given for our correction, reproof, instructions in righteousness and is profitable for our own growth so that as men of God we maybe perfect in all good works (2 Timothy 3:16-17). Lastly, Christians study God's Word because we are disciples/learners of Christ and the more we study the deeper our knowledge becomes of His eternal truths.
   Study God's Word it will lead you into all truths.

Sept 27

Sanctification: 1 Timothy 4:5

For it is sanctified by the Word of God and prayer.

The term sanctification is defined as being set apart, concentrated, separated and or called out. In regards to believers we have been separated from the world for an intimate relationship with God so that we can love Him with all our hearts, soul and mind (Matthew 22:37), live in perfect holiness, have a charitable and compassionate heart like God the Father and His Son Jesus Christ. Believers being sanctified are made free from sin, which rendered us servants of righteousness (Romans 6:18) because we died to sin with Christ (Romans 6:2).

Believers receive sanctification by the following
(a) Faith in Jesus Christ and in union with Him in His death and resurrection (Acts 26:18; John 15:4-10; Romans 6:1-11; 1 Corinthians 1:30).
(b) By His shed blood (1 John 1:7-9).
(c) By the Word of God (John 17:17)
(d) Lastly, the regenerating and sanctifying work of the Holy Spirit in the hearts of all believers (Jeremiah 31:31; Romans 8:13; 1 Corinthians 6:11; Philippians 2:12-13; 2 Thessalonians 2:13).

It is noteworthy to say that sanctification is a lifelong process as believers put to death the temptations and grow progressively in the likeness of Christ. God the Father and all heaven rejoice when a lost soul come to Christ as this is another member of His body-the church (Ephesians 5:25-27).

Believers we are a spiritually separated people with blessings galore-eternal life.

Sept 28

Settled In Christ: 1 Peter 5:10

...The God of all grace, who hath called us into His eternal glory by Christ Jesus, after that ye have suffered a while, make you perfect, stablish, strengthen, settle you.

The first eleven verses of this chapter deals with Christians' life in God's care; with that being said brings this question to mind, What does it mean to be "settled in Christ"? Supplying my own definition of the word "settled" is to bring finality to a situation, or something. Therefore, to be settled in Christ means our lives are completely entrusted to Christ as He is the source of all our needs, cares and desires. Christ died for us; He rose for our justification and is now seated at the right hand of the Father making intercessions for us. *What else can we ask for?*

As we hurt so does Christ, He is sympathetic to our needs, cares, concerns, and asks that we cast all our cares upon Him (v. 7). He is more than able to take care of the situation. Another point to being settled in Christ is that we have the finished product-Jesus Christ nothing to be added nor deducted.

It is noteworthy to say that by the grace of God who is all sufficient we have perfection in Him as we are made perfect in His Son Jesus Christ.

Settled in Christ there is nothing missing, nothing lacking.

Sept 29

Perseverance: Ephesians 6:18

Praying always with all prayer and supplication in the Spirit, and watching thereunto with all perseverance and supplication for all saints;

When we think of the term perseverance what comes to mind is endurance, lasting, not giving up or giving in to something, or remaining committed to the task at hand. Given those associated words to perseverance and the believer's spiritual journey, we then are encouraged and outfitted for the spiritual warfare that we are waging with Satan.

God has given His followers all the necessary equipment for perseverance as He has given us faith, salvation, the gospel of peace, His truth, and His righteousness and most of all His Word-the Bible as well as the Holy Spirit to aid in our quest to reach the finish line-heaven.

Allow this writer to say that in our prayer lives we commune with God as He knows all about our struggles on this journey and is close by to pick us up when we falter or get tired on this journey.

Persevering in Christ is one of endurance likened to that of a marathon runner where the winner completes the race. It's not a matter of who gets to the finish line first but finishing the race. Therefore, perseverance in Christ is not giving up as Christ refused to give up dying for humanity's, but instead persevered to the end. *Thank God He did!*

Perseverance is our steadfast commitment enduring until we see our Savior face-to-face.

Sept 30

Purification: Titus 2:14; 1 Peter 1:18-19

Who gave Himself for us, that He might redeem us from all iniquity, and purify unto Himself a peculiar people, zealous of good works.

Purification is the process of making clean or removing corruptible; in today's discussion the focus is on purification of man by the precious blood of Jesus Christ.

Let's look at what Jesus' blood did in the purification process; first His blood was shed on the cross at Calvary to redeem us from all wickedness as it cleanse us from all the negatives brought on by sin. While in this state of mind we had a desire to deify God's law and His holy standards (1 John 3:4). Once the believer is redeemed, sanctified, and justified those desires changed from disobedience to obedience. Also, there is a heart-felt love and devotion to God as well as a desire to live to please Him by being living sacrifices unto Him.

The second act in the purification process was to make us a holy nation that is separated from the world and its systems. We became a people consecrated to God as His own possession. As a consecrated people we have the seal of the Holy Spirit who keeps us in the family of God. In purification we become a holy people who will stand and tell the world *"yes I have been born again."*

Thanks God for Jesus and His precious blood that cleanse my soul from sin and iniquities and have washed me wither than snow.

Jesus our purifier; His blood the purifying agent in the purification process. What a purifier!

Communication With God Through Prayer

Oct 1

What Is Prayer?: Psalm 17:1, 6

Hear the right O Lord, attend unto my cry, give ear unto my prayer, that goeth not out of feigned lips....I have called upon thee, for thou wilt hear me, O God; incline thine ear unto me, and hear my speech.

The Student Bible Dictionary (P. 191) defines prayer as talking and listening to God, an intimate fellowship with God. 1 Kings 8:28 and Matthew 21:22 support this definition of prayer. Prayer includes faith in God and our prayers are establishing a relationship with God.

Prayer includes praising God, thanking Him for all His goodness, confessing ones sins, and interceding for others as well as receiving prayers from others on our behalf.

The Bible uses various adjectives to describe prayer; such as calling on God (v. 6). Genesis 4:26 describe prayer as calling on the name of the Lord. Psalm 3:4 describe prayer as crying with one voice to the Lord, while Psalm 25:1 look at prayer as lifting ones soul to the Lord. Isaiah 55:6 says that prayer is seeking the Lord, while Hebrews 4:16 describe prayer as approaching the throne of grace with boldness, and lastly Hebrews 10:22 say that prayer draws us closer to God.

Whatever adjective used to define prayer it all means our communication with God and exercising our faith in God for answers to our prayers. For me, I begin and end my day with prayers of thanksgiving and praises to God for His goodness, grace and mercy.

Just simply pray!

Why Do We Pray? : Ephesians 6:18; Hebrews 10:22

Praying always with all prayer and supplication in the Spirit, and watching thereunto with all perseverance and supplication for all saints (6:18). Let us draw near with a true heart in full assurance of faith, having our hearts sprinkled from an evil conscience, and our bodies washed with pure water (10:22).

Answering our topical discussion question we find several blessed reasons as to why we pray; one is that we draw near to God as our faith is at work believing God for answers to our prayers.

There are blessings in drawing near to God in faith through Jesus Christ; we find grace, mercy and God's goodness as well as help through prayer (v. 1; 4:16; 7:19). Also, there is salvation (7:25) in Jesus Christ, then there is sanctification (v. 14) as all believers are a set aside people. Lastly, there is cleansing (v. 22) as we have been washed in the blood of Jesus Christ. We pray because we are communicating with God our Father through Jesus Christ our Lord and Savior. Christ often prayed and often spent time alone with His Father and we as believers are to follow in Christ's footsteps in our prayer lives. We pray because we are in a spiritual warfare with Satan. Prayer is our offensive weapon as well as our strength to persevere in faith in this conflict. Prayer is an intricate part of the conflict itself, but it is through prayer we have victory for self and others by working together in unity with other believers and God Himself. It is noteworthy to say that with constant prayer for all situations we are serving notice to the enemy that we will not surrender to his attacks and lies.

There are many reasons why we pray and some are intercessory prayer, prayers of supplication, healing prayers and prayers of thanksgiving. The question now becomes, What is the purpose of each stated reasons we pray? An intercessory prayer is one where the prayer is making intercession to God for another. It could be a love-one, or just simply interceding for the sins of the world. A prayer of supplication is making a humble appeal to God with honesty and in faith for others knowing that God hears and answers our request. It is noteworthy to say that all prayers are to be made in humble submission to God for who He is and what He can and will do for His children.

A healing prayer is considered a specialty prayer because a special request is made to God for a particular reason whether it's for a love-one or society as a whole or divine healing(Psalm 103:3).

The last mentioned prayer is thanksgiving that expresses gratitude of thanks to God for His goodness and mercy as the two is ever present in our daily lives. Psalm 100 is commonly known as a prayer of thanksgiving as an expression of our thanks to God for His blessings. We sing praises with joy for the blessings He has bestowed upon us.

There are many reasons why we pray; whatever the reason is simply talk to God through prayer. He is listening.

Come Boldly To God In Prayer: Hebrews 4:16

Let us therefore come boldly unto the throne of grace, which we may obtain mercy, and find grace to help in time of need.

There is an implied question in today's topical discussion that is answered in our lesson text, which also implies that in our weakness we are made strong through Christ who strengthens us (v. 15). Christ our high priest sympathizes with our weaken conditions as He wants us to have confidence in our prayers and approach God's throne of grace with boldness and assurances that He hears and will answer our prayers.

What gives us confidence in our bold approach to the throne of grace is that we have a heavenly Father who cares for our every need and encourages us to cast all our cares upon Him (1 Peter 5:7).

In approaching God's throne of grace we find, His love, mercy, forgiveness, His wisdom, spiritual power and gifts as well as the fruit of the Holy Spirit all of which we need in any and all circumstances. One of the greatest blessings that flow from God's throne of grace is Christ our high priest who makes intercession for us as He opened the way for us to come to our heavenly Father with all confidence in every area of need in our lives. *What a Mediator!*

With that being said, let's come boldly to the throne of grace in prayer with assured confidence.

God is an approachable God.

Oct 4

Effective Prayers: Mark 11:24

...I say unto you, what things soever ye desire, when ye pray, believe that ye receive them, and ye shall have them.

If the question were raised, What make for an effective prayer? The best answer to the question is that one must first believe with sincere faith in what we ask God our Father for that He will grant our request. Our scripture text supports this answer as expressed by Jesus Himself. To further authenticate that faith holds the key to effective prayers is stated in Mark 9:23, "All things are possible to him that believeth." Allow me to clarify something on the "all things" phrase is that the prayer of faith must be based upon the will of God; meaning not "asking amiss" (James 4:3).

As stated in Hebrews 10:22 that we draw near to God in prayer with a true heart in full assurance of faith is another ingredient to effective prayers. What this is saying is that faith is necessary in coming to God in prayer and believing Him for His goodness (Hebrews 11:6). God plants faith in the hearts of faithful believers who live faithfully according to His will. Another ingredient to effective prayers is never waver in our faith (James 1:6 cf. 5:15).

To conclude this discussion on effective prayers is to say that we must believe in sincere faith, align our will with God's will, and ask in Jesus name (John 14:13-14).

Faithful prayers are effective prayers.

The Power Of Faith In Prayers: Mark 11:20-23

...Have faith in God; For verily I say unto you, That whosoever shall say unto this mountain, Be thou removed, and be thou cast into the sea; and shall not doubt in his heart, but shall believe that those things which he saith shall come to pass; he shall have whosoever he saith.

For the past several days we have been discussing prayer and its effectiveness, but for today's discussion our focus is on the power of faith in our prayers. What we know about faith is that it is our belief with all sincerity without a shadow of a doubt; however, the faith in this scenario is a God-given faith that enables the prayer to totally trust God for whatever asked for, but must align with God's will.

In our scripture text we see Jesus making a compelling case for faith in our prayers when He used the illustration of speaking to the mountain to be moved into the sea and believing it to be moved. Another school of thought in our faith and the power therein speaks to our trust in God as He has proven Himself to be trustworthy. In other words we cannot ask God for something in prayer and then proceed to doubt Him. Sometimes God answers immediately, sometimes He will tarry with His answer as His tarry is preparing us to receive what we asked for; then there are times when God gives us what we need instead of what we asked, because He knows what best. *What a good God?*

Have faith in your prayers. God will answer.

Unified Prayer Warriors: Acts 1:14

These all continued with one accord in prayer and supplication, with the women, and Mary the mother of Jesus, and with his brethren.

The scene of today's discussion is the promise of the Holy Spirit before Jesus was taken up into heaven and His followers gathered together in prayer. These prayer warriors was on one accord petitioning God for the outpouring of the Holy Spirit's power as they realized the need for His power if they were continue to spreading the gospel of Christ. These prayer warriors avail themselves to God's Spirit with a commitment to do His will. This same principle applies to believers today as we must remain steadfast in prayer on one accord in our prayer requests.

What else can be said for unified prayer warriors is that just as when the Holy Ghost came at Pentecost God's Spirit will move in a mighty way when we come together in sincere prayer. His presence may not be manifested in such manner as on the Day of Pentecost, but His presence will be greatly felt. Have you ever been in the presence of worship or a revival meeting when the deacons and the mothers of the church began to sing and pray from their hearts? Something begins to happen; it appears as though the entire church would catch on fire for God. God's present was felt.

It is a known fact that when prayer warriors come together on one accord God's Spirit will be in the midst.

Oct 7

Results Of Unified Prayer: Acts 1:8; 2:1-4

But ye shall receive power, after that the Holy Ghost is come upon you; and ye shall be witnesses unto me both in Jerusalem, and in all Judea, and in Samaria, and unto the uttermost part of the earth...And they were all filled with the Holy Ghost, and began to speak with other tongues, as the Spirit gave them utterance.

Two factors are at work in our lesson study, and they are (a) the promise of the coming Holy Ghost/Spirit as Christ followers were gathered together in one place on one accord praying. God kept His promise of sending the Holy Spirit so that Christ's earthly ministry could continue winning souls for Him. The second factor at work here is that the Holy Ghost came and manifested Himself in three ways; (1) audible, (2) visual and (3) speech manifestations. The results of this group of believers, they received power to boldly witness Christ, drive out demons, and anointing to heal the sick. Believers today have the same power to boldly witness Christ the world over so lost souls can be saved.

Bold witnessing power weren't just given to believers during the time of Pentecost, but to all who come together in unified prayer with a sincere heart for God and to do His will. It is noteworthy to say that as prayers of the righteous come together in unified prayers things change. Just as Daniel (9:3) prayed for the sins of his nation so are believers today praying for the conditions of our nation and world.

Prayer changes things--believers lets continue in prayer.

Oct 8

Intercessory Prayer: Daniel 9:3-19

And I set my face unto the Lord God, to seek by prayer and supplication, with fasting, and sack cloth, and ashes. And I prayed unto the Lord my God, and made my confession, and said, O Lord, the great and dreadful God, keeping the covenant and mercy to them that love him, and to them that keep his commandments; We have sinned, and have committed iniquity, and have done wickedly, and have rebelled, even by departing from thy percepts and from thy judgments.

The entire ninth chapter of Daniel is known as his prayer for the people of Israel. Our scripture texts outlines why intercessory prayer was necessary as the people had turned their backs on God and His righteousness. Also, in our scripture verses we see that Daniel was severely troubled because (a) there were no indication of the prophesied restoration of Israel (Jeremiah 25:11-12; 29:10-14), and (b) Daniel being a man of God had compassion for the nation and went to God in prayer on behalf of the people.

Just as Daniel's intercessory prayer demonstrates his love for God and the nation while taking aggressive action to intercede with prayer. Daniel recognized the awesomeness of God as well as God's love, faithfulness and covenant mercy shown to those who love and obey Him. With that being said, intercessory prayers are being made for others and our nation. We know that God hears the prayers of His people and He does answer. God responds with great mercy and compassion as He fulfills His promises.

God is a good God who hears prayers of the righteous.

Oct 9

Prayer Establishes Relationships: Exodus 33:11

And the Lord spake unto Moses face to face, as a man speaketh unto his friend. And he turned again into the camp; but his servant Joshua, the son of Nun, a young man departed not out of the tabernacle.

Studying the life of Moses we find that he walked closely with God and in doing so he established a close relationship with God so much so that God called him friend. Verse 11 supports the fact of God and Moses' close relationship and God talked to face to face.

If the question were raised, What brought on this close relationship? It was due in part to Moses' sincere devotion to God and His cause, desire and purpose. God's desire was for the nation of Israel to be His chosen people whom He would shower with His love and blessing as they would be an example for the rest of the world to see and get to know God. It was God's desire and purpose for Moses to lead the nation of Israel out of slavery in Egypt as Moses was the human instrument that God worked through in delivering the nation of Israel. The other factor in this close friend relationship between God and Moses is that Moses was one with the Spirit of God to the extent that he shared God's feelings. He grieved at sin just as God did and suffered when God suffered over worldly conditions. What does this say for you and I today? It says that every believer through prayer and scripture reading should know the ways of God and have the desire to grow into a profound union with Him and His purposes for our lives to the point that every believer becomes God's friend.

There are many other notable biblical characters who established a close friendly walk with God with a committed desire to know and do the will of God. The common thread of those biblical characters was their prayer lives were profound; their love for God and their desire to do His will while humbly submitting to Him. From personal knowledge there are many believers today who possess the same qualities and have established a friend relationship with God. *There is no better friend than God.*

If the question were raised, When must one began building a close relationship with God? Again, verse 11 provides the answer by highlighting Joshua who began at an early age (youth) spending time alone with God and developing a personal union with God. This verse underscores the spiritual growth of every believer as it should begin very early in ones life just as our physical lives. See, God has a purpose and a plan for each of us. Joshua and Samuel were prepared early and each fulfilled their called mission according to God's plan. The same principal applies today.

A good relationship is a godly relationship.

Oct 10

Believers' Prayer Intercessions: James 5:13-18

Elias was a man subject to like passions as we are and he prayed earnestly that it might not rain; and it rained not on the earth by the space of three years and six months. And he prayed again, and the heaven gave rain, and the earth brought forth her fruit.

Today's topical discussion deals with the different kinds of intercessory prayers brought by believers. As noted in our scripture text there is intercessory prayers for afflictions, sickness, sins and worldly conditions.

Whatever the condition we find ourselves in we are encouraged to seek strength from the Lord through prayer. As we draw near to God, Christ our mediator will present our condition to God the Father as Christ make intercession for us (Hebrews 7:25) God will give grace and mercy in the time of need (Hebrews 4:16).

If there are anyone who is sick among us he or she is to call for the pastors, leaders of the church to pray of his or her healing; this prayer must be one of faith and according to James it will heal the sick (v. 15).

We are also encouraged to pray for the sins of the world both confessed and unconfessed (v. 16), because when the righteous pray good things happens. Verses 17-18 are prime examples of a righteous man-Elias praying for a condition; first prayer no rain for three years and six months. Elias' second prayer the rain came. Elias was a man of God who had great faith in God and his prayers.

What does this say for intercessory prayers of the righteous? They availeth much (v. 16).

Oct 11

Intercessory Prayer Purposes: Genesis 18:22-23

And the men turned their faces from thence, and went toward Sodom; but Abraham stood yet before the Lord. And Abraham drew near, and said, With thou also destroy the righteous with the wicked?

The background of today's lesson study is that sin and wickedness had become so prevalent and perverted that God was going to destroy the entire city of Sodom. Abraham a righteous man who was very concern for his relative Lot and other righteous so much so that he went to God in prayer asking Him not to destroy the entire city (vv. 22-23). God answered Abraham's prayer by sparing the city and destroying the wicked that was within the city.

From our illustration, an intercessory prayer serves specific purposes made by God's people. With that being said, then our intercessory prayers serves a purpose in that God-fearing believers pleads with God to turn aside His judgment (Genesis 18:22-23). Intercessory prayers help to restore God's people (Nehemiah 1; Daniel 9). Intercessory prayers deliver individuals from danger (Acts 12:5, 12; Romans 15:31); also, intercessory prayers are prayed to bless God's people (Numbers 6:24-26; 1 Kings 18:41-45; Psalm 122:6-8). There are intercessory healing prayers (1 Kings 17:20-21; Acts 28:8; James 5:14-16), prayers for the forgiveness of sin, Christian growth, for the Holy Spirit's power to come, effective leadership and ministry work, salvation of others and for people to offer praises to God.

Therefore, intercessory prayers are both powerful and purposeful; prayer warriors-pray on because your prayers are making a difference.

Oct 12

Christian Growth Through Prayer: Philippians 1:9-11

And this I pray that your love may abound yet more and more in knowledge and in all judgment; That ye may approve things that are excellent; that ye may be sincere and without offence till the day of Christ; Being filled with the fruits of righteousness, which are by Jesus Christ unto the glory and praise of God.

What is Paul saying to the Philippians believers? Paul is saying that true Christian love is not just mere words, but is sincere that begins in the heart and is predicated on the God's love. Neither is it head knowledge but spiritual and involves a personal relationship with God. This relationship begins with a fervent prayer life. We are taught to love one another as God first loved us. We are also taught to love our enemy because God loved us while we were His enemy. It is hard to love someone who hates you or do not give love in return, but through prayer and asking God to give each of us the ability and desire to love as He love-then there is growth.

Another point of view on Christian Growth through prayer is that while being taught biblical theological facts we gain a deeper meaning of God's Word and knowing His will while gaining a desire and commitment to do His will. This desire is gained through being in constant communication with God through prayer. As our relationship with God grows we become more Christ-like.

Through prayer we develop a closer walk with God.

Pray ye therefore the Lord of the harvest, that He will send forth labourers into His harvest.

Verses 35-37 stress the need for ministry workers in God's vineyard as there is much work that needs to be done as Christ's mission of kingdom building continues.

Our lesson text expresses the importance of prayer as this is one of God's spiritual principles. We witness on many occasions Jesus praying before undertaking a task; believers are to do likewise. God wants His people to pray before undertaking any works because when we pray we invoke the power of the Holy Spirit to become an active part of our ministry as He will be our guide in the works of Christ.

Why is prayer so important in ministry? It is because if we are to carry on Christ's work of healing the sick, driving out demons, and preaching and teaching His gospel then we must be empowered by the Holy Spirit to ensure effective ministry. As promised in Acts 1:8 we are empowered to do great things in the body of Christ. Being empowered with the Holy Spirit's power we can boldly preach and teach Christ where souls will be saved. Another point on the importance of prayer for effective ministry is that we are in union with God through prayer. Lastly, prayer is our offensive weapon in this spiritual warfare.

Prayer is essential to effective ministry in God's vineyard; therefore always pray.

Oct 14

Salvation Of Others: Romans 10:1

Brethren, my heart's desire and prayer to God for Israel is that they might be saved.

Our scripture text takes me back to my childhood days when an unsaved person were pondering salvation, the person were asked to sit on the mourner's bench in church as the elders and mothers of the church prayed for the person asking God to come into this person's heart. The person would also be taught about God and salvation as well as what was necessary for salvation. All unsaved are to confess with his or her mouth that Jesus is Lord while believing in his or her hart that God raised Him from the dead then thou shall be saved (v. 9). John 3:16 were explained to the unsaved and that they were included in "the whosoever".

Another point of view on praying for the salvation of others is that sincere prayers for the unsaved has a positive effect in that it releases the convicting working of the Holy Spirit in the person's life. Still another point worth noting is that it sends a powerful message to Satan saying no this soul belongs to God. Each time the unsaved joins God's army heaven rejoices and Satan is angry. This is the power of intercessory salvation prayers. *What strength we have in prayer?*

Let's close with this statement, lost souls are coming to Christ as prayer warrior continues to pray for lost souls and the sins of this world.

Prayer warriors pray on.

Oct 15

Praising God Through Prayer: Psalm 67:3-5

Let the people praise thee, O God; let all the people praise thee. O let the nations be glad and sing for joy for thou shalt judge the people righteously, and govern the nations upon earth, Let the people praise thee, O God; let all the people praise thee.

How do we praise God through prayer? In our prayer of praises we give thanks to God for His presence, guidance, love, grace, healing power, salvation and the fullness of the Spirit. Given all the blessing that God has bestowed upon us is reason enough to praise God through our prayers. God is worthy of our praise prayers because He imparted His Spirit into each of us as He lives in each believer. God worthiness of all praises is exhibited in His love act of giving His only Son to be man's propitiator.

If the question were raised, Who should praise God? As stated in our scripture text all people and nations should praise God and sing for joy that God is the righteous judge who will judge all nations fairly. How often should we praise God in our prayers? God is worthy of our daily prayer praises because prayers is our communication piece with God and the more we pray the closer our relationship with God becomes. Daily praising God assures us of His many blessing that He so lovingly showers upon His people. God is a loving God who loves to shower His people with His blessing.

Praise God in prayer in good and bad times.

Oct 16

Model Prayer: Matthew 6:9-13

After this manner pray ye; Our Father which art in heaven, Hallowed be thy name. Thy kingdom come, Thy will be done in earth, as it is in heaven, Give us this day our daily bread. And forgive us our debts, as we forgive our debtors. And lead us not into temptation, but deliver us from evil; For thine is the kingdom, and the power, and the glory, for ever. Amen.

This prayer has been called the Lord's Prayer and the model prayer as Christ was instructing His disciples on how they should pray. This model prayer contains areas of concern expressed by Christ that all believers should be concerned with. Three petitions expresses concerns with the holiness and will of God and the second three petitions expresses concerns for our daily needs as God has promised in His word to supply all our needs. God know what we stand in need of before we ask, but by asking God for our daily needs expresses a spirit of humility while trusting God as He is faithful to His promises.

Let's look at these verses and expound each; verse 9 acknowledges who God is and where He is as we give adoration to God because He is worthy of all praises. In praying to a holy God we are involved in worship with Him developing an intimate relationship with our heavenly Father. God loves us so that He cherishes our fellowship and intimacy through Christ as each believer has access to God and He is never too busy to commune with each of us. It is noteworthy to say that God is the only one worthy of our utmost reverence and exaltation.

The prayer encourages us to be concerned with God's kingdom here on earth as well as in the future while acknowledging that God's will must be done. Doing the will of God fulfills His purpose for our lives. We are also acknowledging that Christ is sure to return and establish His kingdom here on earth and true peace will be once again be restored. Also, we pray for the spiritual presence of God now by asserting His power among His people as we do battle with Satan that we may destroy his evil works.

In praying for our daily needs is invoking the promises of God to supply our every need as He has lovingly made provisions (Philippians 4:19).

In all believers' prayer we must be concern with the sins of this world and display a willingness to forgive those who sin against us as our heavenly Father forgave us. Our Lord and Savior Jesus Christ died for the sins of the world and all who come to Him has been forgiven. Therefore, we are to emulate our Savior by forgiving others.

Lastly, we are to ask God for help in leading us against temptation as Satan is constantly trying to tempt God's people. With the aid of the Holy Spirit believers has the ability to combat Satan's fiery darts of evil. God has dressed His warriors with defensive weapons for just such purposes (Ephesians 10-18).

Let us close this discussion by saying that our model prayer contains the important areas of concerns.

Pray, God is listening.

Oct 17

Holy Living: 1 Peter 1:13-15

Wherefore gird up the loins of your mind, be sober, and hope to the end for the grace that is to be brought unto you at the revelation of Jesus Christ. As obedient children, not fashioning yourselves according to the former lusts in your ignorance; But as He which hath called you is holy, so be ye holy in all manner of conversation.

Why must believers live in holiness? Believers are to live in holiness because believers are born into the family of a holy God; therefore His people must be likewise holy. Furthermore, being holy carries the mandate of being separated from the world and its systems as the world is an enemy of God. It is required that all believers must separate themselves from this world as it is currently ruled by the prince of darkness. Believers are set apart for love, giving service to God and worshipping Him.

Therefore, being holy and living holy lives is the goal and purpose of the believer's election in Christ. Holy living means being dedicated to God so that all believers can and will live to please Him (Romans 12:1).

Believers are made holy by the sanctifying work of the Holy Spirit (v. 2) and the power of the cross through Jesus Christ who delivered us from sin. Thereby we were renewed in the image of Christ our Lord and Savior and infused with God's grace to obey Him and live according to His Word.

A transformed (sober) mind leads to holy living.

Oct 18

Revelations From God: Ephesians 1:17-18

That the God of our Lord Jesus Christ, the Father of glory, may give unto you the spirit of wisdom and revelation in the knowledge of Him; The eyes of your understanding being enlightened; that ye may know what is the hope of His calling, and what the riches of the glory in his inheritance in the saints,

The term revelation mean to uncover what was hidden or making known the unknown (Romans 16:25). God has revealed Himself through His written word-the Bible and His Son Jesus Christ who was the final revelation of God the Father. With that being said, Paul's prayers for the Ephesians believers is that God through His spirit of wisdom and revelation make known just who He is and His will and purpose for His people. It is important that all believers know the will of God and His redemptive purposes for salvation and to experience a more abundant power of the Holy Spirit in the lives of all believers (vv. 19-20).

Each believer has been given a specific calling in Christ's church and with the revelation of this gift through the Holy Spirit and His power then believers become more effective in the believer's ministry building God's kingdom. As recorded in Acts 1:8 we receive power to boldly witness Christ with such effectiveness that souls will be saved. Another important factor in receiving revelations from God is that believers come to know that God has outfitted each with His body armour for this spiritual warfare (Ephesians 6:11-18).

God reveals His will and purposes for man.

Know And Do The Will Of God: Ephesians 5:17

Wherefore be ye not unwise, but understanding what the will of the Lord is.

In Paul's writings to the believers at Ephesus contrasting moral and immoral living while enlightening his audience that immoral acts are not in God's kingdom (vv 1-17). Paul was also enlightening the Ephesians the benefits of knowing and then doing the will of God as this applies to all believers today. It is God's expressed desired will that all be saved (1 Timothy 2:4; 2 Peter 3:9) and inherit eternal life. However, God knew that all would not be saved because they would fail to obey His laws.

With that being said, God has a perfect will and a permissive will. His perfect will is His desire and His permissive will is what He permits to happen. For example, God does not force salvation on anyone. He made us a free will agent with the ability to choose Him and be saved or reject Him and be lost.

We learn the will of God from His written word-the Bible, divine revelation from the Holy Spirit. Once we learn what God's will is for us the question now becomes, How do we respond? We can respond by committing our lives to Him and His commandments or we can refuse to commit ourselves to a life of righteousness. Once committed to doing the will of God we have the aid of the Holy Spirit to keep us focus in our commitment.

It's one thing to know the will of God and another to do His will.

Humility: Acts 20:19

Serving the Lord with all humility of mind, and with many tears, and temptations, which befell me by the lying in with of the Jews:

If we were to define humility we would say that it is the absent of pride, and having the right view of self, God and others. It is not seen as a weakness, but instead strength and the ability to trust God. Humility is a Christian character that is praised in the Bible and according to Proverbs 15:33 it is a command.

With that being said, Paul served God with all humility without wavering in his faith and trust in God. In Paul's life he suffered many hardships for preaching Christ, but he remained faithful to his calling. Jesus Christ who is God's Son humbled Himself for the sake of all humanity. He came to earth to serve as oppose to be served neither to be exalted in a prideful manner. Jesus Christ is our perfect example of humility for all believers both then and now to follow in our service to God. Other notable biblical characters served God from a position of humility as do many other true servant leaders today.

Lastly, serving the Lord with humility believers recognize God for who He is and our relationship to Him and His awesome powers. Humility is one of the character traits that all believers must have as believers we are to emulate Christ. Humility is a controlled strength as our strength come from God.

Be humble!

Faith In God: Hebrews 11:1

Now faith is the substance of things hoped for, the evidence of things not seen.

Our lesson text defines faith, but in a short term definition faith is defined as our belief or trust in God (Habakkuk 2:4; Mark 11:22). With that being said, then faith is essential to our salvation. We must believe that Jesus Christ is the Son of God who died on the cross for our sins.

Let's look at some demonstrative acts of faith, and they are
- a) Faith enables the believer to persevere and remain committed to God and His Word.
- b) It is the believer's faith that leads to spiritual realities.
- c) Faith leads to the believer's righteousness (v.4).
- d) Our faith leads us to seek God (v. 6) and believe in His goodness.
- e) Our faith enables us to have confidence/trust in God's Word (vv 7, 11) and then obey His commands (v. 8) which regulate life as He promised (vv 13, 39).
- f) Our faith in God helps us to reject the evil spirit of this present world and refuse the pleasures of sin as they are not of God (vv. 13, 25), but instead lead us to seek our heavenly home (vv 14-16).
- g) Our faith enables us to persevere during times of testing (vv 17-19), and endure persecution (v. 27).
- h) Our faith enables us to perform mighty acts of righteousness (vv 33-35) as we are filled with the Holy Spirit.
- i) Our faith creates a willingness to suffer for God and His righteousness if required (vv 25, 35-38).
- j) Because of Abraham's faith many generations are blessed.

With faith we can do wonders. Have faith.

Oct 22

I Surrender All: Romans 13:1-2

Let every soul be subject unto the higher powers. For there is no power but of God; the powers that be are ordained of God. Whosoever therefore resisteth the power resisteth the ordinance of God; and they that resist shall receive to themselves damnation.

Paul in his writing to the Romans believers is encouraging them to subject themselves totally to God and His commandments so that they may have eternal life. Also, in Romans 13, Paul was instructing the people to obey the government as God ordained governments to provide order to prevent chaos, but by the same token when government go against the ordnances of God then it is better to obey God as He is the supreme ruler of all.

It is important that we have godly leaders leading our government as a godly leader is prone to surrender his or her personal will to that of the will of God. 1 Timothy 2:1-2 encourages all believers to pray for those in authority so that they will hear and adhere to the guidance of the Holy Spirit as He will guide leaders and laity according to the will of God-He is God.

However, on an individual note all believers are to surrender all to God our true commander-in-Chief. It is God who holds all nations, leaders and individuals in the holler of His hands and is present in all.

Let's pray, Lord I surrender my all to You as I go day-by-day as You will lead me in the right way. Amen.

Oct 23

Forgiveness: Colossians 1:14

In whom we have redemption through his blood, even the forgiveness of sins.

What is forgiveness? The Student Bible Dictionary (P. 95) defines forgiveness as "a pardon, or excuse a wrong, to cancel a debt or even give up a claim for revenge or resentment. Forgiveness even reestablishes a broken relationship. Also, it states to forgive is to trust others as if the wrong is forgotten. Forgiveness includes a new start in attitudes and actions."

Given our definition of forgiveness these questions come to mind, Have you ever needed forgiveness? How quick are you to forgive others? Is it easy or difficult for you to forgive others who may have wronged you? When forgiving others do you still hold the grudge or seek in some what to get even? *If so that's forgiving.* When ask to forgive what is your answer? Allow me to supply some answers to the above questions, first we all needs forgiveness and have been forgiven by God because we were born with a sin nature because of Adam's disobedience. Therefore, God sent His only Son Jesus Christ to atone for the sins of the world through His shed blood, and if you accept Jesus' atoning work at Calvary you have been forgiven and your sins have been placed in the sea of forgetfulness. It is worth me asking you to look through the telescopic lens of time and reflect on the magnitude of what God done in the redemptive process of humanity's sins. Only a God who loves unconditionally could and would perform such magnificent act of love. *He forgave and He is still forgiving sin.*

Second, we should readily forgive others as we have been forgiven by God our Father. Third, forgiving others should be an easy task given what our heavenly Father and His Son done for all mankind. Just as we want forgiveness we should be willing to forgive others. No grudges should be held if there is to be true forgiveness nor should we seek revenge because God said that vengeance is His and what is just He will repay. *Remember God is the righteous judge.*

Reflect with me for a moment to the time you needed to

forgive someone and the moment you forgave the other person a weight was lifted from your shoulders. *What a relief!* It was if you had been relieved from a pounding toothache. Then, my advice is to forgive and free yourself from the weight of sin. Also, it is better to forgive and be forgiven than to hold the grudge and miss your blessings.

    We can conclude that forgiveness is a powerful tool in receiving salvation, because God forgave us of our sins and we are to forgive others who have wronged us. All forgiveness is to be done in love to emulate God's love.

    Forgive! Forgive! As we all has been forgiven.

Oct 24

Faithful To God: Proverbs 28:20; Luke 24:50

A faithful man shall abound with blessings; but he that maketh haste to be rich shall not be innocent (28:20). And He led them out as far as to Bethany, and He lift up His hands and blessed them.

If we were to define the term faithful one definition is steady, steadfastness or true; however in today's topical discussion the focus is being faithful to God and the blessing from doing so. Both scriptures support each other when describing the blessings received from God as a reward to His people who have committed themselves to holy living while abiding by His commands.

Let's look at the blessed rewards received from God for being faithful to Him and His kingdom building. Some are, (a) we receive divine gifts that cause our work to be successful. God's kingdom building is sustained by blessing His faithful followers. (b) We are blessed with God's presence at all time as He is working through us to produce good work. (c) He gives us strength and power to help others.

Just as Jesus blessed His faithful followers prior to His ascension, believers today are blessed for being faithful to Christ's ministry. In order for us to receive Christ's blessings we must look to Him for our blessings while remaining in communion with Him through prayer, loving and obeying Him.

Let's close with this thought provoking question, given the promised blessings from God why not remain faithful to Him?

Faithfulness is essential to receiving God's blessings

Oct 25

Reflection Of God's Glory: Ezekiel 1:26, 28; Ephesians 3:21

...Above the firmament that was over their heads was the likeness of a throne, as the appearance of a sapphire stone; and upon the likeness of the throne was the likeness as the appearance of a man above upon it...As the appearance of the bow that is in the cloud in the day of rain, so was the appearance of the brightness round about. This was the appearance of the likeness of the glory of the Lord. And when I saw it, I fell upon my knees, and I heard a voice of one that spake.

What is God's glory? God's glory can best be defined as God's splendor and majesty (1 Chronicles 29:11), something so great that no man can see it and live (Exodus 33:18-23), therefore it is described as the "appearance of the likeness of the glory of God." God's glory can also be termed as His presence among His people and His holy presence and power.

When God revealed Himself to Ezekiel He was preparing Ezekiel for the work he had been called to do during the Jews exile. Ezekiel saw God sitting on His throne in the form of a man. When God reveals Himself He does so as a man just as He revealed Himself through His Son Jesus Christ. God reveals Himself to us today through the Holy Spirit and His Word; this is so that we may experience His presence and power to do the work He has assigned us to do.

God is still revealing Himself in visible form; "in the church by Christ Jesus throughout all ages, "world without end" (Ephesians 3:21).

Living In God's Care: 1 Peter 5:1-11

Casting all your cares upon Him; for He careth for you.

What does it mean to live in God's care? First, we must recognize just who God is and His all sustaining powers with the ability, love and compassion to handle any situation. God in His infinite wisdom has made provisions for any situation known to man as He has a perfect solution. God asks us to bring our cares, concerns and problems to Him and leave them with Him.

Second, living in God's care mean that we have entrusted our lives to God our creator and sustainer as God has proven Himself to be trustworthy. God promised a Savior, in His time He provided Jesus Christ who died on the cross for the sins of the world.

Third, God promised to supply all our needs according to His riches and glory through Christ Jesus (Philippians 4:19). God says in Psalm 23:1 that He is our shepherd. The "is" in this verse denotes presently, not was or will be but currently. Also, this verse says that God's help is ever present. In John 10:11 Jesus tells us that "He is the good shepherd who giveth His life for His sheep." ***What a shepherd!***

Lastly, in God's care means that He overflows our cup with His love, joy while dispatching His angels of goodness and mercy who will see us through this life and its cares.

Blessings abound from living in God's care.

Oct 27

Accessing God's Supply Line: Philippians 4:19

But my God shall supply all your needs according to His riches in glory by Christ Jesus.

In Paul's writing to the believers at Philippi he provided them with the assurance that God will meet all their needs both physically and spiritually. This assurance holds true for believers today.

What one must do to access God's supply line is to seek Him in sincere prayer while having faith that God hears and answers the prayers of His people. We are to make our petitions known to God; He will answer and meet our needs through His Son Jesus Christ. Believers are in union and fellowship with Christ and we will experience God's provision that He has so lovingly prepared for us. Believers have God's guaranteed promise of providing for all our needs and He has proven to be true to His word.

In 1 Peter 5:7 God ask that we cast all ones cares upon Him. Would God make such request if He weren't going to take care of the problem? *I think not.* If one needs comforting, God is there through the presence of the Holy Spirit, if you need a lawyer in a court room, He is there, if you need bread He supplies that as well. Remember the young nation of Israel when God fed them Manna from heaven while they journeyed in the desert. When Israel needed water to drink, He supplied water from a rock. God supplied all their needs and He will do the same for you and I today.

Just ask Him.

Oct 28

Refreshed By God's Spirit: Job 32:8, 18

But there is a spirit in man; and the inspiration of the Almighty giveth them understanding...For I am full of matter, the spirit within me constraineth me.

The scene for today's discussion is that during Job's affliction and he was visited by his three friends and they insisted that Job had sinned and was refusing to admit to the sin. What the Bible does say about Job is the he was an upright man who eschewed evil. When Job had lost all his worldly possessions even his children he continued trusting God for his deliverance. He continued trusting God when his wife told him to curse God and die. What Job knew was that in God's time all his troubles would be over and that he would not take anything with him out of this world.

In times like these, What must a person do? Like Job continue trusting God because God's spirit who lives in each of us is bigger than the spirit in this world. Yes, we like Job will become weary at some point, but we must connect to God's Spirit as He will refresh us and give us the strength to persevere to the end. See, what Job valued most was his right standings with God and we too must possess the same value system. This is because God's Spirit refreshes us daily because of His love for us.

Being refreshed by God's Spirit is like fresh morning dew.

Oct 29

Led By God's Spirit: Romans 8:14

For as many as are led by the Spirit of God, they are the sons of God.

If the question were raised, Why is it important to be led by the Spirit of God? God's Spirit lives in each believer to lead, guide, instruct and protect us.

In each of the Holy Spirit's functions has a specific purpose in the lives of all believers, and they are (a) the Holy Spirit leads believers by prompting believers to do God's will and mortify the deeds of the body/flesh (v. 13) and oppose sinful desires that can and will cause the believer to stumble. (b) He guides believers to live in harmony with God's Word and His instructions are designed to teach us how to live according to God's Word. God's Word is designed for reproof, correction, and instruction in righteousness (2 Timothy 3:16). Believers are to live according to God's righteousness and standards. (c) God's Spirit will aid the believer in persevering in faith and protect believers by warning them of Satan's hidden snares that will result in the believer falling away. Lastly, God's Spirit protects believers from all hurt harm or danger as He sees what's ahead.

Believers are led by God's Spirit by allowing Him to become an integrate part of ones lives through daily scripture reading, meditating and applying God's Word to ones daily life as well as desiring and valuing the manifestation of His presence.

Yield to God's Spirit as He leads the way.

Oct 30

Died With Christ Raised With Him: Ephesians 2:5-6

Even when we were dead in sins, hath quickened us together with Christ, (by grace ye are saved;) And hath raised us up together and made us sit together in heavenly place in Christ Jesus.

Our lesson text carries a profound message regarding the atoning works of our Lord and Savior Jesus Christ. The message from our text is that all who believe in Jesus Christ died with Him to sin and was raised with Him to a new life of righteousness where the believer's final destination is heaven where we will see Jesus face-to-face. *What a glorious time that will be?*

Our lesson text also bring into focus the believer's salvation that is by God's grace through faith in Jesus Christ. Faith in Jesus Christ is what God requires to receive salvation because salvation is His free gift to mankind. Faith is what we as believers believe about Jesus Christ. The question now becomes, What do we believe about Jesus Christ? Do we believe that He is God's Son who was born of a woman lived as both God and man for the sole purpose of redeeming humanity back to God with His shed blood on Calvary's cross? Do we believe that Christ was in the beginning with God? Do we believe that Jesus was slain from the foundation of the world to be man's redeemer as man were going to sin and become separated from God our creator? Do we believe that Jesus Christ was actually crucified on Friday and was raised by God-the Holy Spirit on Sunday morning? Do we believe that Christ has all power? Can He seal the sick, give sight to the blind, raise the dead and most importantly, that He is coming back one day for His bride-the church? Do we believe that the only way to the Father is through Jesus Christ? Do we believe that the actions taken by God the Father and God the Son was the greatest love act ever staged? God the Father willingly gave His Son who willingly gave His life for mankind's sins. In doing so all who believe in Jesus Christ received the greatest gift that has ever been given and will ever be given. *What a gift?*

Believers' gift of salvation is based on God's grace which has mercy written all over it when justice demanded punishment for man because of his sins. Because of the new life in Christ we now live a life of righteousness where the believer has a new found devotion and obedience that leads to a life of holy living one that is pleasing to God. Being raised with Christ to a life of righteousness believers then manifest the holiness of God daily so the world can and will see His glory and love through His people. It is noteworthy to say that being raised to a new life in Christ we become new creatures in Him. The old life of sin had been put to death and in this new life we see things differently.

Being raised with Christ is the result of a mind transformation based on our faith.

Oct 31

Prayers Of The Righteous: James 5:16

Confess you faults one to another, and pray one for another, that ye may be healed. The effectual fervent prayer of the righteous availeth much.

The phrase "prayers of the righteous availeth much" is a popular but true saying in that when the righteous go in prayer things change.

Let's look at some positive outcomes from righteous prayers (a) righteous prayers draws the prayer and the prayed for closer to God (Hebrews 7:25). (b) Righteous prayers opens the door-way to a Spirit-filled life in God (Luke 11:13; Acts 1:14). (c) Righteous prayers make for powerful ministry as believers are to pray to God before beginning any ministry (Acts 1:8; 4; 31, 33). (d) Prayers of the righteous brings about a greater Christian devotion (Ephesians 1:19). (e) Prayers of the righteous give the prayer insight to Christ's provision for them as well as aiding them in overcoming Satan and his schemes. (f) Righteous prayers clarify the will of God for the believer as well as enabling the righteous to receiving spiritual gifts. (g) Righteous prayers bring a closer fellowship with God as well as brining them God's grace, mercy and peace. (h) Righteous prayers help bring the lost to Christ as believers make intercessory salvation prayers on behalf of the lost. (i) Righteous prayers make Christ real in the lives of believers. Lastly, (j) prayers of the righteous glorify God by offering prayers of praises and thanksgiving.

Prayers of the righteous work wonders; pray on.

Harvest Time

Nov 1

Christian Workers: Matthew 20:1

For the kingdom of heaven is like unto a man that is a householder, which went out early in the morning to hire labourers unto his vineyard.

The 20th chapter of Matthew is a parable dealing with Christian workers in God's vineyard. Being a worker in God's labor force is a matter of privilege, not merit because no one can earn enough merit points to earn his or her salvation. Salvation is a free gift from God which comes through our faith in Jesus Christ.

The saved believer has an assigned duty to God and His kingdom building; this duty is to tell others about the goodness of the Lord. The need for all believers to witness the gospel of Christ is greater than ever. It matters not when one come to Christ the pay is the same-salvation.

All believers are gifted with a spiritual gift that is to be used to edify the body of Christ. All believers are encouraged to refrain from developing a superior attitude because of the position one serves in the body of Christ. Also, believers are to avoid the spirit of envy to fellow believers because of what we may perceive as superior positions or blessings, because God our Father blesses whom He pleases, when He pleases and to what extent. The most precious blessing one can receive that is equal to all which is salvation. All believers will one day spend eternity with God.

Christian workers, grapes-lost souls in the vineyard are ripe for harvesting. Witness! Witness!

Nov 2

A Time Of Harvesting: Revelation 14:14-20

And I looked, and behold a white cloud, and upon the cloud one sat like unto the Son of man, having on his head a golden crown, and in his hand a sharp sickle. And another angel came out of the temple, crying with a loud voice to him that sat on the cloud, Thrust in thy sickle, and reap; for the harvest of the earth is ripe.

What is the meaning of these verses? The phrase "like unto a man" represents Jesus Christ Himself who is preparing to reap the harvest of the earth. Some popular beliefs is that in verses 14-16 represents God's wrath on the earth while in verses 17-20 is a different harvest because it make mention of another angel. God's harvest of judgment is the greatest as it will be His judgment on all who followed the beast as described in chapter 13. The grain harvest in this section is the great end-time harvest of salvation (Matthew 13:24-30, 36-43).

Verse 19 further explains the judgment that will take place during this time as it talks about the great winepress. From Biblical OT reading the treading of grapes is used as an illustration to express how the execution of all unbelievers by God Himself. They will be cast into the Lake of Fire for eternal damnation.

What all this means is that all believers who have remained steadfast to Christ will be included in the grain harvest and will rule with Christ when He establishes His kingdom on earth.

The time of harvesting is near; which harvest will you be in?

Labourers Needed: Matthew 9:37-38

Then saith he unto his disciples, The harvest truly is plenteous, but the labourers are few; Pray ye therefore the Lord of the harvest, that he will send forth labourers into his harvest.

During Christ's earthly ministry He preached about the kingdom of heaven and what it is like as well as what is required to get there-repent and be saved. However, during Christ's ministry He saw the lost conditions of this world and saw the need for more believers to proclaim the gospel message so that the unsaved will believe and not spend eternity in hell. The harvest fields in our lesson text represents the lost souls of the world and it is God's desire that all be saved as Christ expressed the need for more believers to obey the Great Commission (Matthew 28-19-20) of preaching and teaching Christ.

Verse 38 plainly expresses Christ's desire and prayer petition that God the Father would send more labourers into the world who would preach and teach the gospel of the kingdom (9:35); seal the sick and drive out demons/evil spirits (9:35; 10:1,8).

Just as Christ gave His disciples power against all unclean spirits and to heal the sick, would He not give us today the same power as this would represent God's kingdom presence here on earth? Another question that comes to mind, Are we as Christians being too silent in the midst of a corrupt society? Also, How bright is our light shining for God?

Let's stand up for Christ for we are His workers.

Nov 4

Wheat And Tares: Matthew 13:36-38

Then Jesus sent the multitude away, and went into the house; and His disciples came unto Him, saying; Declare unto us the parable of the tares of the field. He answered and said unto them, He that soweth the good seed is the Son of man; The field is the world; the good seed are the children of the kingdom; but the tares are the children of the wicked one.

Our lesson text makes it crystal clear the difference of who are the representatives of wheat and tares-saved and unsaved. All believers are children of God who has been equipped with God's suit of armour to fight this spiritual warfare that has been raging since the beginning of time all because Satan wanted to be above God his creator and was cast out of heaven. Satan vowed to destroy God's kingdom, but he is a defeated foe as this victory was won at Calvary.

Nevertheless; Satan continues to sow his seed of destruction alone side the good seed-the true Word of God. God in His due time will instruct His angels to destroy Satan and his followers once and for all (vv. 30, 38-40).

It is noteworthy to say that all believers must be aware of Satan's subversive tactics in planting or infiltrating God's Work as many of Satan's followers will look like Christians when in actuality they are as raving wolves in sheep clothing. When this happens we are to stand firm on God's Word and principles.

Wheat and tares will grow together and God will separate in the end.

Nov 5

End-Time Reapers: Matthew 13:39-43

The enemy that sowed them is the devil; the harvest is the end of the world; and the reapers are the angels. As therefore the tares are gathered and burnt in the fire; so shall it be in the end of the word.

What we see in today's discussion is that there will be a separation of wheat and tares after the return of Christ at the end of the tribulation which occurs at the end of the age (Revelation 19:11-21) when the harvesting of both righteous and wicked will occur (vv. 30, 40-42). The wicked will be the first to be harvested/taken out of the earth from among God's people, and then the righteous will be taken "out of His kingdom." What happens to the righteous; "The righteous will then shine forth as the sun in the kingdom of their Father" (v. 43 cf. 25: 31-34).

If the question were raised, Who are the reapers in this story? The reapers are Christ's angels who will be with Him when He returns to begin His thousand-year reign. The faithful of Christ's church will reign with Him (Revelation 2:26-27; 3; 21; 5:10; 20:4). Other saints that will reign with Christ will be the Old Testament resurrected saints, martyred tribulation saints, those faithful to Christ during the tribulation and those born during the millennium (Revelation 14:12; 18:4; Isaiah 65: 20-23). Satan will be bound during this time (Revelation 20:2, 3).

Knowing who the reapers are and that all will be harvested to either spend eternity with Christ in His kingdom or separated from Him; therefore, it behooves all to get right because harvest time is coming.

Christ and His angels are coming to reap the harvest.

Nov 6

Dwell In Zion: Isaiah 1:27-28; Hebrews 12:22

Zion shall be redeemed with judgment and her converts with righteousness. And the destruction of the transgressors and of the sinners shall be together, and they that forsake the Lord shall be consumed (1:27-28). But ye have come unto mount Sion, and unto the city of the living God, the heavenly Jerusalem, and to an innumerable company of angels.

The term Zion has a rich history in relation to Jerusalem as it means a fortress which was named for Jerusalem (Psalm 2:6; Revelation 14:1). Zion was first mention in the Old Testament as a Jebusite fortress (II Samuel 5:6-9), but when David captured this city he later named it the City of David. Zion's location makes it perfect for defensive purposes as it is located near the only known spring. Archeological remains indicate that this was the original Zion long before David's time. When King David brought the Ark of the Covenant to Zion then the entire hill became sacred (II Samuel 6:10-12). When King Solomon moved the Ark to the temple near Mount Moriah the name was extended to include all of Jerusalem (II Kings 19:21; Psalm 48; 69:35; 133:3; Isaiah 1:8). It was later used figuratively for the Jewish church and polity-a form of government of a religious denomination (Psalm 126:1; 129:5; Isaiah 33:14; 34:8; 49:14; 52:8) and our scripture texts portrays Zion as the entire nation of Israel and heaven as some refer to Zion as the City of God in the age to come.

It is noteworthy to say that Israel is figuratively known as God's people-all believers; therefore to reside in God's dwelling place is heavenly by itself because where God is all believers will dwell with Him one day.

What does it mean to dwell in Zion? It means that all believers have had their robes washed in the blood of Jesus and have persevered in faith unto the end. Zion dwellers have presented themselves faultless before the righteous judge-Jesus Christ who redeemed all believers from the clutches of sin as all believers died to sin with Christ and rose with Him to a life of righteousness. Another meaning to living in Zion is that all believers are the grain harvested crop of the Lord-harvested unto salvation. Living in Zion also means that believers will shine bright as the morning sun as each will bask in the glory and brightness of God. Living in the Zion there will be no more sorrow, pain and suffering, no more tears, no more dying, no more crying as all will be immortalized for ever as all Zion residents will have eaten from the tree of live. Living in Zion means our Shalom/peace is restored. Residents of Zion have golden slippers to wear, a white robe and a crown of live just waiting for each believer upon arrival. Living in Zion means that all believers will be in the constant presence of God our creator, Jesus Christ our redeemer and Savior, the Holy Spirit our keeper.

Zion dwelling is a place for the redeemed where joy reigns supreme. What a dwelling place!

Nov 7

Witnessing For The Lord: Isaiah 55:4-5

Behold, I have given him for a witness to the people, a leader and commander to the people. Behold, thou shall call a nation that thou knoweth not, and nations that knew not thee shall run unto thee because the Lord thy God, and for the Holy One of Israel; for he hath glorified thee.

What are these verses saying? A case can be made that the meaning of these verses is that God the Father gave His Son Jesus Christ as a witness unto Him and as the final revelation of Him. It is well documented in the New Testament during Jesus' earthly ministry that He made it known that He was doing the will of His Father-God. He was sent by God to preach repentance for the kingdom of God was at hand. Christ's earthly ministry is the highest form of kingdom witnessing recorded.

Who did Christ witness to? He preached to all who would hear and repent unto salvation. He publically stated that He came to seek and save the lost. In essence Christ witnessed to the lost souls of the world. The question becomes, Who must we witness to? Believers are to witness to the lost souls just as Christ did. The nations that knoweth not are the lost souls, and those are the nations that will adhere to believers proclaiming the gospel message and repent because of the convicting works of the Holy Spirit.

Regarding the phrase "a leader and commander to the people" represents that Jesus Christ is our Commander-in-Chief of God's army in this spiritual warfare. Christ promised to be with us during our witnessing unto the end of the earth.

Witness! Witness! Witness because there are many waiting to hear the word.

The Great Invitation: Isaiah 55:1

Ho, every one that thirsteth, come ye to the waters, and he that hath no money; come ye, buy, and eat; yea, come, buy wine and milk without money and without price.

Why this scripture is considered the Great Invitation? Well, let's look at what is being said, it is all inclusive and carries a prerequisite of a genuine spiritual hunger and thirst for forgiveness and a restored right relationship with God. This equates to salvation through Jesus Christ. See, sin broke our right standing with God and our redeemer is Jesus Christ as He paid our sin debt on Calvary's cross. Jesus Christ is the living water and bread and all who eat and drink of Him will thirst and hunger no more.

Another point of fact in our lesson text is that our money is no good with God as we cannot purchase our salvation. Our account has been stamped PAID IN FULL. Why, because Jesus paid it all on Calvary. See, our salvation invitation is free to us, but it cost God the Father His Son and Jesus Christ His life all for the purpose of restoring a broken fellowship between God and man. This invitation remains open to all throughout the ages as it is God's desire that all be saved and sit at His heavenly feast table and enjoy the goodness of His presence and glory. Only the true and living God would make such an invitation.

The greatest invitation one can receive. Accept and be saved.

Nov 9

The Great Commission: Matthew 29:18-20

...Jesus came and spake unto them, saying, All power is given unto me in heaven and in earth. Go ye therefore, an teach all nations, baptizing them in the name of the Father, and of the Son, and of the Holy Ghost: Teaching them to observe all things whatsoever I have commanded you: and lo, I am with you always, even unto the end of the world.

Why these scriptures are considered the Great Commission? First, these are the words Christ Himself gave to His disciples and all followers for generations to come. These verses explain Christ church's goal, responsibilities in its missionary task, which is to make coverts through spreading His gospel message. Second, the church is to preach the gospel of Christ to all nations according to the New Testament revelations of Him and the apostles' eye-witness accounts. Third, preaching the gospel centered on repentance and the forgiveness of sin as Christ Himself has paid our sin debt. Fourth, we are commissioned to make disciples, not just converts who will in turn make other disciples. Fifth, we are to preach and teach Christ to all lost souls as this is a mandate from Christ Himself. Six, all who believe in Christ are to be baptized with water as a symbol of the covenant pledge to live in obedience to God. Seven, Christ promised to be with His followers to the ends of the world through the presence of the Holy Spirit.

As followers of Christ obedience to the Great Commission is essential to our Christian walk.

Obey and serve.

Nov 10

Reap Eternal Life: Galatians 6:7-10

Be not deceived; God is not mocked; for whatsoever a main soweth, that shall he also reap. For he that soweth to his flesh shall of the flesh reap corruption; but he that soweth to the Spirit shall of the Spirit reap life everlasting.

I have always heard and been taught from a little girl that you reap what you sow; the meaning was explained to me that if you do good then good will come back to you, but on the other hand if you do evil to someone then it too will come back to you. Whether you do good or evil when reaping time come it will be double; therefore, the message behind this saying was it is prudent to do good all the time. Another saying that parallels this saying is treat people like you want to be treated.

With that being said, our lesson text is the basic for my childhood teaching in that we cannot fool God by professing to be a Christian and continue living in sin. Those who attempt to fool God will surely reap a life of eternal separation from Him at harvest time whereas those who live according to His righteousness will reap the harvest of eternal life.

Let's close today's discussion with this thought provoking question, Why would anyone try to fool (mock) God who sees all, knows all and is in all? My advice, don't live a lie; God knew each of us before there was a when or where.

Sowing into the Spirit equals a harvest of eternal life.

Nov 11

A Mind Transformation: Romans 12:2

And be not conformed to this world; but be ye transformed by the renewing of your mind, that ye may prove what is that good, and acceptable, and perfect will of God.

What is Paul saying to believers everywhere? Paul is encouraging all believers both then and now to resist the temptations of this world as it is hostile to God and His people. This world is built on human wisdom and values as they too are contrary to God's standards and wisdom. This world sports an unbiblical view of things which is filled with darkness, deception, corruption, humanistic thinking, political maneuvering for power, lust, greed, ungodly entertainment and all things naughty, whereas God's view of things is truth and light.

While Paul points out all the negatives of this world he also provides positives of having a transformed mind which leads to a transformed life one in Christ and His Word so that our views and everyday thinking is governed by the Holy Spirit. A transformed life is one that causes all believers to live to please God and manifest His goodness as believers conforms to His likeness. With that being said, having a transformed mind believers embrace God's will and His ways as the best way of life. It is noteworthy to say that a transformed mind seeks to do the will of God. Also, believers are called to a higher calling which requires spiritual separation.

Be ye transformed, but never confirm to this world.

Believe Unto Salvation: Romans 10:9-10

Thou if thou shalt confess with thy mouth the Lord Jesus, and shalt believe in thine heart that God hath raised him from the dead, thou shalt be saved. For with the heart man believeth unto righteousness; and with the mouth confession is made unto salvation.

In yesterday's discussion we discussed the pros and cons of having a transformed mind which leads one to a life of righteousness. In today's discussion the theme is continued in that our focus is on believing unto salvation. The first step to salvation is admitting that we are sinners and in need of saving while acknowledging that we lack the ability to save ourselves. Next we must confess that Jesus Christ is Lord who died for our sins and that God raised Him from the dead. Once this is believed we are saved. Everything begins in the heart as it is the epicenter of all thoughts, feelings and desires; our thoughts resonate into actions. The heart is the inner being or whole person as it is essential for believing which comes from the heart.

Make note here that our belief is our faith which is vital to all believers' salvation in Jesus Christ. Also, faith is a required component in salvation because it requires placing our complete trust in Jesus Christ. God's grace is at work in the process because it was His grace and mercy that resulted in Him giving His best for man's eternal destiny.

Let's close today's discussion by asking, How is salvation possible without believing? ***It is impossible; so believe.***

Believe Thou Art The Christ: John 11:27

She said unto Him, Yea, Lord; I believe that thou art the Christ, the Son of God, which should come into the world.

The setting for today's topical discussion take place in Bethany where three of Jesus' good friends lived, and the brother of Mary and Martha had died. Jesus tarried where He was to demonstrate His deity in order to express two points, (a) that He was God in the flesh, and (b) that all who accept Him as Savior and live with and in Him even though they may die will live again with Him in heaven.

Verses 25-26 supports these findings; when Jesus made this statement "I am the resurrection and the life" expresses the fact that all who die in Christ, then physical death is not a tragic end, but the beginning of a new life in eternity. The "shall" in verse 25 is His guarantee of what will happen. What we know that is God cannot lie and He keeps His promises. The phrase "shall never die" in verse 26 is another assured promised that all believers can trust God with confidence.

Given the conversation between Martha and Jesus and her profound statement the questions that come to mind is, Did Martha really understand that He was really the Christ, the promised Messiah, God in the flesh? Did Martha really understand that Jesus was and is the resurrection of life? Did the Holy Spirit reveal to Martha that Jesus was in fact the Christ? Would we have believed that Jesus was the Christ who came to save the world of its sins? Lastly, today do we believe that Jesus is the Christ? If so, are we willing to trust Him with our lives?

Allow me to answer the last two questions by saying yes Jesus is the Christ, the Son of God and the Savior of the world. Again, yes we should trust Him with our lives given all that He has done for all humanity only if you believe-salvation is your.

What other profound facts that we can believed about Christ? He is the living water and bread and all who eat and drink of Him shall never thirst again. Christ is the only one who was raised from the dead with all power in His hands both in heaven and earth. Christ is the Word of God as well as the light of the world that shines to dispel the darkness of man's heart. Yes, Christ was in the beginning with God and the world was formed by Him. Christ is the head of His church and He is coming back for His church-His bride. Will you be in the marriage to the groom-Jesus? If you believe that He is the Christ, then yes you will be in the marriage.

Jesus is the Christ and there is no other.

Nov 14

Repent, Believe The Gospel: Mark 1:15

...The time is fulfilled, and the kingdom of God is at hand: repent ye, and believe the gospel.

In our lesson study we will focus on repentance as it relates to turning from a life separated from God to one with Him. The first step to becoming a Christian is repentance in doing so each person follows these steps, (1) admit that I am a sinner, (2) confess his or her sins, and (3) accept Jesus Christ as Lord and Savior and His atoning works on Calvary's cross. No one becomes a follower of Christ without repenting his or her sins.

What gospel was Christ preaching during His earthly ministry in asking His hearers to repent for the kingdom of God was at hand? It carries several lessons, which are (1) the kingdom in Israel was God's redemptive action within Israel preparing the way for salvation of the human race. (2) The kingdom in Christ were its power which were present in Christ Himself and the work that He did (Luke 11:20). (3) The kingdom as it relates to the church is that the manifestation of God's power and rule takes place in the hearts and lives of all who repent and believe the gospel (John 3:3,5; Romans 14:17; Colossians 1:13). (4) The kingdom of God in its presence came with great spiritual powers to assert itself against Satan and his evil deeds. Christ followers are equipped to fight Satan on his turf-this world. (5) The kingdom in the consummation in this Messianic kingdom that was foretold by the prophets (Psalm 89:36-37; Isaiah 11:1-9; Daniel 7:13-14). When Christ returns to reign in His kingdom the church will be with Him. Lastly (6) the kingdom of God as it relates to eternity will come into existence after the termination of the Messianic kingdom then God's eternal kingdom will be established in the new heaven and new earth (Revelation 21:1-4), Jerusalem-the Holy City.

Repentance carries bountiful blessings.

Nov 15

Pray For The Unsaved: John 17:20

Neither pray I for these alone, but for them also which shall believe on me through their words.

Our lesson scripture text makes a profound declaration as to why we who are saved and are proclaiming the gospel of Christ should not only pray for self but for the unsaved that they will hear the gospel and upon hearing gospel come to Jesus and accept Him as their Lord and Savior. *What power in proclaiming the gospel of Christ! Yes there is power in prayer; Holy Ghost saving power!*

We are to pray for our saved sisters and brothers as we all sometimes become weary on this Christian journey simply because Satan's body blows can become overwhelming, but thank God for His armour. Our prayers keep us in communication with the Father as we make intercessory prayers for others.

Another underline factor in this message is faith as it is at work from the prayer's perspective and the one being prayed for. The prayer has to believe in his or her prayers as well as the gospel message being proclaimed while the hearer must believe as well.

As we continue proclaiming the gospel of Christ to lost souls we must have confidence because Christ is present as promised through the Holy Spirit; He will and is convicting hearts. Just as the Holy Spirit was at work on the Day of Pentecost He remain so today as the gospel is proclaimed.

Pray, proclaim; lost souls are coming to Christ.

New Creatures In Christ: 2 Corinthians 5:17

Therefore, if any man be in Christ, he is a new creature; old things are past away; behold, all things are become new.

In yesterday's discussion we discussed the unsaved believing in Christ as the result of believers proclaiming the gospel of Christ. Today's discussion is a continuation by focusing on those persons who have come out of darkness into the light of Christ and become new creatures in Christ. Again faith is on display as new believers join the body of Christ as those persons have accepted Christ and His atoning work and been made totally new in the spirit realm. They are no longer enemies of God and Satan can no longer blind the person with his lies as the truth of God and His glory has pricked the hearts of the new converts.

The new creatures take on the image of God and begin to grow in the knowledge and likeness of Him. New creatures in Christ begin to tell others about the goodness of God and how He delivered them from eternal damnation to everlasting life. *What a deliverance!*

One final note on becoming new creatures in Christ is that the old man has become passé and has taken on a life of holiness as things are seen and done from God's perspective. Given all that the Godhead has done and continues to do in the life of humanity shouldn't mankind live in Him?

There is no life like a life in Christ. Join Him and live life to the fullness.

Nov 17

Members Of The Faith Community: Mark 1:1-8

The beginning of the gospel of Jesus Christ, the Son of God...And there went out unto Him all the land of Judea, and they of Jerusalem, and were all baptized of Him in the river of Jordan, confessing their sins.

A bit of background on our topical discussion is that John and Jesus were cousins and John the Baptist came before Jesus preaching repentance. John was preparing the way-the hearts of men asking them of confess their sins and he would baptize with water. Water baptism is symbolic of what has occurred in the believer's heart. This was because the promised Messiah would follow John who would baptize all believers with the Holy Ghost.

If the question were raised, What does it mean for believers becoming members of the Faith Community? Becoming members of the Faith Community has several meaning all of which mean the acceptance of Jesus Christ as ones personal Savior. Therefore, the believer is no longer living in the darkness of sin bound by Satan's dominion. Also, the person has heard the preaching of the gospel of Christ and with the convicting work of the Holy Spirit has repented and has joined God's family and become children of the light. Lastly, believers have a future hope of spending eternity with God.

It is noteworthy to say that as the Faith Community grows so does the kingdom of God. This growth is the result of preaching and teaching repentance and the hearer believing.

Which community do you belong? Faith Community is best.

Nov 18

New Values In The Faith Community: Matthew 5:1-16

And he opened his mouth, and taught them; saying, Blessed are the poor in spirit; for theirs is the kingdom of heaven. Blessed are they that mourn for they shall be comforted.

Today's lesson text is commonly known as the Beatitudes or the Sermon on the Mount. Jesus preached God's principles of righteousness which all Christians are to live by in faith in God's Son (Galatians 2:20). Believers can accomplish this task with the help of the indwelling Holy Spirit. Members in the Faith Community have a new value system.

Let us look at the believer's new value system after repenting, and they are (a) first, the term "blessed" is happiness or well-being because of the believer's relationship with God through Jesus Christ where believers experience God's love, care, salvation and daily presence. Second, believers are guided by God's principles as outlined in scripture as oppose to those of the world. (b) To mourn is to grieve over our own weakness compared to God's righteous standards. Believers also grieve over the sins of this world. (c) Meek referrers to a humble and submissive spirit as all believers are to submit to God as believers are no match for Satan. (d) Hunger and thirst after righteousness is that believers no longer have the desires of this world. (e) Being merciful is having compassion as God had compassion on humanity. (f) The "pure in heart' aspect is that all believers have been delivered from sin's powers through the God's grace. (g) Believers are peacemakers because all believers have been reconciled back to God and are no longer enemy with Him and seek to live as peacemakers. (h) Lastly, believers will be persecuted for living in harmony with God and His right standing.

God's value system is everlasting.

Nov 19

Proclaim The Good News: Matthew 3:4-10

Then went out to him Jerusalem, and all Judea, and all the region round about Jordan, And were baptized of him in Jordan, confessing their sins.

It is well documented how John the Baptist preached repentance and water baptism. Today's lesson setting is highlighting the results of John's preaching as many came from far and near to be baptized in the Jordan River.

Our scripture text is evidence of what will and can happen when the gospel is preached and preached with such conviction that Satan and his workers cannot stop lost souls from coming to be saved. There is power in the gospel message as well as in the name of Jesus Christ; the one who died for humanity's sins, and then rose from the dead for our justification with all power both on earth and in heaven in His hands.

While proclaiming the gospel should we be afraid? No, because Christ is presence as promised through the Holy Spirit. Also, believers are commissioned to proclaim the gospel the world over. Proclaiming the gospel of Christ, we as believers are seasoning the earth/world with the salt of God's Word. If the gospel is not proclaimed, then this world would be in total chaos. Therefore, proclaim the gospel for it is taking root as the fruit is more converts are joining the Faith Community believing that Christ is the Savior who can save anybody.

Preach! Preach! Preach the word!

Point Others To Christ: Matthew 3:11-19

I indeed baptize you with water unto repentance; but he that cometh after me is mightier than I, whose shoe I am not worthy to bear; he shall baptize you with the Holy Ghost, and with fire.

John the Baptist provides a perfect example of pointing others to Christ, in that he preached repentance as he would baptize all who came with water. John made it perfectly clear that he was not the promised Messiah (v 11) and he was preparing the way for the Christ who would then baptize all believers with the Holy Spirit. John's dedication and commitment to preaching repentance is evidenced by him standing firm in the face of opposition (3:7). See some of John's opposers did not believe what John was preaching. These were Jewish religious groups who believed the Old Testament as they adhered to the OT and their human interpretations of the OT. The Sadducees rejected the teachings/doctrines of resurrection, angels, miracles, immorality and the coming judgment. Jesus did not come to destroy the law but to fulfill the law.

The question now becomes, What must we do today when faced different doctrines? Believers today must do just as John did he stood firm on the doctrine of Jesus Christ and that He is the Son of God. The truth about John's doctrine/preaching was authenticated when all members of the Godhead presented themselves at Jesus' baptism in the Jordan River (v. 17).

It is very important for believers to know the truth about God's Word (2 Timothy 2:15) and knowing God's Word come by studying and meditating on His Word. Upon learning the truth about God's Word we then can point others to Christ as we have the indwelling Holy Spirit who empowers us to boldly witness Christ the world over (Acts 1:8). Another point to knowing the scripture it is the holy inspired Word of God and its purpose is for reproof, correction and instructions in righteousness (2 Timothy 3:16-17) so that all who proclaim the gospel will be perfect in his or her works (v. 17).

How must we point others to Christ? This is accomplished

through our witnessing Christ in both word and lifestyles. Living holy lives before men then the world can and will see Christ in us. It goes without saying that the believer's lifestyle may be the only Bible others are reading. Therefore, it behooves all believers to live according to God's righteousness. Pointing others to Christ believers are compiling a positive service record as it will one day be read and believers will have to give an account for what was done while in this world. With that being said, these questions come to mind, Are you pointing others to Christ? Does your lifestyle reflect Christ?

Bringing others to Christ we build His kingdom.

Believers Empowered To Witness: Acts 1:8

But ye shall receive power, after that the Holy Ghost is come upon you; and ye shall be witnesses unto me both in Jerusalem, and in all Judea, and in Samaria, and unto the uttermost part of the earth.

  Christ gave His followers a commission which is to witness Him the world over. Christ did not nor would He send His followers into a world laden with sin without power to be effective and successful. What did Christ do? He said, "I will empower you with the Holy Spirit who will be with you to the ends of the earth." Believers cannot witness absent of the indwelling Holy Spirit. This is because Satan and his warriors are simply too powerful. There is no need for believers to fear because the God in us is greater than the god-Satan in this world.

  During Christ's earthly ministry He performed many miracles such as healing the sick, casting out demons and He proclaimed that the kingdom of God was at hand. Therefore, He empowered His followers to continue His ministry of witnessing to the lost so they too can come to know Christ; to love, obey and praise Him. This adds to God's kingdom. The Holy Spirit is at work while the believer is witnessing to the unsaved in that He is making real Christ's atoning work at Calvary.

  Believers, you are not alone while on your witnessing mission. You are empowered with the Holy Spirit to boldly witness Christ as never before.

  Witness! Witness! Witness!

Nov 22

Servants Of God: 1 Peter 2:11-25

Having your conversation honest among the Gentiles; that, whereas they speak against you as evildoers, they may by your good works, which they shall behold, glorify God in the day of visitation...As free, and not using your liberty for a cloke of maliciousness, but as the servant of God.

Our lesson focus is on Christian submission to God as all believers have been called out of darkness into the light of Christ and have been set aside as a royal priesthood, a holy nation for the purpose of doing the will of God. Being that believers are a set aside people, then our conversation must be godly so that it will glorify God our Father and Creator. Also, believers are not to live as the world does because of our sanctification by Christ even though we as believers remain in this world we are not to conform to this world and its systems, which are contrary to God. With that being said, believers are servants of God as He is our Lord and Master; therefore, all believers are to humbly submit to God's ways as believers have been made right with God through Jesus' shed blood.

The importance of being servants of God is that believers are sanctified for God and His kingdom to proclaim the gospel of salvation to His glory. Jesus Christ is our perfect example of being a servant of God as Christ humbly served according to the will of His Father God until the end, and is still serving at the right hand of God on behalf of all believers.

True servant is serving others.

Nov 23

Believers Are Sons Of God: 1 John 3:1

Behold, what manner of love the Father hath bestowed upon us, that we should be called the sons of God; therefore the world knoweth us not, because it knew him not.

For our lesson study today, let's answer John's question as asked in the text, first only God could love to the magnitude that He gave His only Son Jesus to die for the sins of the world. God did what He did so that all who believe and accept Christ as his or her personal Savior will become God's children. This makes all believers sons and daughters of God the Father. **What a royal family to belong?**

Second, being adopted into God's family through Christ Jesus is the highest honor and privilege of our salvation (Ephesians 1:5; John 1; 12; Galatians 4:7). Believers then become God's property as believers have God's identifying mark of the Holy Spirit. God wants believers to become aware that we are His children through the Spirit of Adoption (Romans 8:15). This gives believers the desire to be led by the Holy Spirit (Romans 8:14) and cry Abba, Father (Galatians 4:6) which gives believers the feeling of belonging. Abba is an Aramaic term meaning Father.

Third, our trust, faith and our future hope is the basic for believers becoming a child of God (Matthew 6:25-34). Being a child of God believers become heirs of God and co-heirs with Christ (Romans 8:16-17; Galatians 4:7).

Fourth, as children of God we are disciplined by Him because we belong to Him as any good parent disciplines his children (Hebrews 12:6-7, 11).

Lastly, God's goal is for believers to be saved forever as it is His desire that all be saved (John 3:16) and conformed to the likeness of His Son Jesus Christ (Romans 8:29).

Believers, we are blessed.

Nov 24

Commit Thy Works To God: Proverbs 16:3

Commit thy works unto the Lord, and thy thoughts shall be established.

If the question were raised, Why would King Solomon encourage us to commit our works unto the Lord? Can't we just get approval from man think our own thoughts and everything be alright? Well, I can think of several reasons why we are to commit our works unto the Lord; first, He is the supreme ruler, creator and sustainer as He is the essence of our lives from beginning to end. Furthermore, scripture encourages us to always trust and acknowledge God and allow Him to direct our paths (3:6). If we want God to bless us in our endeavors then we must seek Him first. With that being said, then everything we do should be to His glory and honor.

Second, His thoughts and ways are much higher than those of man. Psalm 37:5 states, "Commit thy way unto the Lord; trust Him; and he shall bring it to pass." If we want our endeavors to be successful then the motive behind our works must be right; then we must commit it to God while trusting Him. God does not bless wrong motives and self-righteous endeavors. God has given each of us an assigned task, but how we receive the task depends on our relationship with God; Him first and me second.

We can conclude then that committing our works to God is a good thing as we are emulating Christ because all He did was to please the Father; so should we.

Let your works glorify God.

Nov 25

Faith Counted As Righteous: Romans 4:5

But to him that worketh not, but believeth on Him that justifieth the ungodly, his faith is counted for righteousness.

Faith has been defined and written about numerous times and it all comes down to what one believes. However, the term "believe" is trust or confidence or having faith in or to make a commitment to something. According to James 2:19 faith is to simply know. In biblical terms we then have faith in God and have entrusted Him with our eternal lives through His Son Jesus Christ as we live in total obedience to Him.

The question now becomes, What do we know about Jesus and our righteousness? We know that Jesus Christ is God's Son who died on the cross for man's sins and rose for our justification. In justifying the believer Christ gave us a right standing with God the Father. This means that we have been pardon of our sins or declared "not guilty" before a righteous God. This is because "all of our righteousness is as filthy rags before God" (Isaiah 64:6) as we lack the ability to atone for our sins. Therefore, the ungodly being justified is based solely on God and His grace gift that flowed from His nature, love and mercy (v. 16). It is ones faith that is counted as righteous that brings forgiveness through Christ's atoning death (Romans 3:24-26).

Because of our faith we have been made right with God, our sins pardoned and set apart from sin by God to have an intimate fellowship with God and to serve Him in total obedience.

Our faith has made us righteous in God's eyesight.

A Crown Of Life: Revelation 2:2, 10

I know thy works, and thy labour, and thy patience, and how thou canst not bear them which are evil; and thou hast tried them which say they are apostles, and are not, and hast found them liars...Fear none of those things which thou shalt suffer; behold, the devil shall cast some of you into prison, that ye may be tried; and ye shall have tribulation ten days; be thou faithful unto death, and I will give thee a crown of life.

Chapter two of Revelation deals with Christ's message to the seven churches in Asia Minor (Revelation 1:4) issuing exhortation, warnings and edification for throughout the church age (2:7, 11, 17, 29; 3:6, 13, 22). False prophets were among Christ's believers and church and this was a threat to the churches and had caused some to turn from its first love-Christ. Each of these seven churches was at different levels of spirituality.

Therefore, when Christ states that He know "thy works" He does because He is the head of the church and set standards for which the church is to operate. With that being said, our text picks ups with Christ instructing His church to reframe from falling away by tolerating false prophets or teachers and or all who were distorting His Word and thereby becoming weaker and losing some of its authority. Christ instructs His church to test all who claim to have spiritual powers as this would authenticate their true identity. Christ further tells of the reward for all those who persevere in righteousness until the end-*a crown of life.*

Persevere a crown of life is waiting.

Nov 27

Believers Salt And Light: Matthew 5:13-14

Ye are the salt of the earth; but if the salt have lost his savour, wherewith shall it be salted/ it is thenceforth good for nothing, but to be cast out, and to be trodden under foot of men. Ye are the light of the world. A city that is set on a hill cannot be hid.

Jesus is using one of His many parables to teach His audience/disciples regarding believers and their lifestyles as well as the believer's commitment to witnessing to others. Salt is a household commodity that is used to season food and preserve food; therefore, when salt has lost its usefulness it is thrown out.

Let's look at the spirituality of salt as it relates to believers; believers as salt are to season the world by witnessing God's Word the world over. When believers fail to witness then believers are no longer useful as a spiritual seasoning. Also, believers are to use the Word of God as preserve which will keep the believers from becoming corrupt in this world. Believers must defend his or her faith by resisting society's moral decay that existed then and still exist today. When the church and individual believers fall prey to the wickedness of this society then the Holy Spirit's power is quenched and then believers and the church has no powers in which to draw others to Christ. When this happens the world sees believers and the church as one of them. This is the *trodden under foot of men* meaning.

Christ used the same analogy with believers being light, as light dispels darkness wherever it shines. Therefore, believers are the light of the world whose responsibility it is to shine the light of Christ in a sin darkened world. This is accomplished through the believer's lifestyle as it is to authenticate what the believer speaks. Verse 14 also presents an implied question by stating that a city that is sitting on a hill cannot be hidden. This holds true for the church and individuals believers. Christ left His church and individual believers in the world just for such purposes of brining others to Christ.

Therefore, when Christ returns for His church it will be His unblemished bride arrayed in her white dressed for her husband. White represents the holiness of God.

These questions come to mind, Which salt are you? Useful or of no use? Are you part of the city with no lights or the city whose lights are shinning bright? A city that travelers can see miles away?

Believers, we are members of Christ's church and are to season the world with our witnessing while being separated from the moral decay of this society. Our lifestyles are the light spoken of in our text.

Season on and keep your light shinning brightly for Christ.

Call To Repentance: 2 Peter 3:9

The Lord is not slack concerning His promise, as some men count slackness; but is longsuffering to us ward, not willing that any should perish, but that all should come to repentance.

The verb form of call is to invite (Student Bible Dictionary P.55), but for the purpose of our discussion we see call as an invitation from Christ for humanity to become His followers. This invitation has been extended from the ages and remains in effect today so all can be saved. This is the perfect will of God; however, many will refuse the invitation and be lost. The result of those refusing the invitation/call will suffer eternal damnation, but all who accept the call will repent and be saved and will spend eternity with God.

The profound notion by some men who count God's tarrying as Him being slack is making a gross error in judgment. I have often heard people say they have time to come to Christ, when it is well document that no man knoweth the hour when Christ will return, but one thing for sure is that He is coming back again. This question begs an answer, If Christ returns today have you repented? The call is open. He said "come as you are" and He will wash you whiter than snow. Christ died for your sins and mine; therefore, no man can cleanse his or her sins.

Just repent and be saved.

Nov 29

Salvation To All Believers: 1 Peter 1:3-5

Blessed be the God and Father of our Lord Jesus Christ, which according to his abundant mercy hath begotten us again unto a lively hope by the resurrection of Jesus Christ from the dead. To an inheritance incorruptible, and undefiled, and that fadeth not away, reserved in heaven for you. Who are kept by the power of God though faith unto salvation ready to be revealed in the last time.

Today's lesson study expresses the works of God the Father and our Lord and Savior Jesus Christ in providing salvation to all who believe on Him in faith. God's grace and mercy is on display by His act of love that He would give all that He had for all believers to become begotten Sons of God.

What all believers' salvation means is that we have been delivered from the bondage of sin where corruption prevails to a life of righteousness. Also, believers are no longer defiled by sin and have been begotten to receive an inheritance of incorruptible. The believer's inheritance is sure and will last forever as it is currently being reserved for all believers in heaven. *What an assurance of a well kept blessing?*

Only God has the power, love and willingness to provide salvation through His Son Jesus Christ and Christ left the Holy Spirit as the believer's guide and protector while here on earth. The Holy Spirit will guide believers all the way to heaven where believers will meet Jesus face to face.

Salvation is the believer's freedom from sin.

Nov 30

Obedience To God: Romans 5:18-19

Therefore as by the offense of one judgment came upon all men to condemnation; even so by the righteousness of one the free gift came upon all men unto justification of life. For as by one man's disobedience many were made sinners, so by the obedience of one shall many be made righteous.

Our lesson text makes a profound statement regarding man's condemnation as the result of Adam's disobedience to God's command, but through the obedience of Jesus Christ God's Son all men are justified upon the acceptance of Christ. To Reject or accept Jesus Christ as ones personal Savior as reveal in the person's heart and through the written Word is a personal choice and if the decision is rejection then at that time condemnation becomes real; while on the other hand if accepting Jesus as Lord and Savior then justification becomes real and obedience to God becomes a way of life.

With that being said, then justification is being made right (as written earlier) with God through the death and resurrection of Jesus Christ. Also, justification is grounded in the finished work of Jesus Christ as man had no means of making himself right with God as justification comes by the grace of God.

Therefore, given all that God the Father and God the Son-Jesus has done in the redemption process of man then all believers are obligated to obey God and His righteous standards. Christ is our perfect example of obedient living.

Obedience to God brings righteous living.

The Joy Of Christmas

Dec 1

The Promised Messiah: Matthew 1:18-21

Now the birth of Jesus Christ was on this wise: When as his mother Mary was espoused to Joseph, before they came together, she was found with child of the Holy Ghost...And she shall bring forth a son, and thou shalt call his name JESUS; for he shall save his people from their sins.

As we begin the month of December with the climax being the birth of the promised Messiah-Jesus who came into this world to bring salvation to all who believe on Him. What so significant about the birth of Jesus our Lord and Savior is that He was prophesied about many years before His birth became a reality. Prophecy was fulfilled just as promised in Isaiah 7:14 as there were many other prophecies that were fulfilled on Jesus' birth.

Jesus' name mean He is the one who God promised to send some forty-two generations earlier and He would be the Savior of the world. Also, the name Messiah literally means Anointed One or coming Savior. Christ's name means Anointed One. Jesus Christ is God's Son sent from God to be the Savior of the world as He was conceived by a virgin impregnated by the Holy Ghost who is God. God fulfilled His promise.

However you celebrate the birth of Christ let it be with thanksgiving and praises for God clothing Himself in humanity to fulfill all requirements to bring salvation to His people.

Jesus' birth a promise made, a promised fulfilled. Hallelujah!

Immanuel: Isaiah 7:14

Therefore the Lord Himself shall give you a sign; Behold, a virgin shall conceive, and bear a Son, and shall call his name Immanuel.

In yesterday's discussion we discussed the fulfillment of prophecy, but today's our focus is on just what was prophesied by Isaiah many years earlier. The prophet Isaiah prophesied that a virgin would bring forth a child and what His name was going to be-Immanuel. The significance of the virgin birth is that Mary was to be married to her husband Joseph and they had not come together prior to the marriage and did not until after the birth of Christ. The birth of Jesus was a miraculous one in that this was the work of the Holy Spirit and not the act of man. Isaiah's prophecy was very detailed down to the naming of the child authenticating that He was the promised Messiah and His name meant so.

The term "Immanuel" means God with us as supported by scripture texts (Isaiah 7:14; Matthew 1:23). However, the name Immanuel took on a much deeper meaning when God's only Son came into the world (John 3:16) to save the world from its sins. The "whosoever" includes all humanity, but we must believe that He is God's Son our Savior.

Another thought on Immanuel God being with us is that just as Jesus was present during His earthly stay He remains with us in the presence of the Holy Spirit who abides in each believer.

Immanuel God with us then, now and forever.

The Incarnated Christ: John 1:14

And the word was made flesh, and dwelt among us, (and we beheld his glory, the glory as of the only begotten of the Father) full of grace and truth.

What do we understand about the Incarnated Christ? Biblical doctrinal teachings teach that Jesus Christ is the eternal Son of God who became human, but did not diminish His divine nature. Jesus Christ is fully God, the Second Person of the Godhead in bodily form (Colossian 2:9), but at the same time He was fully man. With being said, Jesus Christ who being the eternal Son of God became man and continued to be both God and man, in two distinct natures and one Person forever.

Christians are encouraged to understand two facts about Christ and they are, "the importance of the unity that exits in Christ in that His personality means that He was, in Himself, in His ego, the nonmaterial self, the same numerical identity, the same person who was God and with God "in the beginning" before the created universe, is the same person who sat wearily at the well at Sychar, the same person who said, "Father forgive them," on the cross. Second, the distinction of His natures means, and has always meant to the church, that Jesus is just as truly God as the Father and the Spirit are God, and at the same time without confusion or contradiction. He is just as truly man as we are men. (His humanity as the "last Adam" is perfect sinless, yet genuinely human as was Adam before the fall" (Zondervan's Pictorial Bible Dictionary P.373).

The Incarnated Christ is God in the flesh.

The Virgin Birth: Matthew 1:22-25

Now all this was done, that it might be fulfilled which was spoken of the Lord by the prophet, saying, Behold a virgin shall be with child, and shall bring forth a son, and they shall call his name Emmanuel, which being interpreted is, God with us.

What is the importance of Jesus' virgin birth? First, prophecy had been fulfilled just as God the Father had promised a Savior. Second, the Savior of the world had to meet certain requirements in order for His shed blood to atone for the sins of the world. To atone the world's sins once and for all, our redeemer had to be sinless, one person who was fully human and divine at the same time (Hebrews 7:25-26). Therefore, Jesus' birth had to be conceived of a virgin and have God as His Father. Also, the mother Mary had to be without any previous sexual intercourse; this represents purity as God is pure and holy.

The third importance of the virgin birth is that it met all God's requirements and they are: (a) to be become human Jesus had to be born of a woman. (b) To be sinless Jesus had to have God as His Father and be conceived by the Holy Spirit who is God. (c) For Jesus to be divine God had to be His Father. Therefore, Luke 1:35 state it this way, "that holy thing which shall be born of thee shall be called the Son of God." what Jesus' virgin birth revealed to humanity is one divine person with two natures-divine and human.

The fourth importance of Jesus' virgin birth is that being the Son of God He has the power to deliver us from the bondage of sin (Acts 26:18; Colossians 2:15; Hebrews 2:14; 7:25).

The fifth importance of Jesus' virgin birth, Him being God in the flesh renders Him qualified to be the sacrificial lamb of atoning all sins and to serve as our high priest interceding for all who come to God in faith (Hebrews 2:9-18; 5:1-9; 7:24-28; 10:4-12).

Now that we have discussed the importance of the Jesus' virgin birth, we can say that it paved the way for salvation because He is God in the Second Person. With that being said, without His birth there would be no death on Calvary's cross and certainly no resurrection. Without the birth, death and resurrection there would be no hope of salvation and or expectation of living eternally with God, but glory be to God in His divine love He made provisions for man's salvation and the plan of salvation was in place from the foundation of the world because God knew man would sin and Jesus His Son would have to atone sin. With that being said, Jesus' virgin birth wasn't an after thought, but part of God's divine plan.

Jesus' virgin birth was an essential part in the grand scheme of things.

The Anointed One: Acts 10:38; Luke 4:18

How God anointed Jesus of Nazareth with the Holy Ghost and with power; who went about doing good, and healing all that were oppressed of the devil; for God was with Him (10:38). The Spirit of the Lord is upon me, because He hath anointed me to preach the gospel to the poor; He hath sent me to heal the broken hearted, to preach deliverance to the captives, and recovering of sight to the blind, to set at liberty them that are bruised (4:18).

These scriptures verses make it clear that Jesus Christ is the Anointed One from God the Father and what His mission was while here on earth.

If the question were raised, Why Jesus had to rely on the Holy Spirit being that He is God? Yes Jesus is God, but He was also human and while here on earth (I Timothy 2:5) Jesus had to rely on the Holy Spirit's power to successfully complete His mission. Jesus as God-man He live, served and proclaimed the gospel as assigned by God the Father (Acts 10:38).

Luke 4:18 gives the details of Jesus' earthly ministry, which were (a) preach to the poor, the destitute, the afflicted, the humble, those whose spirit were crushed, those who were brokenhearted, and those who gave reverence to His word. (b) Reflect on who Jesus ministered to or healed some physical diseases in order to heal their spiritual disease. Jesus healed the whole person. For example, Jesus opened physical blinded eyes to open the person's spiritual eyes so the person could see the need for salvation.

Jesus-the Anointed One!

Dec 6

The Righteous Lamb Of God: John 1:29

The next day John seeth Jesus coming unto him, and saith, Behold the Lamb of God, which taketh away the sin of the world.

In today's lesson study we fast forward to John who is the forerunner of Jesus and John recognizing Jesus as the Lamb of God and what Jesus' ministry was as well as Him being the Savior of the world. Jesus is the righteous Lamb of God as He was slain from the foundation of the world to be the human sacrifice for the world's sins.

Jesus is the Righteous Lamb of God simply because He is God who was in the beginning with God as the Word and the Word was with God as all things was made by Him (John 1:1;3).

Jesus came to earth preaching repentance for the kingdom of heaven was at hand because God's kingdom was wrapped up in Him because He is God in the Second Person of the Godhead. Therefore, Jesus came to die to take away the guilt and power of sin and provide a way back to God as He is the only way back to God the Father. Jesus Christ is our bridge that connects man and God through His righteousness.

Given all that Jesus done for humanity, with your spiritual eye do you recognize Him as the Righteous Lam of God? John did as he saw Jesus with his physical and spiritual eyes this is what caused John to say, "Behold the Lamb of God is coming to take away the sins of the world" (v. 29).

He is worthy of our recognition.

Dec 7

Salvation: Isaiah 12:2

Behold, God is my salvation; I will trust, and not be afraid; for the Lord JEHOVAH is my strength and my song; He also is become my salvation.

In the study of salvation much have been written and discussed about salvation, but salvation is the deliverance from harm or danger or to bring one safely through.

With that being said our lesson text outlines why God is our salvation and deliverer. Isaiah like others who recognize who God is and His supreme powers is adequate for all our trust and confidence and there is no need for fear as we are encouraged in 1 Peter 5:7 to cast all our cares upon the Lord.

Throughout the Old Testament God has revealed Himself as the deliverer for His people (Psalm27:1; 88:1). Salvation is a gift of God's grace that He freely gives through His Son Jesus Christ (Romans 3:24); it is based on Christ's death burial and resurrection (Romans 3:25; 5:8; 5:10) and Christ's continued intercession for believers (Hebrews 7:25). Believers receive salvation through faith in Jesus Christ.

There are three stages of salvation and each carries its own significance in the lives of believers. In the past stage believers receives forgiveness of sin as a free gift from God, when justice demanded punishment. In the present stage salvation gives all believers a on-to-one relationship with God as salvation saves us from the bondage and power of sin. Lastly, the future stage of salvation it saves believers from the oncoming wrath of God.

Salvation is God's free gift accept it and live forever.

Dec 8

Manger: Luke 2:7

And she brought forth her firstborn son, and wrapped him in swaddling clothes, and laid him in a manger; because there was no room for them in the inn.

Reflecting on the birth of our Lord and Savior Jesus Christ and the humble way He made His entrance into the world. The birth of Christ is the greatest event that has occurred in our history and it was done in such humble fashion which gives all believers the spirit of humility as Jesus is our perfect example of humility. Jesus as King of Kings and Lord of Lords and being born in the animals' stable makes a profound statement of humility. All God's people are kings and priests and we are to live lives of humility as we have the right view of God, self and others.

If the question were raise, Why was Jesus born in a manger? One could say that because of society and its outlook on life there were no time or available rooms in the inn for our Lord to be born as everyone during this time of the year was primarily concerned with life's temporal enjoyments. Also, one could say that being born in a stable was part of God's divine plan as nothing happens outside of God's control. Then one could ask the question, Was being born in a stable part of prophecy? Probably, but regardless of the answer what we know for certain is that Christ's birth was carried out as plan. Therefore, being born in a stable and being laid in a manger did not render Christ from being God.

Manger the earthly bed of our Savior!

Dec 9

Shepherds: Luke 2:8-10

And there were in the same country shepherds abiding in the field, keeping watch over their flock by night. And lo, the angel of the Lord came upon them, and the glory of the Lord shone round about them; and they were sore afraid. And the angel said unto them, Fear not: for behold, I bring you good tidings of great joy, which shall be to all people.

From yesterday's study of the baby Jesus' birth to today's discussion where we see angels of the Lord notifying the shepherds of the good news. The joy of Jesus' birth and His mission here on earth were to be for all people.

The shepherds abiding in the fields tending their sheep and behold there came this grand announcement from God's angels was enough to frighten these men. The angels calmed the fears of these men by telling them what was happening in Jerusalem. It appears that all believers during this time and the heavenly angels welcomed the birth of God's Son so much so that spontaneous worship and praise began (v. 13). Jesus' birth had been much anticipated by all who believed so when the news of His birth came there was great joy by the angels and shepherds even the heavenly host joined in the praise and worship of this great event (vv. 13-14).

The joyful shepherds left their sheep and traveled to where the baby Jesus and His mother were to see God's promised of a Savior fulfilled.

What a glorious event to witness, the birth of our Savior.

Dec 10

Heavenly Host: Luke 2:13-14

And suddenly there was with the angles a multitude of the heavenly host praising God, and saying, Glory to God in the highest, and on earth peace, good will towards men.

Scripture has it that when baby Jesus was born there were praise and worship by the angels of the Lord, the shepherds abiding in the fields and they too were joined by the heavenly host singing praises to God because He had brought peace to this earth for all who would believe on Him.

If all heaven and its host can offer praise and worship to God for the birth of His Son Jesus our Savior what about you and I? He is worthy of all praises because He is our Savior, our high priest, and most importantly He is God's Son. Jesus is worthy of being first in our lives. Just as the shepherds made the sacrifice to travel to see the baby Jesus; believers today are encouraged to make similar sacrifices to worship Jesus on Christmas morning as a memorial to His holy birth and the sacrifices He made for the entire human race-**providing salvation**.

These questions come to mind, How will you praise our Lord and Savior this Christmas and the entire holiday season? What gift will you give to honor our Lord? Remember Jesus Christ was born to die in order to bring salvation to all who believe in Him and accept Him as our personal Savior?

Join the heavenly host in praising God.

Dec 11

Christ The Savior: Luke 2:11

For unto you is born this day in the city of David a Savior, which is Christ the Lord.

Today's lesson study bring to a close previous discussion on the birth of Jesus Christ our Lord and Savior as His prophesied birth had been fulfilled just as predicted and the shepherds abiding in the field tending their sheep and the angels of the Lord announced to them of Christ's birth in Bethlehem. The shepherds were told by the angels why they were making such announcement and then worshipping the new born king began with the heavenly host joining the service.

If there were any wonderment of why all the praise and worship, verse 11 provides the answer by saying "*for unto you is born this day in the City of David a Savior, which is Christ the Lord.*" Yes, He is worthy of all praises because of His birth peace came to earth. Jesus' birth as our Savior was so that He could free mankind from the bondage of sin, it condemnation of man's transgressions. For mankind to have freedom from sin all men must believe in Him as Lord and Savior. Jesus as our Savior He was anointed by God Himself as the Messiah and Lord to rule over His people (Matthew 1:1). It is noteworthy to mention that no one can have Jesus as his or her Lord without submitting to Him as such.

These questions beg personal self-evaluating answers, Who is Jesus to you? Is He the promised Messiah? Is He Lord of your life? Have I totally committed myself to Jesus? How will I celebrate His holy birth? Do I understand the magnitude of His birth and that He came into the world to die for my (our) sins so that I (we) may have eternal life through faith in Him? Aren't you glad that Jesus Christ limited Himself to human limitations to become our Savior by become the human sacrifice as we lacked the ability to pay our sin-debt? Only Christ's blood was found worthy to be shed for all mankind.

Given the fact that Jesus Christ God's only Son who is God willingly did what He did because of love for the human race and to restore a broken fellowship, What is our response of gratitude? Can we and will we join the heavenly host and the angels in singing praises to our Lord and Savior Jesus Christ? Will we shout glory hallelujah to God for His Son Jesus Christ who was humbly born in a stable and wrapped in swaddling clothes all just for men? Praises should be on-going as Christ the Savior is born.

Hallelujah! Hallelujah! Praise God in the highest!

Dec 12

Joy To The World: Matthew 2:10

When they saw the star, they rejoiced with exceeding great joy.

When God does something He does with grandeur that there is no mistaking His message. I make this claim because the writer Matthew presents Jesus' birth (2:1-10) with the wise men asking, "Where is he that is born King of the Jews? For we have seen his star in the east and are come to worship him." The wise men were the religious learned men of the region and King Herod himself were troubled of the news and sent the wise men to search for the new born King. As God would have it these men returned to their respective homes a different way to keep from giving King Herod his answer as to where Jesus was. The king had ill intentions for wanting to know the whereabouts of baby Jesus, but the wise men intentions were different. *God always has a master plan which will be carried out.*

God's grandeur in this scenario is that He used a star to guide the wise men to baby Jesus so they too could worship Him with great joy as they brought gifts of honor for the new born king. We have seen three sets of worshippers worshipping Jesus, the shepherds who were abiding in the field, the heavenly hosts and now the wise men who represented the Christians of their day. With that being said, let's join in the celebration of worshipping Jesus' birth, then we too can sing *Joy to the World Christ the King is born.*

Jesus' birth is a joy like none other.

Dec 13

Christ My Redeemer: Jeremiah 50:34

Their redeemer is strong; the Lord of host is his name: he shall thoroughly plead their cause; that he may give rest to the land, and disquiet the inhabitants of Babylon.

What is the prophet Jeremiah saying? Jeremiah was prophesying about the Jews captivity and offering hope that the Lord would redeem them form captivity. This is based on two factors; one is the Jews would repent and turn to God. The second factor is the Babylonians would be punished for their sins as they rejoiced over their defeat of Judah and Jerusalem. The Babylonians is looked upon as the prideful who defied the Lord and His righteous standards and lived as they pleased. The destruction of Babylonia is what happens to all ungodliness in the last days (Revelation 18:2-21), but thank God for our redeemer Jesus Christ.

See, God does not tolerate sin, but He is longsuffering giving time for repentance; however, if no repentance then punishment is certain. God is also true to His word, He promised a redeemer and Christ came as the Savior of the world. Just as He came to redeem mankind from the sins of the world He is sure to return to rule this world with all power and all believers will be with Him when He establishes His earthly kingdom. *Will you be in the number?*

There is no greater redeemer than God Himself in the form of His Son Jesus Christ who was born to die for the sins of the world.

Christ our redeemer. Praises! Praises!

Dec 14

The Word: John 1:1

In the beginning was the word, and the word was with God, and the word was God.

The gospel of John presents Jesus as the personal word of God who was in the beginning with God as Jesus Christ is the final revelation of God Himself other than in the Holy Scriptures. Jesus Christ is the manifold wisdom of God (Hebrews 1:1-3) as God had spoken many times and different ways to His people; therefore, it was necessary for Jesus-God to speak to mankind in the flesh as God. Jesus reveals the nature and person of God (John 1:3;-5; 14, 18; Colossians 2:9). This is the same as a person's words reveals his or her thoughts that stems from the heart and mind of the person this is the way it was with Jesus.

John presenting Jesus as the "word of God" authenticates Jesus' deity and being preexistent "with God" before the creation of the world (Colossians 1:15) and Jesus' existence did not begin with His virgin birth. Jesus Christ is a person existing from eternity, but having fellowship with His Father. Jesus as "the word" sustains the world as it was through Him that the world came into existence. Lastly, Jesus being presented as "the word" in relationship to humanity is that He became flesh (v.14) through the gateway of a human birth. Even though He became flesh He is still God.

Jesus Christ is my all-in-all; thank God He is.

Dec 15

Jesus The Light Of The World: John 1:4; 1 John 1:7

In Him was life, and the life was the light of men (v. 4)…But if we walk in the light, as He is the light, we have fellowship one with another and the blood of Jesus Christ His Son cleanseth us from all sin (v. 7).

What does it mean "in Him was life"? It means that all life is embodied in Christ, which is true genuine life as Christ is the light for everyone to see God and His truth, power and nature. This is seen in God's love, grace and mercy; simply because of what God the Father done through His Son Jesus Christ.

John 14:6 further authenticates Jesus as the light of the world when Jesus states, "I am the way, the truth and the life, no man cometh unto the Father, but by me." This verse gives credence to man's salvation as Jesus is the way back to God as sin destroyed man's fellowship with God the Father. Again in John 8:12 where Jesus further states that He is "the light of the world" and all who follows Him shall not walk in darkness, but "will have the light of life". What this means that all who follows Jesus will not be deceived by the deception of sin and will be able to see the truth from God's point of view. This is because what this world has to offer leads to destruction. 1 John 1:7 sums up Jesus as the light of the world in that our broken fellowship is restored through His shed blood.

***Jesus, what a light dispeller and a wonderful fellowship to have?**

Prophecy Fulfilled: Luke 1:26-38; 2:7

And in the sixth month the angel Gabriel was sent from God unto a city of Galilee, named Nazareth, To a virgin espoused to a man whose name was Joseph, of the house of David; and the virgin's name was Mary. And the angel came unto her, and said, Hail, thou art highly favored, the Lord is with thee; blessed are thou, among women......And she brought forth her firstborn son and wrapped him in swaddling clothes, and laid him in a manger, because there was no room for them in the inn.

If the question were raised, In what way was prophecy fulfilled? First, the prophet Isaiah prophesying about the virgin birth of Jesus Christ and it happened as predicted. Second, the angel Gabriel visiting Mary informing her of what was about to happen to her while she was engaged to Joseph. Her cousin Elizabeth being six months pregnant with John the Baptist the forerunner and cousin of Jesus Christ and when Mary visited Elizabeth John leaped in the womb of his mother rejoicing at the coming event-Christ's birth; Joseph maintaining his cool and continued with the wedding as plan.

Third, on the day of Christ' birth the angels made the announcement to the shepherds abiding in the fields tending their flock-sheep.

Fourth, the heavenly host joined in the praise and worship service of the baby Jesus.

Fifth, a star led the wise men to where the baby Jesus lay in the manger and returned home another way instead of returning the same way to keep from telling King Herod where the baby was as the king had decreed that all boy babies be destroyed.

Prophecy was fulfilled as God planned.

Dec 17

Mary The Mother Of Jesus: Luke 2:16

And they came with haste, and found Mary, and Joseph, and the baby lying in a manger.

What do we know about Mary? We know that she was a virgin used by God to bring forth His Son Jesus Christ. Mary was a young Jewish girl who was a virgin at the time of Jesus' birth and she was engaged (espoused) to Joseph as both Mary and Joseph came out of the linage of David (Matthew and Luke). Mary was the cousin of Elizabeth as was Jesus and John the Baptist who was the forerunner of Jesus. Mary was also found to be highly favored by God for such an awesome task one which she took with honor and grace.

What else we know about Mary is that both she and her husband obeyed the law in that they traveled to Bethlehem for taxation and the census count before the birth of Jesus. Mary was present with Jesus at a wedding ceremony and instructed the wine bearers to do as Jesus said. She was present during Jesus' crucifixion. Mary knew in her heart that her Son was special in that He was conceived of the Holy Spirit and He was God in the flesh who came to be the Savior of the world. Mary like many others believed on Jesus as the Son of God and personal Savior.

Mary the mother of Jesus our Savior was blessed and highly favored. Believers likewise, are blessed and highly favored as sons of God.

Dec 18

Swaddling Clothes: Job 38:9; Luke 2:7, 12

When I made the cloud the garment thereof, and thick darkness a swaddling band for it...And she brought forth her firstborn son, and wrapped him in swaddling clothes.

What are swaddling clothes? The student Bible Dictionary P. 215 defines swaddling clothes as a long piece of linen used to wrap babies. It also states that this kind of clothing was used to tightly wrap babies to prevent movement and quite possible to make the baby feel secure or comfortable. Zondervan's pictorial Bible Dictionary support the above definition of swaddling clothes. Newborns were place diagonally upon the cloth and then wrapped over the baby's sides and feet; then a band would be wound around both cloth and baby.

In our lesson study today we see God speaking to Job asking him a litany of thought provoking questions to rekindled Job's awareness of His awesomeness and God used the metaphor of saddling band to illustrate how He set things in place and nothing moves without His giving the order. God tells Job that He used the cloud as a garment band for security for the earth. God further tells Job that He and He alone break up the cloud when He see fit.

Now that we have looked at our scripture text and how God uses this piece of cloth as a security blanked when referencing the cloud; let us speculate on Mary's use of the cloth to wrap her new born baby. Being that Jesus was born in a stable and laid in an animal feeding trough, Mary probably felt the need to make her baby feel as secure as possible. We know that feeding troughs is a hard rough surface and the need for comfort was paramount in the young mother's mind. Therefore, this piece of clothing provided both for baby Jesus and His parents provided the rest. We can further speculate that this type of clothing was smooth and soft so as to provide warmth to a new born baby's skin. Wrapping newborns in smooth soft blankets as well as bassinets are symbolic of the swaddling clothes and manger used by Jesus' parents during His birth.

In retrospect to Jesus' birth and God metaphorically using swaddling cloth when speaking to Job represents security as Jesus is our security blanket. It is in Him that we move and breathe. Our total existence is wrapped up in Jesus Christ; therefore, let's praise Him for being so and sing praised to both heaven and earth for Jesus.

Just as the swaddling clothes that were used to wrap Jesus at birth, now He is our covering for all who believe and have accepted Him as Lord and Savior.

Jesus Christ our swaddling cloth.

Dec 19

Jesus Christ Our Servant: Philippians 2:7

But made Himself of no reputation, and took upon Him the form of a servant, and was made in the likeness of men.

What is this verse saying to us? We can interpret this verse to mean that Jesus Christ our Lord emptied Himself of His deity and glory (John 17:4), His position in heaven (John 5:30; Hebrews 5:8) and His eternal riches (2 Corinthians 8:9), His rights in heaven (Luke 22:27; Matthew 20:28) and His divine attributes (John 5:19; 8:28; 14:10) to become man with human limitations, temptation while remaining sinless as Christ our servant knew His assigned mission, which was to die on the cross for the sins of the world. It is noteworthy to say that Christ was not forced into laying aside His deity, but did so voluntarily because of love for mankind. True servantship can be seen in Christ's suffering the cruelty of the cross because being hung on the cross in Christ's day was the cruelest form of death.

Matthew 20:28 makes a profound statement of what it means to be a servant in that He states that "He came not to be ministered to, but to minister, and to give His life a ransom for many." This scripture bring these questions to mind, even though we will not have to be a ransom for others, but how are we serving God through serving others? Are we serving because of the position in which we hold in the church or community or the mission itself?

Christ our true servant.

Dec 20

Jesus The Temple: John 2:19; 21

.....Destroy this temple, and in three days I will raise it up...but He spoke of the temple of His body.

The common definition of "temple" is a place of worship or the house of worship. It is also referred to believers or a group of believers which for Christians means where God resides. With that being said, Christians must remain morally pure as our Lord and Savior Jesus is. During Jesus' early ministry He cleanse the temple of all wrong doings which can be interpreted as how all believers themselves are to be as well as Christians' place of worship as it is God's dwelling place and He cannot dwell in an unholy place whether it the individual believer or the local congregation-the church.

In this scenario when Jesus spoke of the temple being destroyed in three and in three days He will raise it up He was speaking of His death and resurrection. Christian worship focus was shifted from the temple itself to Christ as He is God in the flesh (John 1:14) and dwelt among His people. It is in Him that the fullness of God lives being that He is God in the second Person.

Therefore, being that Jesus Christ embodies the temple and the church is His body made up of baptized believers we then are temples of God His dwelling place.

Jesus Christ the temple; He in us and we in Him; reside therein.

Dec 21

Worship: John 4:23-24

But the hour cometh and now is, when the true worshippers shall worship the Father in spirit and in truth; for the Father seeketh such worship of Him. God is a Spirit and they that worship Him must worship Him in spirit and in truth.

What is worship? Worship is being in the presence of the Lord to give praises, reverence, adoration and honor to a sovereign God who created both heaven and earth and all therein humanity alike and sustains it with His mighty hand. When God breathed the breath of life into man he became a living soul. Man was created in the likeness and image of God to worship Him and be in fellowship with God.

How do we worship God? We worship God in spirit and in truth. Believers' expresses worship by serving others as Christ is the perfect example of worshipping through serving. Also, worship can be seen in Christian's obedience to God and His moral attributes. We can also worship in private and in public. Private worship is going one-on-one with God our Father. This form of worship is free of distractions just you and the Holy God. However we worship God it must be done in spirit and in truth as God is truth. This is the truth as revealed by God the Holy Spirit who is God. It is noteworthy to say that all who set aside the truth and the doctrine of God's Word in his or her worship has in fact set aside the foundation for true worship.

Worshipping God in spirit and in truth is the highest form of praise given to a holy God.

Worship! Worship!

Dec 22

Wise Men: Matthew 2:1

Now when Jesus was born in Bethlehem of Judea in the days of Herod the king, behold, there came wise men fro the east to Jerusalem, Saying, Where is he that is born King of the Jews? For we have seen his star in the east, and are come to worship him.

Who are these men that traveled so far to see and worship the baby Jesus? History say that the wise men were both learned men and of the religious class from around the region. See, there had been much prophesy about the birth of the Messiah-Jesus and that He would be born of a virgin and this prophecy was being fulfilled. God His own divine advertising method; He used one of His heavenly stars to lead these religious men to where the baby was with full knowledge that they would worship the true King of the Jews.

History also records that the time of the wise men's visit was when Jesus was from 40 days to 2 years of age (Luke 2:22; v. 16). The important fact here is that Jesus is worthy of all honor from the entire human race and both Jews and Gentiles was included in God's redemptive plan of salvation (8:11; 28; 19; Romans 10:12).

These questions come to mind, considering the purpose of Jesus' birth and His mission is the Lord worthy of your worship? How far are you willing to travel to worship our Lord and Savior?

No distance is too great to worship our Savior.

The Messianic Era: Luke 2:25-26

...Behold, there was a man in Jerusalem, whose name was Simon; and the same man was just and devout, waiting for the consolation of Israel; and the Holy Ghost was upon him. And it was revealed unto him by the Holy Ghost that he should not see death, before he had seen the Lord's Christ.

What do we know about Simon who was waiting for the consolation of Israel? We know that Simon was a righteous man, which means that he was right with God both in his heart and action, which translates into not just talk of righteousness but living so that all could see his dedication to the Lord. It is one thing to say that we are Christians, but quite another to live like Christians should, and then the world really see and know who you are.

Another fact about Simon is that he served in the temple daily and was waiting for the consolation of Israel, which is the fulfillment of prophecy-Jesus' birth. Simon was a devout man who was filled with the Holy Spirit as he waited patiently for the coming Messiah. Also, Simon lived during the time in Israel's history when the spiritual conditions were lukewarm at best and the Holy Spirit revealed to Simon that he would not die until he see the Messiah-our Lord Jesus Christ. Lukewarm spirit conditions will once again appear at the end of time, but just as God always has faithfuls who will remain true to Him.

What is the Messianic era? This period in our history was ushered in with Jesus Christ.

Remain faithful to God regardless of the era.

Dec 24

Jesus Presented To The Lord: Luke 2:22

And when the days of purification according to the Law of Moses were accomplished, they brought him to Jerusalem, to present Him to the Lord.

We see that Jesus' parents Mary and Joseph lived according to the law in their day and were also obedient to God's law as they dedicated their son back to God. Presenting the child to the Lord is for consecration purposes as this was setting the child apart to do God's divine will and live according to His purpose as each person has an assigned mission in life. All parents are encouraged to follow Mary and Joseph's dedication as we are to give our children back to God and pray for the child (ren) daily asking for the guidance of the Holy Spirit to be upon his or her life so the child (ren) can and have the mind to do the will of God with complete devotion. Even though Jesus is God He served His Father in total obedience to the end.

These questions come to mind in regards to presenting our children back to God, Is our presentation sincere or is it out of formality? Is Christ being presented to our children in our homes if so are our prayers that they accept Jesus as their Savior and live accordingly?

Given the fact that our children are gifts from God, then why not give them back to God and ask God for the Holy Spirit's covering upon them?

Consecrate your child (ren) to God Jesus was and He is God.

Dec 25

The Prince Of Peace: Isaiah 9:6

For unto us a child id born, unto us a Son is given; and the government shall be upon His shoulders; and His name shall be called Wonderful, Counselor, The mighty God, The everlasting Father, The Prince of Peace.

From our scripture text we see the names Isaiah associated with the new born baby Jesus and Isaiah's prophesy was fulfilled many generations later, just as prophesied.

Other notable facts in Isaiah's prophesy is that Jesus' birth came at a definite time and place in Israel's history (7:14); also Jesus' birth would be born in a unique and marvelous way in that He was born of a virgin and conceived by the Holy Ghost. This makes Him the Messianic Son of the living God.

Let us look at the above Messianic names Isaiah associated with Jesus Christ that authenticates Jesus as the promised Messiah.

a) Wonderful. Jesus Himself would be a wonder in His supernatural birth as He was both human and God and His deity would manifest itself in His deeds and miracles that He performed while here on earth.

b) Counselor. Jesus as the promised Messiah would be the incarnation of the perfect wisdom of God the Father and the final revelation of God to His people. Also, being the Counselor He would make known the perfect plan of salvation (Isaiah Ch. 11).

c) The Mighty God. Jesus as the Mighty God as He is God in the second Person and in Him all fullness of the Deity of God would exist in human body format (Colossian 2:9; John 1:1, 14).

d) Everlasting Father. Jesus as the Everlasting Father would reveal His heavenly Father as well as His acts of kindness toward His people as a Father would by showing compassion, love, and a father who protect His children, supplying all their needs. (Psalm 103: 13;

Philippians 4:19). Jesus does all things that a father does for his children.

    e) Prince of Peace. Jesus as the Prince of Peace He would bring peace to the human race through salvation for all who believe on Him. As the prince of Peace He would restore the broken fellowship between man and God the Father that was broken by sin (11:6-6; Romans 5:1; 8:2). Jesus as the Prince of Peace would serve as man's redeemer with His death on the cross and Him being raised from the dead on Resurrection Morning.

Total peace/shalom will be fully restored when Jesus return to establish His earthly kingdom where He will rule forever. All believers will be with Him and we will dwell with Him in that New Jerusalem- the City of David.

Jesus our Prince of Peace who brings everlasting peace He is God.

The Way: John 14:6

Jesus saith unto him, I am the way, the truth and the light; no man cometh unto my Father, but by Me.

In this scenario Jesus was with His disciples and was preparing them for His departure, but He promised to return one day and return He will as He did after His resurrection (ch.13). In our lesson chapter, verses 2-3 Jesus is referring to His return to heaven where He is preparing a place for all believers (God's heavenly mansion). What we know about God and His Son is that whatever is promised it will come to pass. Jesus is coming back for His followers so we will be with Him for ever. This is the purpose of His return and it will enable all believers to escape the trials that will exist here on earth during the tribulation.

See, Jesus' disciples had been with Him for three years and where He went they went and the talk of Him leaving them they (Thomas) could not comprehend what Jesus was saying. What Jesus was really telling His disciples that He was the way back to God as no man could come to God without going through Him. He is truth and only His truth will stand. Jesus being the light of the world shines His glorious light of holiness in a sin darkened world. Light dispels all darkness. As believers we are to be the light of this world by letting the light of Christ shine in our lives in words and in deeds.

Jesus is the way truth and light-follow Him.

Jesus The Christ, The Son Of The Living God: Matthew 16:16

And Simon Peter answered and said, Thou art the Christ, the Son of the Living God.

The gospel writers present Jesus in different lights as each writer was writing to a different audience. Matthew presents Jesus as the Messianic King, Mark presents Jesus as the Servant Son, Luke presents Jesus as the Divine-Human Savior and John presents Jesus as the Son of God "the Word" as the final revelation of God Himself to His people. All this does is authenticates Jesus as the promised Messiah-the Christ who is God's Son.

With that being said, then Jesus as the Christ is the Son of the Living God and our Savior He is not dead and is now seated at the right hand of His Father making intercessions for all believers. All believers serve a risen living God-Servant who not only served mankind while on earth but continues to so today. Given all that Jesus Christ has and continues to do on behalf of mankind He is worthy of all praise and honor. We are to serve and worship our Savior not just on Christmas, but daily because He wakes us each morning through the presence of the Holy Spirit and keeps us daily as well.

During Jesus' earthly ministry He told His disciples that He came not to be served, but serve as He is the suffering servant. Why so, because He suffered and died on the cross for humanity's sins, but thank God He did not remain dead. He rose as promised to completely fulfill His mission.

Christ our Savior the Son of the living God.

Dec 28

The Resurrection: John 11:25-26

Jesus said unto her; I am the resurrection, and the life; he that believeth in Me, though he were dead, yet shall he live; And whosoever liveth and believeth in Me shall never die; Believest thou this.

To define the term resurrection is to say that it the reuniting of the human body with its soul and spirit from which it was separated at death. What we know about death is that by popular belief is that death is the end, but for all believers' physical death is the beginning of a never-ending life with Christ. This is because we died with Christ to sin and rose with Him to a life of righteousness so that we may live with Him in eternity.

We as believers must shed these mortal bodies and put on immortality, which is a perfectly designed body that is suitable for a never-ending life with God. In the resurrection, just like Christ's body is incorruptible so will all believers and neither will our bodies decay as it does today.

There are three reasons the Bible gives for body resurrection and they are (a) the body is a critical component to the total human person and humans are incomplete without a body (Romans 8:18-25). (b) The body is the temple of the Holy Spirit (1 Corinthians 6:19). (c) Resurrection will undo sin on all levels and it is the final conqueror of its enemy-death (1 Corinthians 15:26).

There are two resurrections; one for believers-life and one for non-believers-judgment, which will you be in?

Dec 29

Jesus As Lord: Romans 14:9

For to this end Christ both died, and rose, and revived, the He might be Lord both of the dead and living.

The Student's Bible Dictionary (P.146) defines Lord as Master, sir or title of respect. We see that the title Lord is used identifying Jesus as our Lord and Savior, which is essential to ones salvation (Romans 10:9-10). The title Lord is also used when referencing God our Father.

Why Jesus is our Lord simply because He was the only one found worthy or met all God's requirements to atone for the sins of the world. During the Old Testament, the priests atonements were performed annually and he himself had to be cleansed of his sins, whereas Jesus the Christ were both human and divine but yet sinless; therefore, Jesus' onetime sin atonement through His shed blood at Calvary fulfilled God's requirements. Also, Jesus as Lord because He is God's only Son who is God born of a woman to become God required human sacrifice for all humanity as this was part of God's plan of salvation.

With that being said, Jesus Christ is Lord of both dead-unsaved and the living-saved and in that great getting up morning we all will rise either to life everlasting or damnation. Jesus is Lord whether you choose to live in and with Him or reject Him and live out of Christ. For me and my house we choose Christ and will serve Him forever.

Yes Jesus is Lord forever!

Dec 30

The Good Shepherd: John 10:11

I am the good shepherd; the good shepherd giveth His life for the sheep.

What makes Jesus the Good Shepherd? There are several reasons that authenticate Jesus as the Good Shepherd and they are:

a) Because He is God's Son who displayed His love, devotion and care for mankind-the sheep. A shepherd cares for the every need of his sheep; when of the sheep leaves the fold; the shepherd will search until he finds the lost sheep. The shepherd protects his sheep from all danger and will make sure they are in a place of safety. **The Good Shepherd.**

b) Jesus as the Good Shepherd willingly gave His life for the sheep-humanity. It is through His death on the cross and all believers' faith in Him as Lord and Savior we become His sheep. Jesus as the Good Shepherd He will not lead us astray for He is that small still voice that whispers directions in the deep sections of our minds. ***Only the Good Shepherd would give His life for His sheep-Jesus.***

c) Jesus as the Good Shepherd is the bridge that connects sinful man to a holy God.

We can conclude then that Jesus as the Good Shepherd knows the voice of His people and His people know Him and His voice and will not listen to any other voice. All who enters into the flock of Jesus come by hearing the Word of God.

Jesus the Good Shepherd; enter into His fold.

Dec 31

His Name Is Jesus: Matthew 1:21

And she shall bring forth a son, and thou shalt call His name JESUS; for He shall save His people from their sins.

All this month we have looked at the many names associated with Jesus our Lord as well as prophecy being fulfilled and it climaxed with the grand announcement being made by God's heavenly angels. Prophecy was also fulfilled with the naming of the baby Jesus-Immanuel God with us. We have also discussed who worshipped baby Jesus and the distance some travel to see prophecy being fulfilled and worship the promised Messiah. There was great joy in the land because His birth meant that peace had come to earth; therefore, we can sing "joy to the world the Savior has come".

Some of the names we looked at that is associated with Jesus is Wonderful, Counselor, Mighty God, Messiah, Prince of Peace, Immanuel, the Resurrection, Lord, the Way, the Word, the life, Good Shepherd and Lord all of which adds to one name and it is JESUS, which means "The Lord is salvation (Joshua 1:1), which is the Greek form of the name. All of theses names are designed to teach that Jesus is Lord and Savior who is God's Son who was born to die for the sins of the world and all who believe in Him died with Him and rose with Him and will live forever with Him. *O! What a name?*

Jesus is the only name by which all men will be saved. There is power in the name of Jesus. There is no greater name both on earth and in heaven than JESUS.

Bio

Dr. WILLIE B. WHITE holds two Masters of Arts degree in Adult education (MA Ed, MA SED and a Doctorate in Ministry).

Ms. White is a certified Dean and instructor in Christian Education, a college professor and special education teacher K-12.

She frequently publishes articles in The Informer magazine of the SSPB. First book, "The Lord is My Shepherd", (2007) PublishAmerica. "An Expose Of The Holy Spirit", released June 2009, "Heavenly Bread", released July 2009, a monthly devotional.

Ms. White publishes a weekly blog discussion Uplifting Insight- http://willie-writing.blogspot.com.

Works in progress, DVD Who is God? An inspirational video, next books, God's Moral laws: The Ten Commandments, and My Faith Journey with Jesus. All material is available through www.shepherdministries.info. or by writing to 31275 Portside Dr 17109 Novi, MI 48377

www.ingramcontent.com/pod-product-compliance
Lightning Source LLC
Chambersburg PA
CBHW060103170426
43198CB00010B/754